M000286202

In loving memory of my brother, Gary Robert Nelson.

THE TEST GAME BETWEEN GOOD AND EVIL

Do you believe in God? Do you believe in love and the consequences of love and religion? Have you been sucked in by both in this thing called life, and you can only chose one path—a life's journey of love or of religion? Have you tried merging both but failed?

I believed in God and prayed to Him daily, and many times, I just wanted Him to prove Himself to me by answering my sometimes very simple prayers. But let's just say, most times, He didn't. So I cursed my belief and my faith. Doubt eventually consumed me, as there were times when I didn't care about the proof of the existence of God or heaven. I just chose to live life my way, day by day.

Have you ever been there?

And then there were other times when I found myself in bad situations with no other alternative but to beg and pray to God to spare my life and make a way out for me. And He did. Yes! He did! Well, until this one time...

Would you sacrifice a loved one for your faith in God, or would you turn your back on God for the sake of a loved one?

Read Genesis 22:1–18.

What would you do if you were a young church boy whose simple quest was to serve God and find love and then later realized that you found both and had both but then lost both because, even while maintaining your faith, you were sucked in by a third entity called evil!

Wow.

I just wanted to live, but that was easier said than done.

This is my story.

My name is Street, a midteen Jamaican dude, and my story starts in Kingston, Jamaica, back in the mid '80s, as the leader of a popular break dance crew called the Street Boys.

The Beginning

Music was blasting in the nightclub. The Street Boys were all hanging out one Friday. It was past midnight. We just did a cameo break dance performance, as we did most weekends there, and afterward were just chilling. Stoke, a member, was slow-dancing with a girl on the dance floor, although they were playing disco music. Really! Bob, another member, was sitting next to me, making out with his new girlfriend, and Assad, who completed our group, went over to chat with a girl he locked eyes with at the bar.

I scanned the club, and everyone seemed erotic and happy as they danced the night away. But I felt somewhat out of place because I just broke up with my "on again, off again" girlfriend. Again. I finally called it quits.

Have you ever been in that situation where a relationship was going nowhere, so one day you just finally said "Enough" and walked away?

I was single and alone. We have all been there.

But I had no intentions of going home alone that night because who would do that on a Friday night out after the disco? That was unless you had that *love of your life* fast asleep in bed, waiting for you to get back home in anticipation of waking them up in the wee hours of the morning for some half-asleep, drunken love.

I would admit, however, that, with that being said, I had lost count of how many girls I had met up with at the club who straight up told me they had a man yet before the night was over, we were making out at the back of the club or in the parking lot before they left. Cheaters? Not in my book, because who am I to judge, especially when I didn't know their story.

Las Vegas stole our slogan from way back when. As we always said, "What happens at the club stays at the club," because as young as we were, we already accepted the fact that countless people out there were living double lifestyles; being innocent, stay-at-home, or hardworking ladies during the days but "shut your mouth and mind your business" ladies when they hit the road after dark for some *let-your-hair down* fun time.

I had no problem picking up girls but got bored over time with me always making the first move, as guys should, or girls making the first move, which made them too easy to satisfy that conquered satisfaction. So what was my creative plan B? I had lost my faith, but I still prayed (we will get into that later). And being half drunk and almost as a mockery, my weirdest test game came to my mind again, but this time, it was when it came to picking up girls. So I locked eyes on this beautiful girl who was sitting and chatting with some girlfriends.

I could have easily gone over to talk to her, but I wanted to prove something; so after I chugged on my beer and put out my cigarette, I started my test game. "God, if you really do exist, prove it! Let her come over to me," I prayed.

Yes. That was my simple. This was my test game.

Nothing happened.

We exchanged flirty glances as if she was waiting for me to make the first move and come over. But when I didn't budge, in the end, she just gave me a disappointed smile, looked away, and kept on chatting and drinking with her girlfriends.

I played the same test game request to God two more times, and she still totally ignored me.

Forget her then!

I went to the bar, got another beer, chatted a bit with familiar faces, stupidly turned down advances from two other girls to come sit with me, then went back to sit down, lit another cigarette, and scanned the dance floor. Yes, back in those days, we could smoke indoors.

My eyes locked on this girl in a skimpy red dress with an awesome body erotically dancing with her girlfriend. She looked amazing—well, at least from a distance and from my blurred, intoxicated vision.

I could have easily said, "Okay, God, how about her?" But instead, and still playing this silly half-drunk test game of mine, this time, I said, "Devil, if you really exist, let her come over."

Yep, I did whisper that.

Nothing happened.

Several minutes passed, and I had had enough for one night, so eventually, I told Bob to go tell the rest of the crew that I was ready. Yep, I wasn't feeling it that night, so I was about to leave and go home alone. I was the leader of the Street Boys crew, so most times, when we were out partying, I called the shots in when we went and when we left.

They all gathered at my table after a few moments, and just as I finished my beer and stood up to leave, we were interrupted by someone. To my surprise, it was the girl in the skimpy red dress.

"Hey, guys, you all leaving already?" she asked with a half-drunk smiling stare at me. "I was just coming over to ask if you wanted to dance. Damn, you guys were really good earlier, especially you." She nudged me in a half-drunk state.

We all took a quick glance at each other, and by now, I had forgotten about the silly test game.

"Thanks, and yeah, it's almost closing time, so we outa here. Street." I introduced myself as I shook her hand.

"Jess." She smiled. "So where you guys heading next? Me and my girl be club hopping since happy hour. This is our third stop."

"There's an after-party at Street's place if you wanna come," Assad lied as he discreetly kicked my feet to play along.

But before I could reply, she took the bait and said, "Sure!"

To our surprise, she asked for my address and went to talk to her girlfriend briefly.

"What was that, bro?" I smiled half drunk at Assad.

"Your lucky night." He chuckled as he nudged me. "Look at that body, bro! You owe me one! Go do what we do best when it comes to these girls."

Moments later, she came back over and then left alone with us after explaining that her girlfriend was heading to another club to meet up at a fraternity initiation party with some freshmen at her college.

We hitched a cab, and we all chilled at my place for a bit, having more drinks and smoke. Then everyone left, except the girl in the red dress.

Yawn

"Street! Yo, Street, wake your ass up, bro!" a voice said almost at noon the next morning, as the person banged on my bedroom window.

It was Stoke.

"Damn, yo! Okay, okay, I'm up." I yawned and stretched.

"We've been waiting forever to start practice, and now there's some chick in a car outside, asking for you. Says she's here to pick up her girlfriend, Jess."

"What the! Okay, gimme a sec." I exhaled, forcing myself to wake up.

I wiped the sleep from my eyes, rolled over, and there was Jess, still asleep beside me. I put my mind into rewind mode, trying to remember how she got in my bed. I lifted the covers from my chest to get up and realized we were both naked. Although I didn't remember much detail from when we went to my room after everyone left, it was obvious that we made out. Surprisingly, there were no signs of a used condom, as I checked my bedside drawer and saw that the new pack was still intact.

Drunken love, followed by drunken consequences.

I gently woke her and told her that her girlfriend was outside. She started swearing as she dragged herself out of bed and looked angry and cranky as she searched for her clothing. We spoke briefly

9

as we both got dressed, and it was then that I realized that she had issues and a bad attitude. Plus, while she had a great body, she wasn't that pretty. So not my type. Sorry!

"Last night was amazing!" she simply said as she passionately kissed me.

She went to the restroom for a bit before returning, looking a bit refreshed. She wrote her address on a piece of paper and said I could come visit her whenever. She then gave me a long sleepy hang-over kiss at the front door before walking to the car, jokingly arguing with her girlfriend, who seemed clearly frustrated at waiting for her for so long.

I admired her body as she walked away in that skimpy red dress, and it was then that I had a flashback about the silly test game I played at the club last night.

The devil proved his existence, but God didn't! I thought.

Sigh.

At that point, I labeled her as the devil in the red dress.

Although I made use of my wish all night and was satisfied, I was once again left disappointed at who didn't prove Himself to me once again, as Jess walked down my driveway, spun around, blew me a kiss, gave me a devilish smile, hopped in the car, and drove off.

Don't call me mean, but based on her attitude, and even with that great body, she was not the type of girl I was interested in hooking up with again. I gazed at the piece of paper she wrote her address on, crushed it in my palm, tossed it away, and started my day.

Haven't most of us all been there? After a night out, you meet a stranger that made your night, you let your guard down, so the night ended with a kiss or a one-night stand, but thereafter, nothing more.

It's okay to pretend you don't have a clue what I'm talking about.

A Day in the Life of a Street Boy

I got my morning started.

It was summer holidays from school and a typical beautiful tropical Jamaican Saturday afternoon.

My break dance crew, as I said, was comprised of Assad, Bob, Stoke and I. We had this huge cardboard box from that new refrigerator my next-door neighbor purchased recently. We cut it open and sprawled it out on my front lawn as our dance floor. I had my boom box blasting, and we were practicing new break-dance moves while some of our fans—well, more like our neighbors—converged to cheer us on.

We competed in various community break dance competitions. We had many signature dance moves, but on this day, I was practicing the windmill dance. Bob was practicing the head-spin dance, Stoke was practicing the moonwalk, and Assad was as usual being Mr. Smooth and hitting on this neighbor he had a crush on while improvising his own moves.

Don't Take the Bait

I lived on a quiet side street with little traffic and few pedestrians. Bob stopped briefly to speak with the postman about a letter he was expecting, while Stoke, Assad, and I continued our routine until, while cheering each other on, we were all distracted by an oncoming stranger.

She could pass for a model as she casually but somewhat nervously walked toward us in her pretty floral summer dress, carrying what looked like a Bible and pamphlets.

Assad was our trigger man—the self-proclaimed bodyguard for Street Boys, who was always on edge as he thought the world was out to get him. On the contrary, our verdict was that he smoked too much weed (marijuana).

He halted her friendly approach with a "What?" look. He pointed to me as they exchanged a few inaudible words because of the loud music, so I went over and paused the boom box as she approached me.

She introduced herself as Michelle, a Christian, and asked if I was saved, at which I scoffed, and then she started the usual "preaching" about God and getting me "saved." I respectfully listened, but it went in one ear and came out the next. I really didn't care to hear, as I was more mesmerized by her charm and grace.

She noticed.

"I get this every time, Mister… What's your name again? Oh, Street. So please, will you stop undressing me with your eyes?" She sighed.

"What! What am I doing?" I tried to downplay it.

"You are literally undressing me with your eyes! Stop." She sighed and turned my chin away from looking down at her body.

It was a beautiful touch from her hands.

"I wasn't always a Christian. I know the game you boys play, and I live in this neighborhood, so I can tell a smooth talker when I see one, because you guys are everywhere, break dancing on the street and trying to impress girls every chance you get. Funny that your name is, Street." She sighed. "So, Street, can we talk, or should I go?"

I thought, *I'm busted.*

"So we're practicing for a dance contest this weekend. We got the dance floor laid out right here." I pointed. "You say you see us break dancing all the time. So how about you show us any signature moves you got, and then we can talk after?"

She rolled her eyes in disgust. "Okay, it was nice talking to you," Michelle said with a look of disappointment. "I have to go. Here are some pamphlets for you and each of your friends. Just take a moment to read it when you can. We have a one-week crusade starting on Sunday. There's the address." She pointed with her beautiful hands. "Please make some time to attend."

I was trying to calm the situation in player mode: "Hey, I'm sorry. But tell you what. The dance contest is this Saturday at the community center at P-Square, walking distance from here. You know there, right? If you attend to cheer us on, I'll be at your crusade on Sunday."

She gave me a "Really!" smile and said, "God bless you." Then she walked away, much to the horny whistles from my crew.

The minute she took a corner and was out of sight, I crushed the pamphlets up, tossed them aside, and we resumed practicing.

Deal or No Deal

Days passed, and to my shock, sure enough, she showed up with two other male churchgoers at the dance contest that Saturday. I saw her when I went to speak with the promoter.

"So you came." I smiled, cutting the conversation short, as the music blasted in the background; two other groups were competing on stage.

"We were on our way back from visiting a church member that just got released from the hospital. We heard the music and decided to stop in. We are missionaries, remember?"

"So you didn't stop by just for me?"

She shook her head to say no with a smile but gave me a warm look, but the conversation ended as my crew was summoned to the stage for the final battle.

"I'd like to see you again. Wish us luck," I said as I abruptly left.

Long story short, we lost the dance contest, which was more like just a concert with not much up for grabs, because knowing she was watching, stupid me overdid it and flopped doing the windmill dance. Bob was an epic fail with his head spin. And once again, Assad went off cue and tried to do sexy gyrating moves to wow the girls in the audience, but the judges weren't impressed. As for Stoke, never mind. After seeing his moves, we were all like, "Really, dude!"

We never danced as we rehearsed.

Have you ever practiced over and over to do something, but when the time finally came for you to deliver, you did everything else, except what you practiced to do?

Sigh.

So as much as I was into this girl, who maybe likes me too, the first time she came to watch us perform, we were losers! Not cool. Not cool at all!

As if she was waiting, Michelle at the end when we were all filing out to leave the premises met me at the exit.

"Hey, that was fun. I'm sorry, you Street Boys were great, but in fairness, the other group was…were…" she started.

I gave her the "I dare you to say 'better'" look, and she just laughed.

We spent the next minute or so getting to know each other amicably until her other missionaries came over and chatted for a moment, and then they all left.

The Crusade

True to my word, I went to the crusade alone that Sunday, because my crew had no interest and teased that I was only going to church to pursue her. Point!

Most in attendance were looking at me funny as I walked in that huge church tent. I had my break-dance outfit on—graffiti jeans, T-shirt, studded gloves and belts, gold sneakers with neon laces, and all. I did remove my bandana though.

My body was there, but my mind was on how we screwed up the contest last night and planning new dance moves for the big upcoming contest weeks away. And yes! I just graduated from high school and got enrolled into college, so being on summer break, that was all that was on my mind—dancing and winning to earn bragging rights as *the best break dance group* in our community and then the country by winning the coveted Break Dance Championship golden belt.

So forget you, if you would have been focused on something more productive.

The pastor finally got my attention when he went on and on and on about why we needed to throw our tithes and offerings and said he was going to spend the entire sermon preaching on this topic and continue for the rest of the crusade on the same topic.

Really!

I scornfully laughed to myself. I had a part-time summer job working at a shoe store, but there was no way I was going to give this pastor my money, as I was saving to shop for shoes and clothing to be the slickest looking kid at college.

I started scanning the congregation for her as the choir got up to sing as they passed around the collection plate. After everybody settled, the greedy pastor was at it again, complaining that he was disappointed and that God would be disappointed, too, at the little money we all threw as offering, considering there were more than a hundred persons in the congregation. He then had the nerve to reprimand everyone and then instructed his ushers to pass around the collection plate a second time.

Wow!

At this point, I had had enough and proved to myself once more why I didn't attend church. I thumped my chair between my legs and stood up and stormed out because of this dude—oops, sorry—this pastor, who was only here to preach, "Show me the money." I turned a few heads as I left the building.

I was at the bus stop across the street, waiting to catch a ride home, when, to my surprise, Michelle ran over.

"Hey!" She smiled with a look of concern. "Thanks for coming. I just saw you leaving, and you looked upset. So I just thought I'd try to catch you to find out what was going on."

I was more focused on my disgust than being happy to see her, so we spoke about it for a couple minutes. She gave her side, which I won't get into, because like most church folks who are devoted Christians, she just simply defended her pastor.

It was at that point that I learned, try as you may; whenever there is a difference of opinion, you will never win in a debate about Religion!

Within the next few minutes we basically respectfully debated and agreed to disagree as my bus arrived. I wanted to skip it and catch the next bus so we could talk some more but she said she had to get back in, promised I'll see her around and left.

The next day, I told my crew what went down at church and basically got the "LOL, told ya!" response.

Days went by, and I never saw her again.

The Main

About two weeks later my crew and I were chilling at a friend's house about a block and a half away on the main street from where I lived, or *The Main*, as we called it. We all went to get beer and cigarettes across the street at the corner deli, and on the way back, there she was.

Assad remembered her too as he and I watched her up the street talking to this couple and handing them pamphlets.

"Yow, there's that b*tch from the other day, bro," he said as she approached us. "Damn, look at that walk and that body."

"Stand down yo," I said.

"You owe me one remember!" he said as he puffed on his cigarette.

"I said stand down!" I replied.

"She's into you," he said as he puffed on his cigarette again then handed it to me. "And you know how we roll with these hoes. Don't let her be the one that got away bro."

The Silver Break Dance Championship Belt

She approached us looking radiant as usual; even a car with two men drove pass, honked their horn and blew kisses at her. We all chatted briefly then Assad surprisingly told her that he read the pamphlet she left that first time and was *curious* to know more about Christ. Liar! He invited her to stop by his house "one of these days" so she could further inspire him as he had never set foot in a church and doesn't even believe in God.

I was looking at him funny as he spoke with the fakest sincere look you could ever imagine, but she actually took the bait and agreed after handing him two other pamphlets and inviting him to church.

Having heard enough, I gave them the hand signal to leave her and me alone, so they eventually went back in the yard to chill.

I then noticed that she was looking at me funny; at my hands specifically. I looked down and realized that I had the half-smoked cigarette in one hand and an almost empty beer can in the next.

"Oops, my bad," I said as I chugged down the last of my beer, took a long puff from the cigarette, and then threw both away.

"I didn't know you smoked," she said as she fanned some smoke from her face and took a few steps back.

"Just socially, and don't start," I defended. "Even Catholic priests smoke because they claim that 'the Bible is silent on the habit,' and the first miracle that Jesus performed was to turn water into wine. Sooo…"

She leaned back with an impressed look. "So, wow, I thought you didn't attend church to know all that."

"I don't. I start college in a month but graduated from St. George's, a catholic high school, where we had to take damn communion every Friday and be preached at."

"I attended Immaculate High School. We are 'sister schools.' Good for you." She smiled. "Which college you heading off to?"

"Jamager Automotive downtown, to be an auto technician, which I bloody hate becoming, but my mom had the final say. You?"

"I was just initiated to be a missionary. My church has affiliates all over the world, so besides nationwide ministry, I am going on church missions to England soon, then Africa this Christmas, and Brazil next spring," she said with an excited look. "I am a full-time missionary."

Rolly eyes. I wasn't impressed.

"Is that what you wanna be when you grow up? My mom is all about me getting this degree to get a good job to support a home, wife, family, and stuff, so how does being a missionary pay the bills?"

"We get sponsorship. And please, I never ever debate religion and my Christian purpose. My dad is a devout Christian who gives me his full blessings, even financially."

"And mom?" I asked.

"She passed away. I don't want to talk about it."

"I'm sorry to hear. But back to our topic: it still sounds lame to me but it's your life following all these lame-ass pastors like the one that night at the crusade who just want to take our money."

"You watch your mouth!" she snapped. "That was my father! And he is not lame, but even with sponsorship, these missions cost money."

"What the…" I started to say out of shock before she shut me down.

"Stop…stop!" she begged as I laughed.

Our conversation was interrupted by a car that pulled up. It was one of the promoters I was cool with, for the upcoming break dance mega final contest that weekend.

"Yo, Street! Bro, you better bring your A game to the finals 'cuz we just rapped the other auditions and some a these crews got mad moves bro." He laughed as I walked over and we dabbed. "You flopped the last time around, but I know you kids. I got some money on you, Street Boys, so you better bring it!"

We exchanged a few more words with me promising to do just that, and then he drove off. When I turned around, there was Assad talking to Michelle again.

"What?" He laughed as he handed me a beer. "We in there chilling, and we sweating 'cuz a the heat, so I just brought you a beer bro and offered your lady a drink. You know I got you!" he said as he smirked and walked off.

"So see, you have your own mission, too, Street!" she said sarcastically. "To win as the leader of *the best break dance group ever* from around here, while simple old me, who doesn't even know how to dance, just wants to win souls for Christ."

"What were you two talking about?" I asked, a bit upset, and she realized all that she just said fell on deaf ears.

"What? You mean your friend? We were just making arrangements for me to stop by his house this weekend." "What!" she again asked when she saw the stone look on my face. "He says he lives right across the street from you, Street. And you and the rest of your friends are free to join us."

Imagine the sounds of crickets besides passing cars, as I gazed into her innocence, yet vulnerability to unsuspecting trouble as a missionary. Because as much as we were cool, I knew the dark hypocritical side that Assad had.

"Okay, I have to go," she then said with a heavy sigh as she attempted to walk off.

I stopped her by gently holding her hand. I've known her over a month and this was the first time we ever touched that long. Surprisingly, she didn't withdraw it but instead squeezed my palm.

"Seriously, Street," she said, "you don't even know my last name yet here you are judging me."

"Luckrisha?" I jokingly replied.

She did a poor job of holding back her laughter, and then she gave me a beautiful look that I would never forget.

"Respectfully, I don't care how popular you are, Street, or what your story is." She sighed. "You are no stranger to God. Your eyes tell a story! God knows you by name and He is saying (searching for words) I don't know what He is saying, but He has drawn me to you for whatever reason." She smiled. "Unlike all these other men I have encountered since I have been doing this street crusade with my colleagues, you, of all the persons, I couldn't have predicted. Don't look at me like a piece of meat anymore," she preached as she released my hand. You have a good soul, but I don't want you to be a distraction," she ended, as it seemed like she was getting a bit emotional as she walked away.

And then I opened my mouth and blew it.

"Are you done?" I scoffed from all the mush that just came from her mouth.

"Seriously!" she said in almost disbelief, let out a heavy sigh, gave me a look of pity, and walked off.

Much to the hilarity of my crew, I spent almost a minute or so keeping up with her pace behind her apologizing as she briskly walked away, ignoring me.

I was futile in trying everything to have her stop and talk to me, so I just gave up and started expressing what I was seeing looking at her body as she stormed off.

"Fine, I'm not gonna chase after you. But go, girl. Work that body," I teased, slowing my pace behind her. "Oh my gosh, look at that walk. Look at those cheeks, and I am not talking about your face. Hmmm, work it, girl. Damn, you're a 10! Oh, and you're not just a piece of meat to me. You're a whole (thinking) damn animal, but which animal? 'Cuz I can't say cow (thinking), a horse, a kangaroo…umm, a goat?"

Eureka!

She finally stopped, turned around, and with the worst display ever of holding back the laughter and still pretending to be mad, she screamed, "Okay, mister, I see you have jokes, but just leave me alone! Or I'm going to scream."

"Yeah, scream my name while I bust a move for you." I smiled before I dropped to a grass covered lawn on the sidewalk and started doing some basic break dance moves.

She was surprised by my actions as if to say "Is this guy for real?" looked around, and covered her face out of humorous embarrassment with both hands.

"Street! Street!' she screamed, laughing. "Stop! What are you doing? I said stop! You're embarrassing us!"

I stood up and adjusted my attire.

"I'm embarrassing *us?*' Now there's an us? Never got that memo." I smiled.

"What's wrong with you?" she asked, still holding back that outburst of laughter. "Look, you came to the crusade." She sighed. "Things didn't go as you expected because my dad disappointed you. It was nice knowing you," she said with a sad smile. "I like you, which I shouldn't, because now you have become a distraction, and I can't do this."

"Did you just say you like me?" I blushed. But her blush after that question was worst.

Not sure what the hell I was thinking in that moment, but I unbuckled my prized silver break dance championship stud belt from my pants and handed it to her.

"What's this?" she asked.

"What matters most to me. We won this belt in the break-dance championship final last November. It made us Street Boys legends and me the king of break dancing in our community. I am *lending* it to you for a bit. It might sound corny but…I want you to hang this belt somewhere in your bedroom so whatever turn you make you will see it as a reminder of, us, so that you won't get me out of your head until you finally say yes, to our first date," I said, as I gazed into her beautiful eyes. "I am not as bad and as lost as you think I am," I added during an impromptu moment of reflection.

Silence.

"Who are you?" she asked with smiling, weary, searching eyes.

Silence.

"I'm just a nobody from nowhere. I like you. You live walking distance from me. We'll talk. I have to go home and do some yard work before mom returns from overseas," I said as I walked off.

I turned around to give my crew the "Let's go!" hand signal, but they were nowhere in sight. No surprise as I knew they were all inside again, watching TV or smoking weed in the backyard.

"Street! Street, wait," she beckoned.

I stopped and turned around with a soft smile, wondering, *Does she like me, or as a single guy, is this the best you can do to win her over?*

"Why are you doing this to me? You seem like a great guy but… but I dunno what's going on here." She exhaled heavily. "I know you are the leader of the Street Boys, the most popular break dance crew around here, but that doesn't matter to me. I don't know you. I don't even know your real name, yet you're giving me this 'prized' possession to do what with it? With this belt! It's just a belt to me, but for you, it might mean so much more. I'm sorry."

Silence.

I kind of had a moment when I compared my *prized* break dance championship belt to an engagement ring. How? Because most women become excited and are as happy as can be, when they are proposed to and have that engagement ring slipped on their finger. It's priceless to them and they happily show it off to everyone. But then if things don't work out and the relationship ends even before the marriage, that prized engagement ring just becomes a stupid ole piece of jewelry, with no significance and with just a story behind it that you would rather not tell. True?

I let out a sad sigh as she tried to hand it back to me, but I refused. I paused for a moment and then slowly walked back to her.

"It's more than just a *belt*. It's to remember me, *us*, regardless of what happens after today." I sighed.

She gave me a warm, curious smile, and for the first time, I sensed that she was relaxed enough to not preach at me but instead have a casual conversation.

"Just make sure you don't lose it. You want to know my real name and what I am and why?" I started happily, before I was interrupted by some guys from across the street that was walking by.

Yup, they were a rival break dance group of around five guys who were feared in the community because they were more infamous for their gang activities than their break dancing.

The Other Side of the Main

Call it ridiculous, but after many street fights with these thugs, we made a simple truce that they would walk on one side of the main, and we would walk on the other, so as to avert a physical in-your-face confrontation.

"Michelle!" one of them shouted. "What did we tell you about walking on that dead beat side of the street? And what you doing talking with that dead-beat punk Street?"

Yep, they knew of us Street Boys, too, because we competed with them in contests many times before.

"You know these punks?" I questioned under hushed breath.

"Yes, it's fine. They live across the street from me and claim they are my protector," she replied somewhat nervously.

"I'm talking to you, girl," he shouted as they now all stopped, provokingly waiting for her to respond.

Their leader, Willy, fresh out of a one-year stay at a juvenile detention center, puffed on his joint and didn't say a word or even looked our way.

"Is that punk ass bothering you?" another asked as he crossed over to our side of the street. "'Cuz just say the word, and the rest is bloodshed!"

"Get back over to your side of the street, bitch," I said to him, "or there *will* be bloodshed."

I held my ground, felt for my switchblade in my pocket, turned it upside down, and slid it open.

She noticed.

"No, stop. You guys just stop! I was just leaving," she beckoned as she tried to diffuse the situation by crossing back over to the other side of the street with him. "I'll see you around," she said with a parting glance.

"Damn, girl. From Bible to the silver break dance championship stud belts? This is a real trophy right here," the leader of their group said as he reached for the belt I gave her. She reluctantly showed it to him as they continued an inaudible conversation as they all walked off.

They all knew the importance of that belt because they were one of the groups we knocked out to win it. But I was outnumbered without my crew, so I stood my ground and just left it alone. One of them spat in my direction as a taunt as two of them had small talk gestures with her, while Willy, his brother, and the others admired my belt.

I was fuming because they just walked off with my trophy—no, not Michelle! My belt!

I looked down my friend's house and wanted to run and summon my crew, but I knew that it would cause a street brawl, but I didn't want to start that and ruin the adoration she now showed signs of having for me. It then became obvious that these punks were looking for trouble as they were all high school dropouts with parents who weren't there or didn't care, so the street life was all they knew.

I knew that life, too, and knew that the minute you back down like I just did you are deemed a coward. I wasn't sure what Michelle was thinking of me now. I wasn't sure how my crew would react when I tell them, but I stood there for what seemed like an eternity weighing the good versus evil options that were now swirling through my head.

What do you do when the one thing that matters most, is taken away from you?

Sigh.

CHAPTER 2

TROUBLE LOOMS

A few nights later, after practicing on our street corner, the rest of my crew were still fuming about the incident after I had finally told them.

"Yow bro, that wasn't just your belt that was *our* belt, and it wasn't just a 'belt' it was the Holy Grail of winning that last break dance competition!" Stoke vented as he took a chug from his beer.

"I still can't believe you didn't come get us. You knew we were out back smoking."

I had no response as I took my t-shirt off, wiped the sweat from my face and chest with it, sat and popped a beer.

"That belt was name brand custom made bro!" Stoke continued to fume. "It's like a boxer who wins the Golden Gloves Award or... or a footballer who wins the Golden Boots for Player of the Year. You think that was just another pair of gloves or boots to them, bro? We were break dance *Champions of the Year!* And they took our trophy... They took our belt. They took our pride!"

I had no words, as everything he was venting was true.

"I told you, you shouldn't be wearing it so often out and about, Street, only on special occasions. And let me lock it away in my dad's safe otherwise," Bob chided. "That was *my pride!*"

"That was my *respect!*" Assad fumed.

"That was my *glory*, which made everyone in our community respect us and all the girls wanna date us." Stoke sighed. "That silver belt got us into the break dance Champion of Champions golden belt finals coming up, to win the golden belt." He sighed. "And if we do win it…"

"*When* we do win it—if we all stick to our dance routine," I corrected him while eyeing Assad, who noticed. "I'll get it back!" I said then took a gulp from my beer.

"You better!" Stoke said as he lit a cigarette.

"Damn skippy! We got this. I got this, because I could sure use my cut a that $10,000 up for grabs to pay off Mr. James for his old car so at least I will hold the distinct honor of being the first dude in the Street Boys to say to my girl, 'No, no, babe, we don't have to take the bus to meet up no more. I'll come pick you up,'" Assad said as he and Stoke chuckled and high-fived each other. "And then I'm gonna get that car turbo charged and just…and just live life in the fast lane."

"I be riding shotgun." Stoke laughed as they both looked at me, as since I was the group's leader, I ride shotgun if not driving. But my mind was elsewhere, so I just smiled and shook my head.

"I'll be going on a shopping spree with my cut of that cash, yo—name brand *everything*!" Stoke said. "Plus, I wanna get that new mega boom box for myself that we all be drooling at in that store."

"Cuz Street's shit looks like it ain't gonna last much longer." He laughed to the amusement of everyone. "Half the lights on this boom box don't even blink to the beat no more."

"Not to mention tape deck A, which we have to slap sometimes to play," Assad upped the laughter.

"That's because a month ago someone was doing the hand spin move and kicked it over!" I scoffed with a grin as I glanced at Stoke. "Maybe I should take a cut out of your cut when we win to fix it since you getting your own brand-new boom box." I smiled as I spread my hands wide to emphasize the size of the boom box.

Bob was distracted by the postman that pulled up at his gate a few houses down.

"I'll be back, yo!" he said as he got up and jogged off to meet him.

"Yeah, yeah! That fool still waiting to see if he got that scholarship," Assad puffed as he put out his cigarette and lit another one and stood up. "Whose turn is it to get some beers, yo? And what we gonna do about getting our belt back?"

"Yo, I got it! I got it!" Bob screamed with delight as he power-walked back to us. "I was accepted! I finally got the scholarship, bro." He hugged me, as I was the only other person in the group that was rooting for him to get it.

"Dear, Mister..." he started as he read the letter aloud to us. When he was done, he was so excited he started to break dance. "Yo, I catch you guys later. I gotta tell this to Grandma!" He ran to his house.

The postman stopped, dabbed us, and handed Assad and me our respective letters then rode off on his bicycle.

"Yup! More bills," scoffed Assad as he sifted through his letters. "I never wanna deal with all this shit. Can't wait to enroll in the army and live on base for the rest of my life."

I had a "Still nothing yet?" look on my face as it was almost the end of the month and my mom—who worked four months in Cayman as a CNA, returned to Jamaica only for a week, then was gone for another four months, and so on—had still not sent the money for us to cover the bills yet.

Who do you blame when the bills are due and you can't afford to pay them? The person you rely on for being late in sending you some cash, the government for not giving you enough in their aid assistance, or yourself, for even as an adult, for whatever reason, you are unable to sustain yourself financially?

The Street Boys

My older brother and I lived together, although he was hardly ever there because he spent half the time staying at his girlfriend's house, on campus, or riding cross country with his huge bicycle crew of cyclists when he wasn't too busy at the Tech University he attended.

He would stop by a few times a week out of the blue to stay the night with his girlfriend, who liked break dancing and came to most of our competitions. But I scoffed each time they told me they were staying the night, because I'd spend most of the night in my room, blasting my boom box to avoid hearing their corny love making sounds.

But other times he would ride in with his crew of almost thirty cyclists. There would be bicycles laying everywhere as they would just ride up, pop his girlfriends car trunk which was stacked high with alcoholic beverages, have a few drinks and get some music going as they just chilled and chatted. Sometimes we would even do cameo performances for them, until one by one, they all eventually left.

That was my living arrangement, but I never complained because most times I had the house to myself. And I enjoyed that because let's just say there were other fun stuff that the Street Boys would indulge in at my crib, like movie nights or house parties, like that night when I got laid by the devil in the red dress. Remember her?

Bob lived alone with his sickly grandma. His parents lived a few hours away. Insurance sales reps. Always on the road and would just check in for a couple days, or sometimes just for a couple hours at a time. They had money, so this was their second house. But instead of having his grandma put in a home for the elderly or a stranger as a live-in caregiver with her, Bob volunteered to take care of grandma. Oh, and yes, his parents okayed it for his girlfriend to come over and stay the night, day, week—anytime. So he and his girl were quite comfortable being his grandma's caregiver. He was the brains of the Street Boys with his genius ideas but was also the most reserved.

Assad was the hot headed trigger man in our dance group; always getting suspended from school for fighting, always trying to start a fight when the decision in a dance contest didn't go our way. He was from a strict military family. His mom worked at our national army headquarters, who was pushing for him to get enrolled, and his, no-nonsense, kick ass dad was again deployed somewhere overseas. His dad was very strict on him, so Assad would be the "recruiting disciplined soldier" whenever dad returned, but the badass gangster when he was redeployed.

Stoke was in *chill mode* since we all met up and became friends a couple years back when us four realized we were "loners." Chill mode as in he was waiting for his filing papers to be finalized so he could migrate to the United States. As such, he didn't care for work, school or anything, as his parents in the United States sent him whatever he wanted, plus the aunt he lived with also spoilt him. Like Assad, all he cared about was the respect from the street and the attention from the ladies. Shockingly, while they were both players, Assad had no baby mamas, but Stoke, at seventeen plus, already had four—yes, four!

We were united by music, as I would always bring my boom box out on my front porch and blast it. One by one, as they passed by, they would stop, and we chit chat until we became friends. Over time, we would get together and compete in dance against each other until I came up with the idea that instead of competing against each other, we should unite and form a break dance group. We all agreed unanimously and being the leader of the crew, we decided to name ourselves Street Boys. We then started entering break dance competitions. We lost many but won most, including the recent grand final for the coveted silver break dance championship belt.

So that was over two years ago as I had a flashback about our beginning, but with us all heading in different directions once adulthood crept in, the days of the Street Boys as a break dance group were numbered.

What I didn't know was that while the clock was ticking until we went our separate ways to pursue our individual careers, it was only going to be a matter of weeks before we transformed from a break dance group to a violent street gang that would see sweat from dancing replaced with blood from fighting.

My beloved boom box that we played around the clock daily would start growing cobwebs from a lack of use, and girls that chased us for sex would be replaced by our rival enemies that chased us for blood.

CHAPTER 3

THE STREET BOYS: FROM GLORY TO GORY

It was a nice day out, and we just finished practicing on the sidewalk.

"Let's go. It's my turn to get beer...again, every other day," Stoke said with a smirk.

"Let me go put this down," I said as I retrieved my boom box and put it inside my house, while Assad folded up our cardboard "dance floor," which was mostly kept over his house.

By the time I came back out, they were halfway up the street, so I ran to catch up.

"So...what we gonna do about our championship belt, Street? We need that shit back. We earned it. These punks declared war by stealing it," Stoke asked.

"She said she'd get it back and return it today," I replied.

"And if she doesn't?" he doubted.

"Bloodshed!" Assad whispered with empty eyes. "News travels fast around here, so people been talking and teasing us about it already. I know you dig that girl, but she left you for them losers, bro! She coming by my house tomorrow to do 'Bible study,'" he said with a smirk on his face while gesturing with his fingers. "So if you don't get even, I will."

It didn't click what Assad meant at the time until the next evening.

Bible Study

It was around midafternoon, and I had just finished mowing the front lawn and was now pruning our flowers garden, as my brother ordered because he was bringing his girlfriend over for the night. It was her birthday, so he wanted everything to look beautiful and perfect from the moment they stepped through the gate. I didn't complain about him bossing me to do so however, because, he did as all cool big brothers did; he paid me.

Assad, Stoke, and Bob were over Assad's house juggling a soccer ball in his driveway.

I was suddenly interrupted by someone who I had not seen in like forever.

"Hi, Street!"

I looked up, and it was Michelle standing at my gate.

She looked stunning, and I was elated to see her, but still upset about the encounter with those thugs the last time I saw her, I shut my glee down and kept on pruning the garden.

"What?" she questioned when she realized my mood. "Say something," she begged as she squeezed on her pocketbook and Bible.

I didn't.

"Listen, I am sorry about yesterday, but those guys and I grew up together, not as friends, but just as neighbors. They respect me and my family because of my father being a pastor. These are very, very, very bad people, Street. I have seen some horrific things they did growing up. I was just trying to protect you."

What the what!

How embarrassing, I thought.

I chuckled, threw my clipper down, and slowly walked up to her.

"Protect me? Protect me!" I scoffed with disgust. "Sounds like you're saying I'm…I'm aah…a li'l pussy who couldn't defend myself against those assholes, who, by the way, I am not neighbors with or grew up with but know a thing or two about," I mocked. "Or are you saying Willy and his boys are just some badass from hell who me and my crew won't stand a chance against if things get ugly?"

She turned pale from concern.

"The latter." She then exhaled heavily. "Look, it's just four of *you*, but these are twenty to thirty guys, Street. They disgustingly brag about who went to jail for what and who served the longest time locked up," she scoffed. "They live in and out of jail and have no respect for authority or anyone."

"So while you say they have respect for your father, how come they have so much respect for you?" I asked, looking at her body up and down. "If these guys are such badasses, you would have been gang-raped by now. Or are you dating one of them?"

"I'm not! Never! Ever! It's because of Willy," she said as her body jerked from getting emotional upset.

My demeanor changed. "What about Willy?"

"I don't want to talk about it," she said, visibly upset as she clutched her Bible and pocketbook and started to walk away.

"Michelle. Michelle!" I snapped.

She stopped dead in her tracks. I opened my gate and walked a few paces to meet her, gently turned her around, and lifted her chin that was now buried in her chest.

I will never forget that look in her eyes as she stared into mine.

Although she held back the tears, all I saw was the face of a mighty woman of God whose faith in Him had been tested and whose eyes beseeched God to maintain His faith in her.

"What about you and Willy?"

She took a deep breath.

"I have not even told my father this as I don't want to start a riot between our families. But Willy always had a crush on me since I was in middle school, but he kept saying he was waiting for me to be *ripe for the picking* before he 'took me,'" she started. "He wasn't biding his time to take me, out of respect. He just didn't want to have another case added to his long list of cases by having sex with a minor or, in my case, rape of a minor. I detest him, but he always warned that he was going to have me by any means necessary. That's why I never travel without this," she said as she half opened her pocketbook to show me a can of mace.

Silence.

"He warned his *boys* not to touch me but instead be my protector as he was in and out of juvenile centers for the last three or four years, serving at least a year at a time and only out for a couple weeks at a time because he just couldn't stay out of trouble," she continued. "They obeyed, because the last time he went back to jail a year ago was because he almost beat one of his...his boys to death because he just...he simply made a cat call at me as I walked past their house. And now...and...and now he's back out, I hear for good this time, and ironically, out early because of good behavior."

"Has he touched you?"

"No!"

"Has he kissed you?"

"No!" she squirmed.

"Has..." I sighed. "Has he... Has he raped...?"

"No!" she said and then became stoned-faced. "I would die first before I allow him to even touch me with a long stick."

"Because your adversary, the devil, as a roaring lion, walketh about, *seeking whom he may devour.* That's Willy and his men." She sighed. "But the Bible also says: 'Be sober, be vigilant; God is with thee, his angels encampeth around thee.' So I fret not, Street. I worry not because even in the midst of trouble, God, my omnipotent protector, will always walk with me!"

"First Peter 5, verse 8," I exhaled.

She looked surprised.

"You know your Bible. Impressive." She forced a sad smile. "So you are a church boy!"

I just replied with a gentle smile. She smiled back.

"Where is she?" She then sighed to herself, looking down the street.

"Who?"

"The other missionary. We do weekly visits for people in this area, especially the elderly from church that request it. Let me go see your friend, Ass...assa?" she said as she looked at her watch.

"You got the first name right." I smiled. "He's right there." I pointed to his house across the street. "And it's Assad."

"We're running behind schedule," she said in reference to her other missionary that she always travelled with. This time, they split up to save time, but now they were nowhere in sight. "Can you come with me? He's kinda creepy."

"Really! Me? I though you just said you had your omnipotent protector."

"Really, Street." She sighed as she slowly walked away disappointed over to his house. "Hey, if you see her, can you tell her I'm over here? Short chubby old lady, glasses, with the biggest Bible you've ever seen." She smiled.

I noticed her handbag.

"By the way," I shouted, "come gimme my belt before Stoke takes it from you and it's gonna be hell to get it back from him," I beckoned.

She stopped, slowly turned around, walked back over to me, had a long pause, and took a deep breath.

"Okay, so…so I kept leaving my room going to my gate looking and looking and looking out for them last night, but there was none a them hanging out at his house."

"What are you saying?"

Heavy exhalation from her.

"I don't have it!"

I was about to snap until she calmed me.

"But listen, hey, Street! Listen. Please. I will look out for them again tonight. You will get it *tonight*! And…and you can come pick it up yourself."

I gave her a hesitant look.

"You say you know my street? I live at number 33. Lime-green house with a big mango tree in the front lawn. It's right on the corner. You can't miss it. I'll tell my dad you're coming. But come *alone* around six to seven because if Willy and his boys are there and they see you guys, there might be trouble because, yes, I know about you boys and your boundaries."

Damn. Did she just invite me over? I blushed, suddenly forgetting everything about my belt.

"Okay, okay. I'll be there…*alone*," I flirted.

34

She gave me a "Just drop it already" look and headed over to Assad, glancing back at me after ever few steps to ensure that I am or would be there for her, if needed.

Have you ever set out on a task or journey alone, but never felt alone because you knew that there was someone on speed dial that would be there for you, if you needed them?

It's a blessing not to be taken for granted to have an emergency contact because countless people, while being processed with paperwork during some situations and asked for their emergency contact, sadly said they had no name to give or didn't fill in that section on the paperwork because they were all alone in this world, because all their emergency contacts had either left them for dead or, just over time, moved on without a trace from their contact list.

Have you ever been there, where you didn't have an emergency contact?

Sigh.

"Hey, Michelle! Tell them boys I'll be over there in a minute. Just let me tidy up here real quick." I smiled in assurance that I got her back in case Assad tries anything stupid.

She smiled back at my assurance.

My boys all met her at the gate and let her in.

I had never packed away gardening equipment so fast in my life. Not for the fact that my brother would be satisfied and maybe even pay me more, but for the fact that my now public crush, Michelle, actually invited me over.

The Lions' Den

In less than a few minutes, I was all done. I took a quick shower, dressed, and ran over, stopping only to look up and down the street for her other missionary. No sign. Oh well.

As I entered Assad's yard, Stoke and Bob were still drinking and smoking while juggling a soccer ball in his driveway. But there was no sign of Michelle or Assad.

"Yo, where they at?" My adrenaline immediately started pumping.

"Assad said he would rather have a quiet sit-down with her solo, so we don't make a mockery of him, Mr. Tough Guy, so they in the living room." Stoke played it down. "She invited us to join them, too, but…really, dude," he scoffed. "Where's the belt?"

"She didn't get it, but I'm going by her house tonight to pick it up."

"What? Double what, because going to pick it up is one thing, but you gonna be on Willy's turf, bro!" Stoke pleaded.

"We'll roll with you. And if it makes you feel any better, go check on them," Bob dabbed as he gave me a puff from his cigarette.

"She wants me to come alone." I exhaled smoke. "So I will," I said as I gave a suspicious gaze at Assad's house.

"Chill, man. I know she's your crush, but Assad is like family. He would never violate." Stoke again played it down in noticing my gaze—until he heard it too.

It sounded like a woman ordering someone on top her voice to stop and to let her go!

I stormed at the front door and banged on it and then shoved it open, only to see Assad trying to pull Michelle into his bedroom while she vigorously resisted.

What the what!

"Yo! Assad!" I screamed.

He promptly let her go.

She ran to me, hugged me with trembling arms for a bit. Still shaken, she then brushed Stoke and Bob aside, who followed behind me, and ran out from his yard.

"Hey! Michelle!" I screamed.

She never looked back but just power-walked, crying while hugging herself, until she took a corner and was out of sight.

We all looked at Assad with shock, but he was so sprung out on weed that he just gave a giggly "What?"

"What? What!" I fumed. "What the hell was that about?"

He made a drunken burp, searched around a bit for his beer, and took a gulp. "Yo, yo, listen, Street. Listen, *bro*." He tried to compose himself. "There is…there was nothing to it, man. She came over, I asked her if she gave you the belt, and she said no!" he continued as he took another gulp from his beer. "So I got mad and didn't want to do *Bible study* anymore," he mocked with his fingers. "I wanted to give her a tour of my house, starting with my bedroom."

I charged at him. Bob and Stoke restrained me and pulled me outside as he and I cussed back and forth.

"That's it, you rapist! You are done! You are officially out of the Street Boys!" I snapped.

But, oh snap, Street Boys were all he got; we were his life. So the next thing I knew was hearing him charging at me and shoving me from behind.

"What you just say, church boy?" he fumed. "We gangbang bitches all the time, and they never complain because we are the Street Boys! So what the hell is your problem, Street?"

Bob was restraining me, but I wrestled him away, took an angry breath, and stormed over so close to him that I realized he had fresh scratch marks on his face, as if she was desperately trying to fight him off.

Heavy exhalation. "I ain't no church boy!" I said, staring him straight in the eyes. "Yeah, we do lots of bad shit on my watch—gang-banging, shoplifting, street brawls. But *rape* was—and will *never*—be on my résumé. You violated us…me! You're out!"

For a split second, it was as if his whole future flashed before his eyes.

"Nooo!" he exploded in a thunderous tone as he grabbed me by my shirt, and we started fighting.

We crashed to the ground, wrestled, and traded some blows.

The Street Boys had always had disagreements over the years, and we agreed on a policy to, as a last resort, fist fight any disparity, with the winner having the final say. However, when Stoke and Bob saw that the fight was growing intensely violent and getting bloody, they rushed in and wrestled us apart.

So no winner, but as leader, I still had the final say.

"You're done!" I panted and spat blood, as Bob restrained me.

"Street, stop!" Bob pleaded. "Assad! Why don't we all just take a timeout, yeah? We do this all the time to settle our differences, so what the hell's up with all this rage today?"

"Why don't you ask church boy love here?" Assad mocked me as he spat blood from his mouth also. "Seems like that bitch Michelle has him love sprung."

I charged at him again but was restrained.

He shrugged Stoke away to let him go, and then he entered his house. Moments later, he stormed out with Michelle's belongings and threw them at my feet. I picked them up, and surprisingly, the mace fell out.

"Here! Your bitch left her shit!" he growled. "And you know what, Street?" He paused and exhaled heavily. "I *am* done! To hell with this! To hell with y'all. To hell with the Street Boys!" He grabbed our cardboard dance floor and sailed it on the sidewalk, then stormed inside and slammed the door. The guys checked if I was okay. I assured them and ran to the street corner to return her stuff, but Michelle was nowhere in sight. I walked back past them to my house, no words exchanged, leaving Bob and Stoke scratching their heads as to what the heck just happened.

Back home, I dropped her stuff on the living room sofa, went to the bathroom, realized I had a bloody nose and lip. I flushed my face with water, took off my ripped T-shirt, and just stared at myself in the bathroom mirror for what seemed like an eternity.

I let out a heavy exhalation, as I wasn't sure what to say to myself. Yes, I always speak to myself in the mirror or shower, especially before a dance competition, but I just kept on staring as something was amiss with my usually happy routine lifestyle. I felt terrible that I was about to lose a best friend, Assad. But then my mind flashed on Michelle, and I wanted to kick his ass all over again.

Trying to shrug off the feeling, I showered, grabbed a beer and some chips, slumped in the sofa, and turned on my television. The news was on.

I was about to quickly change the channel but paused, realizing it was *safe* to watch the news.

Don't pick your brain in what I meant by that; you will get your answer later.

There was boring local news on, so I leaned over to the other side of the sofa to get the remote on the side table to put some music on, and my eyes locked in on Michelle's Bible and pocketbook.

I retreated and, for whatever reason, stared at the Bible.

"I remember when I used to read you daily," I whispered to myself, "for inspiration, guidance, answers, assurance; everything. But…but now you are no longer a Bible. You're just another book."

I took up her Bible and just started fanning through the pages over and over with an empty disconcerting feeling until her book marker fell out along with a piece of paper from a notepad folded in half.

I wasn't sure if it was her grocery list or just notes from church, but I was curious to find out. I stuck the bookmarker back in between the pages, and as much as I was home alone, I literally looked around the room to see if anyone was watching, and then slowly picked up the piece of paper that had notes written on it.

Until…

"Yo, Street!" someone shouted from outside.

I freaked, dropped it, and sat up straight.

"Street! It's Stoke!" He knocked on the door.

I exhaled and opened the door. Bob and Stoke came to check in on me.

"You all right, man?" Bob checked.

"Yeah," I lied, as mentally I was not, with all these recent occurrences.

"He's okay. He's calm now," Stoke reported on Assad.

"Cool." I sighed without a care. "Hey, my brother and his girl are coming over for the night, so I'm trying to get this house in order."

"Need some help?" Bob offered.

"Nah. I got this. Hey, you know the drill. See you guys on the Main tomorrow… Oh and tell Assad, *Street* said to stay away," I ordered, as we dabbed and then closed the door.

I sat back down, lit a cigarette, and chocked on it as I took a chug from my beer. I then took up Michelle's note from the floor and smiled at some of her silly doodles on the back. Yup! I guessed even she thought her preacher father was boring also. But when I opened it, she had a list of names under a heading: "Special People Prayer List."

My eyes scrolled down, and her dad was the first. Other names followed, but one name made the cigarette almost fall from my mouth: "Street!"

Out of the ten or so names, my name was the most recent added, and even in a different color ink, with "Street Boys" in brackets.

I was flabbergasted! No offense, but I was not amazed that she wanted to pray for me but that she labeled me...*special!*

I was tempted to go through her pocketbook to see what church girls carried, unlike typical women who traveled with makeup, mace, condoms, etc., but I felt like I won the lottery, so I left it alone!

Date Night or Fright Night?

"Michelle!" I called from her gate for like the umpteenth time.

I was at her house at around seven as she told me. I wanted to make it quick as I was on Willy's territory, which placed me in the lion's den asking for trouble. So I just wanted to apologize for Assad's behavior, return her stuff, get my belt, and be gone.

"Who's that?" a male voice barked from her front door.

"Hi, good evening, sir. It's Street. I'm here to see Michelle," I said in the fakest, most gentle way ever.

"Michelle!" he barked. "There's a Street standing outside on the street, asking for you."

I heard her voice telling him it was okay and that I was expected. I then heard him remind her that no boys were invited beyond his gate, and then he reentered the house. She slowly walked down the driveway with arms folded. As much as she seemed upset, all I saw was super sexy as she slowly walked to meet me in leggings and T-shirt, with a faint smile, though her eyes were sad.

"That was my dad." She exhaled as we both gazed into each other's eyes for what seemed like forever.

"You okay?"

"I'm fine," she assured me.

"Hey, I apologize for his—" I started before she interrupted.

"Shhh," she hushed. "Never apologize for another man's sin."

"Are you sure you're okay?" I again asked.

She gave a weary chuckle, almost in recollection of how he tried to force himself on her.

"Today wasn't the first or second or third…or fourth time this has happened to me since I became a missionary," she said, stone-faced. "But my God has never left me nor forsaken me, and that's why I am still a virgin."

She said a few more words, but my mind drifted to drown out her words, as all I kept hearing her saying was "I am still a virgin."

"Street. Street!" she snapped.

"Yeah? Yes."

"I said, is that my stuff you have there? I left them at his house."

"Oh yeah. Here." I handed them to her.

Her hands touched mine, and I held them for a bit, gave them a quick stroke, and then handed her stuff over. She made a quick check to see if she was missing anything.

"I let my guard down because I trusted your friends," she said as she checked on her mace. "Lesson learned! Did you go through my pocketbook?" she asked as she checked.

"Really? No!" I assured her while praying she didn't ask if I went through her Bible.

She didn't.

Phew!

"You got my belt?"

"He's not here yet. They live over that house." She pointed.

"*They*, as in Willy?"

"Yes, plus, his little brother. You can know when he's home because that's where the rest of his friends converge."

I knew Willy lived on this street but didn't know which house, as it was forbidden territory, so us Street Boys hardly ever trespassed.

I took a visual photo of the house and had a bittersweet feeling, as here I was across from my enemy's gate yet standing at Michelle's.

"I shouldn't be here." I sighed as a warning to myself. "I should go. Bring the belt tomorrow."

"Street, stop," she said comfortingly. "Stop being so paranoid, okay. I don't know what's going on with you two groups—gangs, whatever you call yourselves—and the boundaries and streets that you shouldn't cross, but all this is just teenage nonsense to me."

"Long story that I don't want to get into," I said, wanting to drop the subject, as I scoffed at her labeling our beef as "teenage nonsense."

We changed the subject. All this time, I was looking over my shoulder. While I knew I was asking for trouble by being here, I wanted to be here with her. She accepted the fact that Assad was a jerk and was comforted that I expelled him from Street Boys and severed friendship.

Minutes flew by as we small-talked while occasionally being interrupted by her father coming out by the door to ask "Where are my notes for tomorrow's service?" which she apparently helped him to prepare or "Did you iron my shirt?" or some other blah, blah, blah.

"I never knew my father." I sighed with a smile.

"I'm sorry to hear that."

"Don't be. I'm over it."

And then as the minutes went by, it changed to small talk.

"So let's cut to the chase. You have a boyfriend?" I asked.

"No!" she asserted. "You?"

"No! I don't have a boyfriend," I joked.

She gently laughed. "So what's your story?" she asked.

"I have an on-again, off-again girlfriend, who just thinks I'm a womanizer because of all the girls that chase us Street Boys. Now we're off *again*—for good this time."

"Are you a player?"

"I was. Now I'm just trying to tame myself by finding that one good girl to settle with. I think I've finally found her," I confessed with a hinting stare into her eyes. "Your turn…"

I was hoping for a blush, but she just gave me a warm stare. "I was dating this guy at church. He's from a rich family, and I soon found out he is spoiled and cocky, so I walked away. Not my type."

"You must have a long list of guys waiting to date you in that waiting room. Just look at you. You're stunning!" I stripped her with my eyes.

"Standing room only in that room." She smiled. "Call me queer, but I don't see the physical in me. I see the spiritual, because I could meet in a car accident tomorrow and lose a limb or an eye or be burnt in a fire and get disfigured and then what? Would you still find me… stunning?"

I didn't see that coming, so I had no response, because she made a great point. Only the blind would not be swayed by those eventualities, if you were attracted by physical beauty.

"Why did you lose your faith?" she then abruptly asked, changing the subject.

"What?"

"You heard me. I sense that you are no stranger to God. So if we are having a moment here, again, tell me, why did you lose your faith?" she gently persisted.

I didn't want to go there, and I looked up and down the street for any sign of trouble to leave, but I just couldn't—or more like, I didn't want to. I recollected, felt a bit empty, and then spoke.

"Homer. He was my best friend from childhood. He grew up in the church. He was such a devoted Christian. He became a deacon, then junior pastor, and then dragged me into church. I was reluctant at first but then loved it, got converted, and was living for Christ. His to-be fiancée, Amy, came down with a strange illness that doctors couldn't figure out. She was his world. She became so sick she was hospitalized for weeks," I spoke dryly with poignant memories. "As a church group, we prayed and fasted and prayed and prayed…and prayed to God, forever, for her recovery. Being a newborn Christian, I even kinda played my test game and asked God to prove His love and existence by healing her." I paused. "But she died. Homer was devastated. He stepped down as a junior pastor and migrated to England. This was about two years plus ago. I never heard from him again, and let's just say I never heard from God again. And I have just lost my way since."

Silence.

I thought I saw a tear in Michelle's eye as she listened attentively. But as soon as she was about to respond, something even more ominous caught my eye. Two cars with music blasting pulled up by Willy's gate.

Damn, it was him!

The Beat-Down

It was about ten of them, all smoking weed, drinking, and chatting until, even though it was dusk so a bit dark out, one of them noticed me—his wannabe gangster piece of shit little brother.

"Yo, bro! Who da hell is dat!" He pointed at me. "On *our* turf, talking to *your* girl!" he incited.

Willy grew so mad he took a final puff from his weed, handed it to one of his boys, and walked over to me. His entourage followed behind him with jeers and comments like "It's about to go down!"

For those of you who are not "street smart," that meant we were about to fight!

Michelle got scared.

"Get in the house!" I ordered.

She didn't obey out of concern for my safety.

"What you doing 'round these parts, dude? We have our boundaries. So if you asking for trouble, you just trespassed into it," he threatened.

"No trouble. I just came to get my belt back. One of your boys took it from her the other day." I backed down, gesturing at Michelle, who was clearly in fear about the confrontation.

"What belt you talking about, fool?" His li'l bro, about fifteen, ran up in my face, trying to play tough guy to Willy.

"Our championship belt, the one that you and your crew couldn't dance for shit to win!" I mocked.

He was about to sucker punch me, but Willy quickly restrained him.

"Chill, bro," he said as he nudged him aside.

"Willy, just give him back the belt, please. This is all uncalled for," Michelle pleaded as she exited her yard and came out to diffuse the situation.

He hugged her as if he owned her, just to mock me.

She cringed, but she allowed him to.

"How did he know where you live, you li'l devil? You finally 'ripe' now, so you inviting men over?" he snarled.

"No, she didn't." I tried to save her ass.

"I wasn't talking to you!" he snapped.

"Well, I'm talking to you, and I know where you live too!" I said as a warning, as I pointed at his house across the street.

"Yo, is that a threat, punk?" his brother stormed in again.

I glanced at his punk ass and gave him a "Really, bitch, just stay outa this" look.

"Listen, I just came to get the belt. Just give it to me, and I'll be outa here." I sighed.

Willy raised both his fists, showing his wrists.

"You mean this belt?" he then said in an evil tone.

His brother also raised both his fist, showing his wrists.

"We had a tug-of-war over it the other night, so to settle, we just decided to chop it up and turn your prized belt into wristbands instead," his brother mocked. "Cool, eh?"

What the what!

I couldn't believe they destroyed our belt, the Street Boys' silver championship belt, and made wristbands out of it as a ridicule. I grew so mad I lunged at his brother but was met with a punch from Willy, which sent me staggering backward.

Michelle screamed.

Willy shoved her aside and screamed that she should get in the house. She obeyed him and screamed for her father.

His brother lunged at me again, and I met him with a knee in his chest, which sent him slumping to the ground. Willy grew enraged and swung at me, but I ducked and met him with an uppercut.

Oh, snap, it was on now!

But then I remembered the golden rule of a street fight—which was, when outnumbered, as it was just me against ten or eleven of them, just stand down and take your ass whooping or make a run for it and live to fight another day. Because if you didn't and tried to be tough and fight back, you might not live to see another day.

"Look! I don't wanna fight, okay? You can have the belt," I tried to diffuse the situation. "I'm outa here."

Too late.

His brother got up and sucker punched me. He punched me a second and third time, and I just stood there with my arms at my side as I played by the golden rule of street fight when outnumbered.

"Fight bitch, fight!" he urged me to fight back.

"You hit like a bitch, and I don't hit girls." I coughed as I spat blood from my mouth.

"What you just called my brother?" Willy said as he lunged at me with a punch that caught me on the chin, as I didn't lean back fast enough to avoid it. I went crashing on my backside.

His brother charged at me again, but just then, Michelle and her dad, whom she ran to summon, came hurriedly walking from the house.

"What is going on here?" her dad snapped. "The cops are on their way! You all get away from my gate or plan to spend the night in jail because I can and will identify all of you!"

Willy froze, petrified. While at that point, he wanted to settle a score with me via fist fight, he knew that if he violated his probation, he would no longer be locked up in juvenile detention centers but instead would be looking at serving a very long prison term.

"Nothing, Mr. Preacher Man. We outa here!" He tried to downplay it. He looked at Michelle with disdain then signaled for the rest of the crew to retreat with him.

"This was round one! I'll be seeing you around," he said to me in a deadly tone, as one of his crew members gave him back his spliff and they walked away.

"Are you okay?" Michelle gasped when she saw my bloodied face, but her dad didn't give me a chance to answer.

"Get inside!" he ordered.

"But, Dad, he's—"

"I said get inside!" he snapped.

She started sobbing loudly and walked back up the driveway, with both hands covering her face, wiping the tears away as she maintained her concerned stare at me.

"Listen, young man—Street, or whatever your name is—you street thugs don't scare me! So if the cops don't lock your sorry asses away and let you rot in jail so our community can be free of this violence, then I will fast and pray for God to heap fire and brimstone on your damn heads until you burn and rot in hell. Stay away from my daughter!" he ordered.

"But, sir—" I tried to explain.

He didn't want to hear it.

"Go!" he again commanded. "And if you *ever* set foot at my gate again…" And then he walked away, shaking his head in anger at what the ominous outcome would be.

I heard the distant approach of sirens. He wasn't kidding; he did call the cops. I staggered off. A voice in my mind said, "Look over your shoulder." I did and noticed Willy pointing and directing some of his gang members in different directions on the block. Some of them were jumping into neighbors yards and running to the back. A few dogs started barking, and I even heard one female voice scream, "Get out of my yard!"

Being street-smart, it was then that I realized this night wasn't over; he and his thugs were trying to flank me as I left so they could finish their beat-down. I slowly walked around the corner so they could all see me *walking* away; but the minute I was out of sight, I took off running like a bolt of lightning. I ran the long way home because I didn't want to take the usual route for them to corner me.

I outsmarted them and finally got home. Although out of breath and still bleeding from my nose and mouth, I was glad that quick thinking made me dodge them and that I made it home safe. Sometimes, based on the situation, it was better to take the long way home. I could hear music and laughter as I slowly walked up to my front porch and slumped into a chair. My brother and girlfriend were home for the night.

He must have heard me slump and almost tumbled over with the chair, so he opened the door.

"You drunk this early, bro?" he questioned, as it was dark out so he couldn't see my face. He then turned the patio light on. "What the…" he gasped. "What happened?"

He knew I had been in street brawls before and at times never got him involved, so knew he wasn't going to get an answer. After asking a few more times and not getting any response, he dragged me up from the chair and pinned me against the wall.

His girlfriend ran out after hearing the commotion. "Oh my god, Street, what happened?" she escalated the situation.

I looked over at her, weary and lost. "Nice dress," I spoke emptily. "See, I kept my promise to you with the gardening today, bro. Plus, I made your favorite for dinner too. Surprise!" I continued lamely as a tear rolled from my eyes.

"Oh my god, should I call an ambulance?" she asked, now visibly shaken.

"No. He'll be all right. Get inside!" my brother ordered.

"Okay, but I'm a student nurse! Just let me take a look at his injuries," she pleaded, looking at my bloodied face and T-shirt.

"Okay, give us a minute," my brother complied.

"Okay. Let me go get my kit," she replied out of deep concern and then ran back inside.

"Who did this to you?"

I didn't reply.

He got even angrier and pressed me against the wall. "I said… who did this to you?"

I just let out a heavy exhalation while maintaining a vengeful, weary, teary-eyed stare into his eyes.

"I know you are a badass, but on my watch, Mom would kill me and then die, if anything bad was to ever happen to you," he gasped. "You're her world! And I've grown to accept the fact that you're her favorite son, whom she constantly begs me to watch over. If she was to just pop up tonight, as she always does to catch us off guard, and see you like this, I would have failed her in my promise to protect you. I would have failed myself! I would have failed you. So again, who did this?"

My brother had fire in his eyes, but he slowly released his grip. Silence.

"Who did this?" he softly exhaled, in revenge mode, pleading with me.

My mind flashed on the fight with Assad earlier, then on the possibility that I might never see Michelle again, and then on that beat-down by Willy and his gang—all in a matter of hours. Not to mention how I ran almost a quarter mile for my life just now. I was drained.

"Willy and his boys," I finally gasped.

My brother looked shocked. He had been in a fight with Willy once before over a break dance contest that we beat them at in the finals, and as usual, as sore losers, they started a brawl. He took a few heavy breaths.

"Let's go inside. Get cleaned up, and you tell me what the hell is going on."

I complied. I showered, got patched up by his girlfriend, had a beer, and told them everything.

"Come here. That wound is still bleeding," his girlfriend noticed as she rose from my brother's embrace and retrieved her first-aid kit.

The television was on; everyone was looking, but nobody was watching.

Haven't you ever just had the TV on but didn't care to watch?

I could tell my brother was fuming, and his girlfriend was beside herself. I sat on the floor back with shoulders between her legs as she dressed me.

"I thought you guys just danced, Street, and fights were far and few," she said as she removed the old bandage, cleaned the wound on my forehead again, and started to apply a better bandage. "What changed?"

I let out a heavy exhalation as I asked myself the same question. Then I answered, "Some people are just sore losers."

"You are so right. So many losers out there," she continued as she nursed me. "I used to be bullied back in nursing school by a bunch a losers in my class, all because I was an honor student and labeled as a prude. I thought being bullied was a way of life and accepted it, praying for the day that I finally graduate so I could be rid of them. But when I told your brother, he refused to accept it."

"Don't ever!" my brother, sitting across from us, playing with my Swiss blade, exhaled as he handed me his cigarette for me to take a puff, which I did and then handed it back to him.

"I still remember that Wednesday evening walking home from school in the rain, and these freaking bullies; about six or seven of them grabbed my umbrella away and started taunting me, until your brother and his friends unexpectedly rode up on their bicycles," she recalled. "He and his boys gave them a beat down so bad I had to beg him to stop. But they didn't, until campus security came driving up and eventually broke up the fight. From that day, the cops got involved, but no charges were filed, and I was never bullied again."

It soon became clear at the point she was trying to make.

"You guys compete every month, and I have been to all your break dance battles. And as much as you try to teach me break dance, I suck." She smiled. "I can count on one hand how many times you Street Boys lost in the past two years in countless competitions," she continued. "But you know why I love and admire you, Street, and the Street Boys? It's because every time you lost a battle, come next competition, you nailed it and won! And then went on a long winning streak after that."

"Because he knew I'd kick his ass if he didn't, 'cuz I bet big money on you guys," my brother added.

"You might have lost the battle tonight, but the war is not over," she said in a serious reflective tone, all done patching me up. "But the next time you see Willy and his boys," she continued as she held my face, turned it to hers, and looked me dead in the eyes, "Nail it! You hear me? Nail it!"

CHAPTER 4

DON'T WATCH THE NEWS

I slept until late the next day. My brother left a note, and he and his girlfriend were gone.

I did my morning routine and went to our friend's house on The Main to chill where I met up with Bob and Stoke.

They saw my bruises, so I told them everything too.

Bob was a bit scared at the escalating developments. He was timid as there was one street brawl a few months back at a dance contest out of town that we won, and like Willy's boys, the sore losers started a brawl. He got beat up bad. I met the same fate too a while back.

It was at that point that we accepted the fact that, even though us Street Boys just wanted to dance and not fight, that choice was not always left up to us.

Stoke swore revenge. Hmm, now I was thinking, *Maybe not revenge because I got beaten up but revenge because his beloved belt got chopped up.*

We were sitting on our usual fence, drinking and smoking and conversing, when a car pulled up. It was the promoter for the upcoming break dance finals competition.

"Hey, bro, you good? What the...?" He then gasped when I approached and he saw my black eye, plus the bandage on my forehead. "What happened?"

"You know what happened." I smiled. "Sore losers' brawl."

"Who did this, bro? Let me go break some bones for you, couz."

"No!" I smiled as we dabbed. "We got this."

"You sure you good, bro?"

"I'm good."

"You better be! 'Cuz you better bring it come next Saturday at the finals. People from all over the country gonna be there. Plus, it's gonna be televised."

"I know."

"Couz, who did this to you? Just give me a name and where to find them, and me and my boys will handle it," he pleaded in an angry, concerned tone, albeit in concern to ensure that we win so he could collect, not about my welfare.

He and his boys had jumped in at our defense at break dance brawl venues before and helped beat the crap out of our opponents, but I didn't want to escalate things.

"It's all good, boss. I'll let you know if things get worst, like that time in Portland." I calmed him down and reminded him with a grin.

"Yeah! We gave them a good ass beaten down," he recollected, rubbing his chin. "Okay, couz. Take care of yourself and get better. You look like you could use a drink," he said as he took a hundred dollars from his wallet and gave it to me. "My treat to you and the boys. See you at the finals next Saturday. Bring it!" he said as we dabbed and he drove off.

I went back to sit with my crew, and just as we were about to walk to the corner deli a half a block away to get some beers, I saw a group of about ten thugs hop off a bus about a block farther and started walking our way.

As they approached closer, I realized it was Willy's brother and some of his gang.

"What do we do?" Bob somewhat nervously asked.

"What we always do?" Stoke said as he put out his cigarette and stood up while gazing at them approaching from the other side of the street.

"Just let them be!" Bob tried to diffuse it. "It's three against one! We will live to fight another day."

"Don't start no shit. There'll be no shit," I said, reminding them of our code—that us Street Boys never started a fight first, but if they did, then it was on!

Stoke was fuming, and Bob was on guard. I was ready for whatever. But instead of minding their business, Willy's little brother started taunting us—well, more like taunting *me*—in telling the rest of the gang how he beat the crap out of me last night.

I tried to stay calm until he shouted something nasty. I shouted something even nastier back at him and gave him the finger. It made him snap and run across the street to attack me. It was then that Stoke got a closer look at the studded wristbands he cut up our championship belt to make and charged at him.

Oh, boy, here we go.

Heavy exhalation.

Fight

I beat him to it and met Willy's brother, who was distracted by Stoke, with a powerful blindsided elbow, which sent him crashing on his backside in the middle of the street.

The rest of the gang charged at us, and a street brawl was on!

Stoke gave one of the gang members a kick to the chest, which sent him flying in the street. Bob took out two guys with a sweeping karate kick. But then another jumped him from behind. I could hear the screeching of tires, as traffic was halted from us fighting in the middle of the street. We were outnumbered and getting a beat down, but at least three of the gang members were already lying semiconscious.

I was getting kicks from all sides as I kneeled on top of Willy's brother, pummeling his face with blows, as he lay in a state of unconsciousness, with blood bleeding from everywhere. I was eventually hauled off him by two of his gang members who came to his rescue, and the fighting continued.

I wish I could say we were winning, but we were outnumbered, weary, and losing until…

Amidst all the commotion, through my bloodied face and motorists pleading with us to stop, I saw a group of cyclists swerving through the now-halted traffic, racing toward us. It was my brother and about fifteen of his crew.

Without saying a word, they tossed their bikes aside and jumped into the fight.

It was a vicious beat-down for Willy's boys.

Within less than a minute, all of Willy's little brother and his gang were sprawled out in the street and sidewalk, bloodied and semiconscious. One was unconscious—Willy's little brother.

I staggered over to him, knelt on top of him, and remembering what he did to me the night before, just started raining powerful punches to his face until my brother eventually dragged me off him.

"He's out!" he gasped as sirens from cop cars in the distance approached. "Go home!" He dragged me to my feet. He summoned his boys to split. Stoke and Bob were also busted up, but I summoned them to split too.

As I staggered off, I looked back at Willy's brother sprawled out unconscious and bloodied in the middle of the street.

"Hey, bro," I said with a bloody smile to my brother as he was heading to his bicycle, "tell your girl, I nailed it!"

He just winked at me and ordered, "Go!"

As all three of us hugged and hurriedly staggered home laughing and commenting on what just went down.

Have you ever found yourself chuckling or even laughing during or after going through a bad situation because if you didn't laugh, you would probably end up crying so instinctively you chose to laugh?

Bob interrupted our celebration.

"Yo! We kicked ass just now, but you know Willy. This is not the end—this is just the beginning."

The laughter stopped. We were passing Assad's house when Stoke stopped and shouted his name a few times. He eventually came out. The look of shock was obvious on his face as he noticed our bloodied and bruised state.

"What the? What happened, yo?" he gasped.

Stoke just stared at him. And for a moment, there was dead silence.

"Don't watch the news!" Stoke finally exhaled.

"Wha…?" Assad asked.

"Don't watch the news!" Bob asserted as he staggered off.

He knew the oath. We all went home leaving a now confused and furious Assad pacing his gate as he angrily kicked an empty beer can away and puffed hard on his cigarette.

"Don't watch the news" was our oath whenever we had a street brawl that ended really bad for our opponents, simply because we didn't want to hear the news report on TV later and have it play on our conscience.

Showtime

My brother and his crew came by, and we talked about the situation. Bob and Stoke also came over that evening. His girlfriend patched us up.

There was no talking as I sat back between her legs as she applied the final bandage to my cheek, kissed me on the top of my head, then playfully kicked me on my hip to get up as a signal that she was all done.

It was an ongoing feud for years between Street Boys and Willy's gang; some days, we licked our wounds and counted our losses, and other days, like today, we celebrated our victory. But it was clear to the Street Boys that this was about to be continued.

The Little Girl

Almost a week passed. I chose to be the bait for any reprisal as was the norm, by going to my friend's house on The Main and chilling out front on his fence at around the same time that we saw Willy's brother and his gang get off the bus that last time. My brother and his crew of around thirty cyclists this time, plus the rest of the

Street boys were all parked up at the corner store deli each evening, and was drinking, chilling and watching for my signals. We created a special hand signal to say "They are coming," and another to say "No sign of them," which I would signal from time to time after a bus passed.

But for the whole week, the prior signal was never made because there was not a sight of Willy's boys on the main all week. We didn't celebrate the fact that they retreated; we braced for the reprisal, as there was an eerie calm.

Before you are quick to say, we were instigating another fight or asking for trouble, the reason for what we did was simple: in those days, back to back beat downs from us with a rival would make them finally call it quits, call it even, or make a truce with us, and the fighting would finally be over.

That was all we wanted—for the fighting to be over.

Haven't you ever been in a bad situation that you just wanted it to be over and done with once and for all, instead of bracing for round 2 or the next episode?

Sigh.

I was sitting on the front fence of my friend's house on the main having a smoke and a beer still doing lookout, when a basket ball flew from over his gate and knocked the beer from my hand.

I thought it was my friend doing the "got ya" horseplay with me as usual, so I just laughed to myself and stooped down to take up the still half full can that was spilling so I could have at least one last sip.

I was about to go get the ball that was now rolling off the sidewalk into the busy street when, through the corner of eyes, I caught sight of his five-year-old daughter dashing through the gate and running to retrieve it.

I screamed her name to stop as, almost at the same time, a speeding car ran over the ball and burst it. She obviously grew sad and was more upset about her ball being busted than the consequences of what could have happened to her also if she had caught up with that ball in the middle of the street.

"Come here!" I commanded her over to me, as I tossed my beer and cigarette in the trash bin. "Don't even start!" I snapped at her as she came over to me and was about to start crying.

She calmed down.

"Don't move!" I pointed at her with a warning finger as I waited until there were no passing vehicles and went and picked up her busted ball. I went back to her, picked her up, sat her in my lap, and showed her the busted ball.

There was a brief silence, as she was still a bit shaken and was holding back tears. So I gave her a moment to calm down.

"Where are your parents?"

"They are in the backyard, gardening, and was coming here next." She pointed at her front garden. "So they told me I could go play with my ball in the meantime."

Silence.

"What did they also tell you about coming outside through those gates by yourself?" I asked as I comforted her.

She hesitated and then spoke. "That I should never." Her cute little voice trembled as she twiddled her thumbs.

"So what was that?" I snapped. "You could have been killed by what you just did. This could have been you!" I said as I showed her the crushed ball.

She started to cry. I tossed the ball aside and hushed her.

"I'm sorry." She sighed as her crying slowly stopped.

I hugged her, and she hugged me back.

My simple lesson to her was that sometimes it was better to stop chasing after certain things and just let it *die* rather than to continue the pursuit and end up dying over what you were chasing after.

I knew her well, as I even baby sat her many times, but I hardly saw her as she grew older however, because her mom owned a hair salon out of town and eventually started taking her to work with her. Yet still, she was my little cutie, and her parents and I were super cool in entrusting her in my care.

She was like the child I never had.

"You know how dangerous that was that you just did? Don't you ever, ever, ever do what you just did again, you hear me?" I warned.

"I'm sorry," she said as she wiped a tear from her eye. "I won't. Are you going to tell on me? Dad will get mad and take away my toys." She started crying again.

I hushed her. She calmed down.

"I won't tell on you if you keep your promise never to do that again." I smiled as I playfully tickled her.

I finally got a happy face and laughter from her as she hilariously twisted her torso to resist my tickles.

"I promise if you stop tickling me," she started laughing even harder. Then she raised her tiny pinky finger.

I stopped so that she could learn the importance of keeping a promise and literally playing it safe. She looked over at the busted up ball I tossed aside, and after a while, she put her pinky finger up to my chest.

"Pinky swear!" She then stared me in the eyes.

"Pinky swear!" I said without hesitation as we hugged pinky fingers, and I gave her a kiss on the forehead.

She hugged me.

It felt strange; here I was as the leader of a street gang now doing a pinky swear with a cute little five-year-old girl. Maybe I wasn't such a tough guy after all.

She relaxed and got cozy in my lap as she just watched cars passing by. She then asked if we could play our car game that I made up a long time ago, where she would choose a color car and I would choose a color car. We started, and as cars passed by we would shout and point happily and count at our respective choices, and the first person that got to ten for the color of their car that passed by, would win. She won.

Her mom and dad came to the gate to check on her whereabouts, and I gave them the signal that all was well and she was fine. They then started tending to their front garden.

She saw them.

"Pinky swear, remember?" she said with a nervous look as she raised her cute little pinky finger up to me again.

"Pinky swear." We hugged. "Just remember, don't ever do that again. The street is a very dangerous place."

"Why?" her curious mind asked.

"Because it is what people use to get from one place to the next, and sometimes they meet into accidents and robberies and all kinds of bad stuff that can happen to them in the streets, because bad people use the street also."

Silence.

"So if the street is so dangerous, why is your name Street?" she asked while picking at one of her fingernails. "Are you dangerous?"

She caught me off guard there, and I wanted to say yes, but this was a five-year-old, so there were some answers that their developing brain was just not ready to handle.

"I'm not. For years, I'd have friends come over, but I'm never home because I'm always on the street, break-dancing or just chilling with my friends. That's how I got my pet name."

"What's a pet name?"

"It's a name you or someone else label you as because of your lifestyle or image."

"What's image?" She went on.

"It's what people see when they look at you as they get to know you and they label you in their own perception."

"What's perception?"

OMG! She was killing me.

I learned while growing up that some of the toughest questions you would ever be asked to find an answer for in your life were from kids!

"A perception is simply what people think about you."

Silence.

Thank God! Phew.

"I'm still winning!" She laughed and pointed as another red car, the color she chose, drove past.

I exhaled with a smile.

Sometimes in life it's okay to lose and let someone else win and just be happy for them.

"Mom says she is taking me to a baby shower this weekend for one of her employees at her salon."

"Oh, cool. That's nice. You will have lots of ice cream and cake and balloons and even bounce about."

I thought she was going to be relaxed and excited about that until she dropped a bombshell.

"Street, where do babies come from?"

What the what!

I was silent as I gathered my thoughts to explain that question to a five-year-old.

"From their mommy's belly. They grow in their mom's belly until when they get old enough, a doctor takes them out at the hospital."

"I know all of that, Street. Mommy told me. But…but how do they get there in Mom's belly?" she frustratingly gestured with her arms.

I almost fainted. I had the answer, but she was too young to know the answer. As 1 Corinthians 2 said: "I gave you milk, not solid food, for you were not yet ready for it. Indeed, you are still not ready."

Always remember—there are some answers that can wait!

I panicked at not daring to answer, so I simply told her to ask her mom and dad how she came into this world. Yeah, I put them in the hot seat, as I tickled her some more and then eventually took her back to them, chatted a bit, and then went to meet up with my brother and the rest of the crew.

Phew.

We chatted a bit, and all concurred that Willy's boys weren't going to show up, so we gradually left for our respective destinations.

All was quiet for the rest of the week.

Let's Dance

Saturday night finally came, which was the big night of the finals of the championship golden belt break dance competition.

Wow!

Everyone was excited and gearing to go but was still nervous as hell; not only was it a packed house, but there were several TV cameras set up. I heard that many entertainment journalists from overseas were present to cover the event, as we had contestants from at least six other countries vying for the coveted belt.

My brother and his whole crew were there as our "security" as we pumped ourselves up to focus on dancing and winning this championship golden belt. We were questioned as to the whereabouts of Assad by the promoters and judges, but Stoke just played it off as him having an emergency so he was running late.

The dance contest started to the uproar of the crowd as the music blasted. I didn't know if it was the magnitude of the moment (with the packed arena and television cameras and all), but a couple of the crews we battled against in the preliminary rounds made it easy for us to win with their simple mistakes and fumbling. I was still sore from a shoulder injury I sustained by a vicious kick from that street brawl, so I was struggling a bit to do my signature dance moves, but we still advanced from round to round. We won all our preliminary rounds and were into the grand finale battle.

Wow!

It was a packed house, and the crowd went wild as both crews took to the stage to do one final battle for the coveted golden belt. Although we were local favorites, the crowd was split in both, screaming for us and the other finalists; a break dance crew from the United States was, I have to confess, quite impressive.

Okay, challenge on!

We took turns going back and forth, sending the crowd into a wild frenzy, until the final performance where each crew were given three minutes to perform alone on stage. They went first and nailed it, and now it was us Street Boys' turn. Bob and Stoke nailed it. Based on the crowd's reaction, all I had to do was likewise, and we'd win! But in a routing, move my shoulder acted up again, and I flopped. I heard the groan and jeers from the crowd as they knew I had to give it another shot and come good, or it was all over. I started dancing again, and just when I was about to attempt my daredevil signature dance move one last time, Assad "moon walked" onto the stage.

What the what!

We were all shocked, as the crowd went wild.

He and I stared at each other for a few seconds.

"What are you doing here?" I asked over the blaring music.

"I didn't watch the news, although I can tell you guys kicked ass," he said in an apologetic way. "I don't know the outcome of that brawl and with whom, but watching you guys break dance one round after the other, I can tell you're all banged up. And it's your shoulder why you couldn't nail that move just now right?"

No answer.

"Tonight has one outcome—we win! Tag me! Not for your sake or my sake but for us Street Boys! Tag me, and let's get this golden belt, Street! Tag me!" he pleaded.

A million thoughts flashed through my head at that split second. I hated him for what he did with Michelle, but I loved him like a brother at the same time. "Tag me" was like wrestling where you couldn't continue, so you tagged your partner to do so. I was still mad at him, but he was a Street Boy; he was still one of us. Pride and bragging rights were at stake over this golden championship belt, so even though I had little confidence in him because he always ignored his signature moves to put on a show for the girls, I tagged him.

"Nail it!" I simply said as the crowd screamed at the tag, and then I danced off.

"C'mon, guys, time is running out. You got less than a minute!" the DJ then shouted over the microphone as he then did a little bit of DJ scratching and then mixed in our all-time favorite break dance rap song. I went to huddle with Bob and Stoke.

Assad took some deep breaths as he scanned the packed auditorium, gave me a glance, and then started to break dance. The crowd went wild, as not only did he do all his signature dance moves to perfection but at the end—and I'm still not sure if he tried to do me a favor or was proving that he was as good as I am—he did my signature closing dance move, which I struggled to do earlier because of my injured shoulder, and nailed it to perfection with my final pose!

In an adrenaline rush, I then danced on stage, did a few break dance moves, and even with the pain from my shoulder, ended by nailing his closing signature dance move with his final pose.

There was pandemonium as the crowd went wild when Bob and Stoke quickly danced onstage, break-danced for a few seconds, and then nailed their signature pose again with pinpoint perfection.

We held our poses for a few seconds as the Toro horn sounded to signal the end of the competition. Reporters and fans alike were scampering to take a photo of us as we were almost blinded by the flashing lights from their cameras.

Nervous moments went by as we then retreated back to our side of the stage. There was no music, just deafening chants from the crowd for their respective crew, as both crews were then summoned to the stage and anxiously watched the five judges as they huddled to vote for their winner. They finally handed a note to the promoters who also did his crowd response vote by ranting up the crowd to cheer their response for their winner.

He first asked for the crowd to scream their vote for the team from the USA. It was loud as hell, which got us all nervous. He then asked for the crowd to scream their vote for the Street Boys. It was deafening as they jumped and screamed their vote for us. We held hands and let out a heavy, joyous exhalation as most in the jam-packed arena now started chanting, 'Street Boys! Street Boys! Street Boys!'

The promoter had a hard time settling the crowd but he eventually did, to announce the winner. He made a few small talks, and then:

"So, ladies and gentlemen," he started, looking at the judges score sheet in his hand, "based on the judge's respective scores and individual final vote, we have a three-to-two winner."

The crowd went wild until he finally hushed them again.

"Wait, wait, it's not over yet, because your vote based off crowd response counts as well," he said.

There were nervous murmurs in the crowd, as he eventually hushed them again.

"Based on your crowd response vote, we could have had a tie leading to one final dance-off or a clear winner. But based on your crowd response vote, ladies and gentlemen, the winner of this year's coveted golden break dance championship belt for a vote of four-to-two is…"

Silence and growing nervousness, as he deliberately took a long pause to ramp up the anxiety of the crowd, until he finally spoke.

"The Street Boys!" he shouted. "Let's hear it for the the Street Boys!" he again shouted, which triggered wild jubilation from the crowd.

First the bronze belt, then the silver belt, and now the ultimate golden belt! We took the triple!

Wow!

We always knew we were local favorites. We just weren't certain for sure that we would win! Have you ever been in that situation?

Security had a hard time clearing the stage from fans and reporters who stormed it to hug and greet us and for photo ops and interviews.

I was given the mike to speak my gratitude after being handed the prized golden championship belt.

I spoke with passion as I huddled with the crew and saw the crowd still cheering as we passed the mike back and forth to each other for everyone to speak their gratitude. My brother and his girl were at one end of the stage with his crew, pumping his fist at our victory, but as I waved thank-you to the crowd, a familiar face caught my eye at the other end of the stage.

It was Michelle.

I tried to go meet up with my brother first but was stalled by several journalists who wanted us to pose for photo ops and interviews.

That was the proudest moment of my life as the leader of the Street Boys break dance crew. We were the best in the island, and we would all be watching the entertainment news the next day. Yep, we'd all be watching the news.

It was a happy moment! But what happened thereafter to trigger a ripple effect of misfortunes in the coming days and weeks after that joyful moment would all change our lives forever.

Jealousy

As we exited the stage to go meet and greet our fans Stoke with his adrenaline still pumped up asked if he could hold on to the belt for the night. I said yes, and handed it to him. Bob went off to celebrate with his girlfriend.

"So are we cool?" a smiling Assad asked as he adjusted his attire.

I sighed in response, as we happily high-fived more fans that came over to us, while trying to have a serious conversation.

Haven't we all been there, whereby, in the middle of a serious conversation, we had to suddenly switch off and switch on a forced happy face because of someone who interrupted us?

"I'm sorry. You're like a brother to me, and I screwed up. Forgive me, and tell her I apologize!" He exhaled. "There she is. Go get your girl!" he then said, gesturing at Michelle, whom he also noticed waiting for me.

I started to walk off the stage but then turned back to him.

"Hey! Yeah, bro. We cool," I said as we dabbed and hugged. "I'll meet up with you guys backstage later."

I was giving high fives and hugs to fans while making my way through the crowd, and after briefly chatting with my brother and his crew, I made my way over to Michelle. But a familiar face took my arm and halted me. It was Jess. Remember her? The girl that night at the club—the devil in the red dress?

"Hey." she smiled.

"Hey." I smiled back, looking at Michelle through the corner of my eye, waiting for me.

"You never did come over," she said as she hugged me around my neck.

"I know. Long story, but nice to see you."

"I've missed you. I can't get that first night over your house out of my head," she then said as she looked over her shoulder and quickly planted a soft kiss on my lips. "Once again, you guys did great tonight! You want me to come over later to celebrate with you all? I can always make up an excuse to him, because I just want you so bad all over again," she said while planting another kiss.

That was an invitation only a devoted Christian would refuse. But before I could answer I heard a course voice shouting her name over the blaring music. We both looked around, and it was Willy.

"Shit! Maybe a next time. I have to go. Come see me," she said as he made his way through the crowd to approach her. She walked off to him through the crowd in frustration.

I stood there, still hugging fans and taking pictures with them with a plastic smile, as I watched Willy and Jess argue back and forth for a moment. He grabbed her. She shoved him off and attempted to slap him, but he caught her arm. She dragged it from his grip and was about to walk off, but he held her back. His demeanor changed, they exchanged a few words, and she stroked his face and kissed him. He held her hand and led the way as they exited, but not before, while his back was turned, she looked back at me and blew me a kiss. He turned around as she looked at me with love in her eyes, but he caught my stare and looked at me with revenge as they both walked off, arguing all over again, and disappeared into the crowd.

Okay, so what the hell is going on here? I questioned myself.

Speaking of disappear, I looked at where Michelle was standing waiting for me, and she was gone.

I hurriedly made my way through the crowd for the exit, hoping to find her. I did, as I saw her leaving with some friends.

"Michelle!" I called.

She ignored me.

"Michelle!" I called again.

"What!" she snapped in an angry tone as she stopped and turned around with arms folded.

"What is this?" I asked, sensing her anger.

She beckoned for her friends to keep walking so we could talk in private.

"What was *that*?" she screamed. "I saw you kissing her right in front of me."

"I wasn't kissing her. She was kissing me," I explained.

She scoffed in frustration and started to walk off. I went after her, held her hand, and she stopped.

"Leave me alone! I know her! Was that your on-again, off-again girlfriend going back and forth with different men, and now you two are on again?" she queried.

"No. Just some chick I was fooling around with. And thanks for the congrats and asking how I'm doing," I said. "The last time you saw me, I was getting a beat-down at your gate from Willy and his boys."

There was a moment of silence as I could tell our minds reminisced back to that night, as our demeanor calmed.

Heavy, calming exhaling from us both.

"I'm sorry!" she said.

"Don't be. She's just a fan," I lied, as I dared not confess that we were intimate after she spent a night at my house. "Just tell me what happened after I left," I then said, trying to change the subject.

"Nothing! I went inside, and I haven't seen or spoken to him since as I left the next morning for an out-of-town missionary conference," she explained. "We just got back in town tonight and came straight here to watch you perform. You guys were great! Congrats!"

Silence.

"What happened after that night between you two? What's going on between you and Willy and his boys, Street?" she continued.

"Nothing," I replied. "They're still mad that us Street Boys were the group that beat them and deprived them of the previous championship belt, I guess. That's why they didn't even bother to compete for this one," I continued, downplaying the seriousness of what was brewing, as it had now escalated from break dance battles on a stage, to fistfight battles in the street.

She was silent as if she was contemplating and then accepted my answer.

"I told my dad what happened, and he's going to speak to the promoter and have him order a new belt for you—on the condition that you leave me alone." She smiled.

What the what!

"In that case, tell him to cancel the order." I forced a smile. "But in all seriousness, tell him I said, 'No, thank you.'" I sighed in thought. "Him sourcing a replica belt from the promoter will be just a belt. What those punks took from us was *the* silver break dance championship belt, which we worked blood, sweat, and tears for. I don't just want a replacement belt. I want *that* belt back! And now I realize we will never get it back because of what they did with it."

Silence and a long stare from her as she exhaled heavily, hugged herself, looked at me out of concern at a possible reprisal from us Street Boys.

"Please tell me you won't start a war with them," she begged. "Street, Street!"

"I…I promise," I said as I snapped back from a premonition of a series of violent events that were about to unfold between us two rivals in the coming weeks and months.

Sometimes, in certain situations, you have to be very careful how you put your questions together, so as to ensure that you get an accurate answer; which is why many times you will see a reporter in an interview read the question from their notepad, instead of asking from memory. So in this case she asked me to promise her that 'I won't *start* a war with them.' That was an easy promise to make. Why? Because guess what, the war had already started, and *they* were the ones that started it!

"I promise!" I again asserted as I held her hand.

"Congrats on winning tonight again, but I thought you said Assad was out of the crew."

"He surprised us all by turning up tonight. He apologized. Everyone deserves a second chance, right? Tell your father I said that."

"I have to go," she then said after a long searching stare at me as she picked something from my hair and flicked it away. Then she started to neatly adjust my attire, as if I was a little boy she was getting ready for school. "What am I going do with you, Street?" she finally ended with a heavy exhalation as she took both my hands.

"Just love me," I said with a gentle squeeze.

We held a long stare into each other's eyes.

"When can you come over? Because I'm not coming back to your father's house and Willy's turf," I asked.

"Not sure. I'm back in town, so you'll be seeing me," she said as she also gave me a gentle squeeze, released our grip, and slowly walked off to meet up with her friends waiting for her. "Oh, and if I were you, I'd stay away from that girl you claim is just a fan! She might be playing both of you, but that's Willy's girlfriend!" she warned as she left.

What the what!

I was stunned. But after thinking about it, I had a devilish grin because of the fact that Willy took my championship belt, but I took his girl!

CHAPTER 5

WATCH THE NEWS

We celebrated, did interviews and photo ops, had a few drinks, and chatted with the promoters, my brother, and his crew, and fans for a bit. His girlfriend gave me a tight bear hug and smothered my face with kisses, as she was so proud of us. We had an afterparty, and it was after two in the morning when we finally decided to head home. We were offered rides from the promoter and his crew who were the last to leave, as everyone else including my brother and his crew already left the venue, but as usual, we decided to take the fifteen-minute walk home to enjoy the night sky and some fresh air.

The street was a ghost town as we walked home, celebrating and drinking. I never dropped the bombshell about sleeping with Willy's girl as I knew that would raise concerns about a reprisal from him, and ruin our celebration.

Stoke was beside himself with our golden championship belt, while humorously negotiating with Assad about their deal to let him keep it if he gave Assad his cut to pay for the outstanding balance so Assad could get his first car.

"That was for the other belt!" I interrupted in a tipsy tone.

"Which is no more," Stoke said, killing the mood, as he remembered seeing how they cut it up to make wristbands. "But now we got the ultimate gold!"

We all cheered loudly and toasted. I was just happy for my crew and that we won the break dance competition and wanted peace of mind, as I was more focused on winning and keeping Michelle than who gets to keep the ultimate golden championship belt.

"What do you say, Bob?" Stoke said as he slumped an arm over my shoulder as we all staggered down the street, drinking. "Should we all vote that I keep the belt as long as I give Assad my cut for him to pay the balance for his ride?"

"Yes!" Assad beat him to the answer. "We just need Street to sign off on it. He's our leader. He has the final say," he said as we knocked beers to say, "Cheers!"

"Yes," Bob said as he took another gulp. "No more bus and cabs. Assad's my new ride."

"Deal," Stoke finally concluded with a glee. "Three to one vote, Street, but you still have to make the final decision. So what say you?"

They all gave me a curious happy drunken stare for my verdict.

"I'll sleep on it." I chuckled.

That prompted a happy horseplay debate as Stoke strapped the belt around his waist and we staggered home, while rapping to that famous break dance rap song we dance to at the end, that made us win the competition.

We got to the main and continued rapping and dancing silly in the middle of the street. We were about five minutes from our house when we noticed a car approaching us from behind. No worries right? Well, until it then killed its headlights and slowly followed behind us. Our merriment stopped, suspicious about the car.

We all glanced at each other to stay calm as we took a turn off the main and were now on Merry Wood Street, which was the last street before we got to our street; and be in our respective homes.

Have you ever been through a long tumultuous journey but made it to the point where you were almost home—whatever home was in your situation—and you were so happy that you didn't even wait to get home to celebrate and you started celebrating on the final lap but then, from out of nowhere, here comes trouble?

Fight or Flee

"I know that car," Assad said under the dim of the streetlights. "I know those blue fog lamps and those neon blue headlights with one brighter than the other and the sound of that messed up turbo engine," he scoffed.

"Yeah, I see them driving up and down the main all the time. It's Willy!" Stoke gasped, knowing what was about to go down.

"I'm gonna race that punk someday when I get my car!" Assad fumed.

"Really, dude? Now is not the time," Bob said nervously. "Or better yet, yeah! Let's race him for home right now—on foot!"

"No, wait!" I exhaled heavily. "You can't outrun a car! Let me think."

"Think? Street, I can see Assad's house from here. That's like a little over a block away. You know the drill. Let's just split up and make a run for it and live to fight another day," Bob pleaded, sensing that I wanted to confront them.

I glanced over at Assad and Stoke. They all gave me a hesitated half-drunk nod of approval, as we were way too tipsy to fight.

We were all nervous, but although we were caught off guard, being in this situation before, we didn't flinch.

The car started to rev its engine as a taunt, causing it to let out a lot of sputtering smoke as it backfired loudly.

"Listen to that piece a turbo junk." Assad laughed. "I can't wait to kick his ass in a drag race."

We all gave him a "Really!" look about his poor timing for talking about a drag race, but knew he always got way off point when tipsy.

"What do we do?" Bob again asked as he quickened his pace even more.

I suddenly stopped.

"Let's live to fight another day," I then finally ordered, in flight mode.

I adjusted our "on-foot bar" backpack I was carrying, which thankfully was no longer heavy from being packed with beer, because we had all consumed the contents in celebration as we walked home, so now it only contained a single forty-ounce bottle of beer that I was saving for when I got home to enjoy and celebrate our victorious night by myself in quiet solace.

And yes, we were kids and couldn't afford the jacked up prices of beer at these break dance competition venues when we compete, so we got that backpack and smuggled in our own drinks. And we were never searched at the various entrances, because us Street Boys were all well-known, so security simply thought that the puffed up backpack contained our break dance costumes. Hush!

Have you ever been there where you wanted to go out to a party or an event to have a good time but couldn't afford to, however, you still went with cash only for the entrance fee but had no worries because you snuck in your own liquor?

Okay, so back to what I was saying.

"Flight mode! You know the drill, guys," I instructed as we all prepared to make a run for it.

"Yeah, we got you now, fools!" a voice, however, shouted from the sputtering car, which prompted loud combative chants and jeers from other passengers in the car.

That was our signal to run off, but just as we were about to, an empty quart bottle of rum thrown from the car struck Assad and shattered at his feet. Another one sailed from the car and barely missed me, as the car doors slowly opened.

"What?" a now fed up and fuming Assad cursed as he turned around to face the car.

Someone in the front passenger seat placed one foot on the ground, took a final gulp from what looked like another quart bottle of rum, and started to exit the car, but made a hasty retreat as Assad aimed and sailed his half-full bottle of beer at our attacker.

Bull's-eye! His beer bottle caught and shattered the rum bottle held chest high in the attacker's hand, causing the bottle to shatter. The punk quickly retreated back into the car as broken splinters flew into his face. In a split second, Stoke and Bob, in knowing the drill, almost simultaneously sailed their beer bottles at the windshield, shattering it in two places.

The car engine revved angrily, as it sounded like the driver was having difficulty putting the gear stick into drive to charge at us. That bought me another split second to, without even thinking, I frantically searched for the forty-ounce beer bottle in our "on-foot bar" backpack, took it out, aimed and deliberately sailed it at the driver's side of the windshield, shattering it completely.

"Run!" I then ordered, knowing that I had obscured the vision of the driver, who I glanced at and saw him frantically brushing splintered glass from his face, as we all took off running.

The driver finally got the car into drive, kicked the shattered windshield out for a better view, floored it and chased after us!

Assad, Stoke, and I ran into the opposite direction of the oncoming vehicle; as was our drill to do when being chased by a car at the start of a street brawl. This was simply to buy ourselves precious seconds before the driver could hit reverse or makes a U turn. But for whatever reason, Bob kept running straight ahead.

What was he thinking?

With all three of us quickly out of sight from the driver's rearview mirror, tires screeched as the fuming driver focused on Bob, who was smartly not running in the street but more closer to neighboring fences. It didn't help, as the car pummeled through a line of garbage bins lining the sidewalks, rode the embankment, and struck Bob, sending him crashing into some other garbage bins, which at least cushioned his impact from hitting the concrete sidewalk.

Stoke, Assad, and I all cowered in shock for what seemed like an eternity as we watched Bob curled up and writhing in pain. The car then screeched into reverse, made a U turn, and came after us, but we were long gone. I was hiding behind a neighbor's fence. Assad was across the street, and Stoke was hunkered behind a dumpster.

The car patrolled the street a couple of times, looking for us, with the passengers shouting threats. It then pulled up at a groaning, bloodied Bob.

Yep, we were right. Willy came out from the driver's side accompanied by some other thugs.

We were like four houses away so couldn't hear their conversation, but although they just hit Bob and he was sprawled out on the sidewalk, all busted up and bloodied, Willy took the lead as they started pummeling him with blows until he lay there unconscious.

I looked at Assad and gave him the signal that it was do or die to go to his rescue, but just when we were about to come out of hiding and charge at them, another car pulled up from the opposite direction next to them, flashing its lights.

We held our ground as I saw Willy give a hand signal.

The other car then pulled up next to theirs, and the passengers exited. It was his brother and some more thugs and, of all people, Jess—yep, that devil in the red dress.

What the what!

"Wait!" I halted everyone in a hushed code.

They were all cussing at how Willy's car was all messed up with a busted windshield and now oil running from below the engine. She pleaded with them to leave, as sirens approached and surrounding household lights started turning on from the commotion.

Some neighbors apparently called the cops.

Willy gave a still unconscious Bob one final kick. Then they all jumped into their respective vehicles. He again had difficulty getting the gear stick into reverse this time but finally did, and both cars sped off, took a turn back onto the main, and were out of sight. His car left a trail of oil, which seemed like he also busted his transmission when he rode the embankment to hit Bob, which meant that his car was now busted up, so we wouldn't have to worry about another car chase from it anytime soon. The sound of their engines speeding off farther into the distance made us all exhale that they were finally gone.

Just as we were about to exit our hiding spot and rush to go check on Bob, another car screeched round the corner from off the main and raced to our location. We thought Willy and his boys were back, but the siren, plus the red, white, and blue flashing lights that lit up the street made us exhale that it was the cops.

We went back to hiding in the shadows out of grave concern for Bob, as another cop car arrived shortly after. A couple neighbors came out and were having an animated conversation with them, but it was inaudible. One cop was administering medical attention to Bob until several minutes later, an ambulance arrived on the scene. He was rushed off to the hospital; the cops took statements from neighbors, one of whom was an old lady who identified Bob as a member of a gang called the Street Boys.

What the what!

Did that ole fart really just label my crew as a gang! I was furious even more.

Everyone eventually left or retreated, and before you knew it, after all that commotion, our poorly lit side street where we remained hunkered retransformed into a quiet ghost town again, only serenaded by the sound of crickets.

I gave the signal for us to leave, and we all slipped away in the shadows.

A minute later, we were all back at my house, breathing a sigh of relief and concerned over Bob's condition.

Why We Love Our Beer

Assad was slouched in the smaller sofa where he lit and had a cigarette in his hand which was almost now burnt out because he still hadn't taken a single puff from it in minutes. Stoke went to my refrigerator and popped a beer, but instead of taking a sip, he just held the cold bottle against the center of his forehead in deep thought as he leaned against the wall. He let out a heavy exhale as he lifted the front of his T-shirt to wipe his face, exposing the golden break dance championship belt wrapped around his waist. I just gave it an empty stare, and he also probably forgot that it was even there.

It's sad that at times we put in so much effort and hard work into achieving or accomplishing an award or a dream. Yet in one sudden crazy twist of fate because of an incident or, worse, an accident that coveted achievement is pushed to the back burner because its value has suddenly been replaced by something, someone, or a situation that has more significance.

Sigh.

I was beside myself also as my eyes stared at the letter of acceptance on the center table that Bob got from the university. We had all come back to my place to celebrate him getting it by having a few drinks, and he left it there as we then went back outside to practice some break dance moves for the finals. Even something as important as that must mean so little to him now, I thought as I pictured him lying all battered and bruised and in pain in the emergency room at the hospital.

"That was quite an aim!" A still tipsy Assad finally broke the silence as he playfully aimed and sailed a cushion at me. "Our beer bottles were like, as Street calls them, 'anointed weapons,' but in this case, missiles, crashing into that fools windshield, and at that punk who came out of the car first," he recalled. "What was Bob thinking, man? He knows the drill! We all have been there before, so we all know the drill!" He sighed. "I really could use that forty ounce now though Street." He chuckled as he got up and went to the fridge to get two beers, dabbing Stoke as he passed him.

"We messed up that piece a turbo junk real good. That fool made it even worst. Did you smell or see the trail of transmission oil that was draining from his car as it drove pass us, because he busted it when he rode the embankment? Good for him! Now he has a busted up car, and we have a busted up..." He stopped, in not finishing the sentence, in referring to Bob. He returned from the kitchen, handed me a beer, slouched in the sofa again, and we all just drank in silence.

There was silence for what seemed like an eternity, as we all tried to process what just happened from us celebrating victory, but then to violence all in a matter of minutes. Everyone was just in reflective mode.

Anointed Weapons

You must be wondering why Assad referred to me calling our beer bottles and cans anointed weapons.

Long story short: We got weary of being stopped and frisked by cops who searched us, took our knives and threatened us with arrest because of our street life and attire. They all thought we dressed like a street gang instead of break dancers, but to be fair, in those days, you could hardly tell the difference. So once in a blue moon we would travel with a knife.

One night while walking home from a rehearsal for an upcoming concert, drinking and chatting, as we walked pass a house, two men standing outside started pointing and laughing at us because of our break dance attire. They obviously weren't into that kind of music so didn't know about us Street Boys. One took it too far when he asked Bob a cynical question twice but got no answer.

That bully made a fatal mistake by storming over to us.

"Hey, I'm talking to you, bitch!" He then barked with heavy alcohol on his breath, as he grabbed Bob by the collar of his jacket and spun him around.

Okay, you asked for it.

He was met by a powerful swing from Assad's beer bottle that broke, splitting his forehead open in the process. Bob then gave him a powerful kick to the groin and as he slouched and screamed like a girl he was met by a powerful uppercut that sent him stumbling backwards before he crashed on his back in the middle of the street. Bob then did his trademark karate poise in combat for retaliation from that fool, but it never came. He was semiconscious.

Listen, Bob could fight and knock you out in a flash before you even saw it coming, because his parents sent him to karate school for years while growing up. But unlike the rest of us Street Boys that were trigger happy, violence was Bob's last resort, as he was always the last to be in fight mode.

The other man ran inside. We were about to run for cover, thinking he went to get his firearm, but stood our ground when he stormed back out and returned soon after with, of all things, a baseball bat.

Really, dude!

I sprung into action by quickly draining my twenty-four ounces can of beer and did a trick I showed the guys on how to stomp on this cylindrical-shaped beer can to make it perfectly flat and then the trick on how to fold it from side to side, then top to bottom. Stomp on the middle even harder to flatten it ever more and eureka: depending on how you hold it, you would now have a deadly three-inch "beer can shank" to defend yourself.

Please don't try this at home. You would never get it anyway because we proved that it only works with the texture of the tin from a certain brand of canned beer, and that brand I am not telling!

The rest of the Street Boys stood their ground as I gave them the signal to.

The man looked scared as he looked at his friend clutching his groin and slowly trying to wobble back to a standing position, before Stoke used his foot to stomp him back to the ground.

"Please!" That's all the tough guy bully that was taunting us earlier squirmed, as he curled up into a fetal position, and raised a trembling hand in surrender in expecting a beat down.

"Stay down!" Bob ordered, to spare him the beat down. "Just stay down!"

The other man hesitated but then let out an angry roar, and in his wounded friends defense swung at me with the bat.

"You sure you want to do this?" I said as he swung again and again, with me dodging the bat each time.

He swung again, I swayed to the side, and in a split second used my beer can shank to give him a deep telephone cut; which in those days got that name because it was a long slice on your face from your ear all the way down to the corner of your mouth.

He immediately dropped the bat, knelt to the floor and screamed like a girl, while holding his face. I then gave him a powerful wind-mill kick to the cheek which sent him crashing to the ground. I swore I saw a tooth fly from his mouth in the process.

It was over as quickly as it begun. I wouldn't even call that a fight because we all left the scene unscathed.

If only they had just left us alone, they would still be having their happy, animated conversation at their gate. But in less than two minutes later, because of their bullying, just look at them now, I thought as I glanced over my shoulder as we walked away.

Let sleeping dogs lie!

We have seen him a few times since he was either at the bus terminal or the store with that unmistakable telephone cut across his face. He was easily recognizable, pot belly, mid thirties, and not just because of the scar, but because of his weird hairstyle. He must have been into rock or heavy metal music as he sported a huge Mohawk hairstyle, which he dyed red.

He never recognized us, and we never made eye contact, said a word, or showed any giveaway emotions or bragging rights, but we just kept on going about our business—well until this one night at the bus terminal.

What Would You Do?

We were waiting for our bus home after performing at a high school outdoor barbeque. We got a decent salary for our performance so as usual we split the money, and treated ourselves to beers and smokes. Our on-foot bar backpack was stuffed with beers. Bob, Stoke, and Assad were all chugging on forty ounce bottles of beers, and I had my twenty four ounce can as usual.

We were all laughing and bragging about how we nailed our performance, to the delight of the packed soccer field and which one of us came out the luckiest for getting a phone number from one of the cutest girls that flocked us back stage after our performance, until we were interrupted by a commotion.

A small crowd had encircled what was going on, so as curious teens we went to take a look. To our surprise, it was the Mohawk bully with the telephone cut that got into a tussle with two half-drunk dudes that were teasing him about his haircut.

Serves him right. I sort of smiled to myself, as here was our bully now being bullied.

One thug kept slapping his Mohawk, while the other teased him about the telephone cut in his face. That scar back then meant that you lost a fight, and it would be your forever reminder. Some people who had gathered found the bullying funny, but others pleaded for the two thugs to leave him alone.

The Mohawk bully got so frustrated at one point that he shoved one of the thugs so hard that he fell backward to the ground. He got up and charged at him as he braced for a fight, and don't ask me what I was thinking, but I suddenly sprung over and stood between them.

"Who you, fool?" one of the thugs asked. "You better get outa the way before you get a ass whooping too."

I didn't say a word, so frustrated and itching for a fight, he swung at me. I swayed back to miss it, and before he could swing again, he was met by a powerful swing from Assad's forty-ounce beer bottle that shattered upon impact with the side of his head. He crashed to the floor.

His other thug friend charged at me from behind which sent us both crashing to the ground. We rolled over a bit exchanging blows until I had the advantage by kneeling on top of him and landed a few powerful elbows to his face.

I looked through the corner of my eyes and saw someone approaching. I thought it was a third thug, but it was Assad. But just when I though he was coming over to assist, he simply unzipped our on-foot bar backpack I was carrying, took out another forty-ounce beer, popped it open, and had a gulp.

I gave him a "Really, dude!" look.

He gave me a "What? You got this, bro!" look.

I shook my head and refocused on the thug I was still kneeling over. He had both palms up in the air as if pleading for, no more.

"So how would you want this to end?" I asked as the rest of the Street Boys surrounded us in fight mode.

He started crying.

What the what!

I got off him, draped him by his collar, and dragged him to his feet.

He sobbed his apology, saying he didn't know the guy they were bullying was with us and that they are just half drunk and acting stupid.

I accepted his apology.

"You got anything to say to this fool?" I asked as I turned to the Mohawk bully.

He was at a loss for words at first until he gathered himself and spoke.

"No. No. Hey, for what it's worth, thank you, guys. I just wanna go home to my wife and kids, yo. I just want to go home. I was just trying to go home," he said, a bit shaken.

I had mixed feelings as I gazed at him. Why? That night, while we were all walking home, as we passed his gate, they bullied us and started a fight. We were all on our way home. We just wanted to get home too.

"Apologize!" I snapped at the bully as the crowd of onlookers swelled. Some in the crowd screamed that they got what they deserved, as they were known to always harass commuters at the bus terminal.

He apologized with a trembling voice as he glanced over at his other thug pal on the ground who tried to get up swinging in fight mode. Big mistake, as he got a good stomp down from Assad and Stoke, rendering him almost unconscious. Bob was standing just behind me and was at the ready to attack, if this other thug tried any sudden moves.

Some in the crowd surprisingly cheered on their ass whooping, until there was silence, as I contemplated my next move.

"Take a good look at his face," I finally said as I grabbed his chin and turned it to the Mohawk bully. "The next time you see him, you look the other way, or you will be seeing us again. Apologize again!"

"Okay, okay, man, I got you. We good. We cool. We cool, right?" he asked the Mohawk bully, who just spat but didn't reply.

"Get outa here, and drag your lame ass friend along with you," I said as cops finally arrived on the scene.

"What's going on here?" one of the cops snapped.

"Ask him!" I said, gesturing to the conscious bully that was dragging his friend up to his feet.

"Aah, nothing. Nothing, Officer. Just horse play that got a bit rough. It won't happen again," he finally answered. "Right?" he then said as he gazed at me.

"Yes, Officer. I apologize for all this, but like he said, it won't happen again," I said with a warning gaze at the two thugs.

The officer had doubts with his curious glances, but let us all go.

Our bus came, but just when we were all about to board, I was halted by a familiar face.

"Hey. Hey, man, I...I...I just want to say thank you for saving my ass just now," the Mohawk bully said, as he tapped my arm to stop me. "I had made up my mind to go down swinging until you boys stepped in. Thank you!"

I didn't reply. I just stared at that telephone cut in his face and realized that he would forever be taunted by it. And it was my fault. I felt bad. I wanted to confess and apologize, but I dared not to!

"No worries, man. Next time, depending on where you go, just wear a hat to cover that cool hairstyle. Too many punks out here looking for trouble." I just smiled.

We actually dabbed with a parting smile. I entered the bus, and we left.

He still didn't even recognize me, but what startled us Street Boys even more as we rode the bus home and chatted was the crazy fact that, one moment, we were being bullied out of the blue by the Mohawk bully and his friend yet today, just now, we ran to the defense of our Mohawk bully, who was being bullied.

How crazy was that!

Wow!

That was one of the many incidents that caused us to start saying "Don't watch the news!" as my recollection faded and I came back to, and just gazed at the TV and then at Assad and Stoke, who were still beside themselves.

I could tell we were all ready to call it a night, so I finally broke the silence.

"We have all been down this road before," I started. "In fact, the last time we were in this situation was when we were jumped by that street mob from that town in Manchester. What was that; like two years ago? We travelled over a hundred miles by bus to enter into that special Best of the Best regional Caribbean finals, and we won! But the hundreds of locals that turned out to cheer on their local break dance favorites didn't like the ruling from the international panel of judges, who had voted that their lousy local team was a close second."

"They shouldn't even have made top ten," Stoke recalled as he removed the golden championship belt from his waist and admired it.

"Remember the riot that ensued while we were celebrating and splashing around beer on stage after being handed the then coveted, break dance championship bronze belt?" I asked. "Scores of sore losing fans suddenly stormed the stage and tried to take our belt," I recalled as I stood and patted Stoke on the shoulder in assurance that Bob would be okay. Then I went to get two more beers.

"They had some cool moves but never nailed the big ones. Not even sure how they made the finals," Stoke recalled, still leaning on the wall before he finally took a gulp from his beer.

"Favoritism. They shouldn't even have qualified for the competition," I scoffed as I toasted Stoke, handed a beer to Assad, popped my beer open, took a long chug, and sat.

There was silence until I broke it again.

"We could have easily handed them the belt and made a run for it, but no! Not Street Boys! As like David in the Bible didn't, who was just a simple shepherd boy standing against the giant Goliath who was armed with a mighty sword, ready to attack and kill him. We stood our ground. Just like David did, who was only armed with a sling and five stones. He only used one to kill Goliath." I sighed heavily as I held up my can of beer as a toast to Bob.

"That night and thereafter, like David, who seemed to have had a petty weapon but still slew his enemy. These beer bottles and cans became our petty weapons. Stoke, you and Bob were swinging your forty ounces like crazy, in self-defense. I lost count how many a those sore losers face and heads you busted open." I chuckled, which triggered a ripple effect.

"I counted seventeen with my forty until it broke on this fools head, and then the sharp edge became an even deadlier weapon that made those attacking me back off," Assad recalled. "You probably took out more than me with your 'beer can shank' before you were clobbered in the head with that speaker box monitor that came flying from nowhere, that blinded sided you."

"The last thing I heard were shots being fired in the air by armed security to disperse our attackers." I sighed. "And then waking up in the hospital early the next morning with you guys next to my bedside, but no break dance bronze championship belt in sight. You all then broke the news that they stole it from us during the melee."

Silence of recollection.

"Hey, for what it's worth, at least we did qualify for the break dance silver championship belt and won that too!" Assad smiled.

"And we all know how that turned out." Stoke sighed sadly. "They stole one and chopped up the other," he continued as he strapped the golden championship belt back around his waist.

He adjusted it even more tightly around his waist, as if to say, "There is no way we are going to lose you!"

"Bob will be fine. It's almost daylight. There's only one hospital around these parts that they could have taken him. We pay him a visit first thing at daybreak, but for now, let's call it a night," I said.

"Willy and them boys might be back out there patrolling. We messed up his piece a shit turbo junk really good, so he might have crossed the boundaries again, circling our territory and looking for us. Imma lay low tonight and crash here, Street," Assad said.

"Don't mind if I do myself," Stoke said as they both made themselves comfortable in my respective sofas.

It was the norm for them to all crash over my crib depending on the occasion.

"Yo, Street!" Assad halted me as I was about to enter my room.

Silence.

"After what happened tonight, should we start arming ourselves again?" he then asked out of concern to upping our armory for defense from just beer bottles and cans.

"No," I finally responded. "For yeah, though I walk through the valley of death, I shall fear no evil, for thou art with me. Thy rod and thy staff shall comfort me…" I recited Psalm 23.

"Oh, Lord, here we go again! Good night, Street!" an unimpressed Assad then said. "I still think we need more than beer cans and beer bottles as 'anointed weapons' of yours, though. Things are about to get worse. Let's prepare ourselves. Until then, church boy, preach to Stoke. They started all this shit," he ended as he positioned himself for sleep and covered himself with a sofa throw.

Silence.

"And we will finish it!" I exhaled heavily.

Stoke was beside himself and was just gazing at pictures I had of us street boys hanging around the room.

"You okay?" I asked him.

No answer. Only a sad contemplative nod in worry for the state of Bob.

I went to my room and didn't even know when I dozed off, as the next thing I know was, it was daylight.

The News

Assad and Stoke were still sleeping. My mind was in a whirlwind; from winning the ultimate break dance Golden Championship belt, to Michelle, my crush, being mad at me for kissing the devil in the red dress, to Bob; my friend, who was also like a brother, in the hospital, and then to Willy, who had declared war.

I went to use the restroom and as I exited, my eyes caught sight of the follow-up letter Bob got from the university, and right next to it was the television remote. Against all odds, I broke our coveted rule and turned the television on and put on the local news, as that was the only way to find out about Bob's state while laying low, if it made the news.

There were commercials on, but immediately after, the anchor resumed by saying, "Back to breaking news we're following..." And then my heart skipped a beat as she gave a report on the incident last night with Bob.

I hurriedly woke the rest of the crew up, and we all watched in anxiety as the anchor lady said there were no suspects in their supposed "hit and run" accident and that Bob was in a stable condition at Kingston Hospital.

We all slumped and exhaled a sigh of relief, followed by dabs all around.

The channel started showing some community residents reaction to the incident, and I'd never forget this same old lady who vented her frustration and thought otherwise by saying that it was probably a hit or a reprisal because all of us youngsters were all street thugs and gangsters who simply masqueraded as break dancers. Other neighbors, including some familiar faces, however, spoke in our defense. It then became clear that while us Street Boys had a huge fan base as break dancers, some people in the community disliked us and labeled us as a street gang.

Those critics had never come out to see us break dance; they only saw us fighting in the streets, and without even caring to know the reason for the fighting, that was all they judged us and labeled us by—the fighting.

Have you ever been judged by your actions by someone who was swift to do so, not caring what the reason or purpose for your action was?

Interestingly, the news went on, and to our surprise, it then showed clips of us Street Boys winning the break dance competition. There was footage of us on stage in high jubilation. Normally, when we saw that, we would be ecstatic for being on TV again, but this time around, we all just sat there in quiet solace.

I turned the TV off. No more watching the news!

Bob

We were happy that he would be okay, and that the cops weren't going to get involved by labeling it as a gang related incident.

All three of us went to visit him at the hospital that afternoon. Surprisingly, we were met by Michelle and some of her church friends at his room, who also went to visit and pray for him. News traveled fast as I wasn't even aware that she knew of the incident. She led me to a private corner.

"What happened, Street?" she abruptly asked.

No answer.

"I'm speaking to you. It's all over the news, and everyone is talking about it. What happened?"

I still didn't answer.

"Street. Street! I'm speaking to you," she said as she thumped me in my chest twice and did a poor job of holding back the tears. "You promised me." She exhaled heavily.

Silence.

"We were simply walking home last night when they drove up from nowhere and attacked us," I finally said.

Silence.

"You just missed his parents. They just left." She exhaled at the thought of the imminent reprisal from us.

I didn't reply, as I just looked over at Bob with rage as he lay there semiconscious in the hospital bed with all kinds of monitoring stuff hooked up to him.

"The news said it was a hit and run, but rumors say it was a hit from Willy!" She exhaled. "What's really going on between you two, Street? Why did he attack you guys?"

"You should go. Give us some alone time with him," I refused to explain as I entered his room.

"Street!" she beckoned.

I ignored her.

"Street. Talk to me," she begged.

I still ignored her until she sensed my mood, and she and her friends reluctantly left. I asked Assad and Stoke to give me a moment alone with him first. They complied.

Bob could barely communicate as he appeared heavily sedated. He seemed to have suffered a fractured leg and some torso wounds. He also had a few bandages on his face and head.

I took off one of my silver necklace and slowly and carefully placed it around his neck. It was a favorite of his that he would always borrow from me for hot or special dates. I also placed the follow-up confirmation letter from the university by his bedside table, which had some of his other personal belongings, which his parents apparently brought.

Yeah, yeah, here we go again. While just sitting by his bedside staring at him, I once again played my test game.

"Satan, you already proved yourself by doing this to my friend. So, God, if you really do exist, prove it! Save my friend Bob, and give him a swift and full recovery," I softly whispered hopelessly under my breath.

Some time passed.

Bob slowly woke up.

Silence.

After a while, he reached out to hold my hand and simply asked "What happened?" as if he was trying to remember how he ended up in the hospital.

Silence.

I held his hand.

Silence.

"Rule number 1 when on foot and being chased by a car?" I finally quietly said with a smile to jog his memory as a tear rolled from my eye.

He let out a heavy exhalation and then turned his head away and sobbed quietly.

Silence.

"Shit. And to think I was the one that came up with that idea." He finally sighed as he wiped tears from his eyes.

"Always remember to practice what you preach!" I said as I clasped his palm with a sad smile. "Sometimes, depending on the situation, it's okay to run in the opposite direction when you're being chased."

Silence.

Assad and Stoke came in, and we all chatted for a moment and embraced him with brotherly love.

"Don't let them win," Bob whispered after a while as he was fading back into sedation. "I love you, guys. Fix this. Win! Lest I be like Brownie." He finally exhaled as he slowly went back into sedation again.

Silence, as we just stood there, talked, and watched him sleep before a nurse entered and politely told us that visitation time was up so we had to go.

Strangely, it crossed my mind there and then watching him fall back into sedation, that we are all lying in the same state or position, whether we are sleeping or dead. The only difference was that one state would have your body buried lifeless six feet under to rot until the day of judgment because you were dead! But the other state was still breathing and would allow for peaceful rest until you woke up and live to enjoy yet another day and another journey in this beautiful thing called life.

Some believers in Christ no longer say RIP as in "rest in peace" when someone passes away. We now say SIP, as in "sleep in peace."

Sigh.

Brownie

So here is why he mentioned *Brownie*.

A couple years back, we were all walking back from a side street break dance challenge, which yes, we won!

I came across this stray brown pup, which barely escaped being run over by a car while running across the street, chasing a butterfly.

I rescued her. She was the cutest puppy ever. After lingering for a while for her owner to come claim her and seeing no one, I took her home with me and begged my mom, who was visiting at the time to adopt her. She reluctantly agreed, and I simply called her *Brownie*.

Really! I just saw that reaction, so forget you then if *you* with your creative mind would have come up with a more creative name.

Rolly eyes.

So anyways, we built a bond together; Brownie and I were inseparable when I got home from school.

She ignored everybody else but me when it came to even feeding time. Back then, dogs were kept outdoors in their dog house, so while my mom, bro, and his girl would get frustrated when they would constantly call her for feeding time and got no response, one call from me, and she would come running like crazy.

They claimed it was the sound of my voice. I told them it was chemistry; that was why a dog was labeled as man's best friend—because it latches on to the love from its master.

The Street Boys were my escape to vent and exhale. Brownie was my pet and playmate when I switched off from dance mode, as back then there were hardly any street brawls, and Willy and his boys and us only competed break dancing on stage.

But Brownie had issues.

Instead of being excited and barking and running around, she showed absolutely no interest when my boom box was blasting as we practiced break dance moves. She would just curl up in the lawn across from us, watch us for a bit, yawn and then fall asleep.

Have you ever been there where everyone is partying and having the time of their life, but you just wanted to find a quiet place to curl up and sleep?

Sigh.

After practice or school, I would relax on my front porch, Brownie in my lap, and I would just exhale while having a beer and smoke. Brownie was my lifeline, and mom and everyone else knew, and accepted it.

Brownie liked curling up in my lap as I scratched the back of her neck. But then out of the blue, she would jump up in high alert, bark, and spring from my lap and dash to the front lawn to chase butterflies. Yes, butterflies.

It was butterfly season, as we called it back then where almost everywhere you went there would be clusters of butterflies in gardens, on trees, etcetera. They were beautiful and a beautiful sight to watch. But for whatever reason, Brownie was annoyed by them. Told you that pup had issues.

She would run around barking in the front lawn as she chased them; which ranged from just a few to as much as twenty or thirty at a time, and would even leap in the air trying to catch one. This would go on for minutes, much to my amusement, until the butterflies all flew away next door or across the street to the next lawn.

Brownie would then give her trademark 'satisfactory bark' as she would look back at me for approval, as if to say, "How was that, dude?"

I would cheer her on and you could tell how ecstatic she became at my approval by how frantic her cute little tail was wagging. At times she wanted to dash through the gate to chase after butterflies some more until I had to scream at her to stop. Sometimes I wonder if that was how she got lost—by going through the gate at her home to chase after butterflies.

Eventually, she would come back and curl up in my lap again and I would feed her dog treats and water, or she would just fall asleep, as I did my homework.

This went on for several weeks, and Brownie made me so happy.

Well, until this one Sunday evening, I had just finished my written closing arguments on a class project final paper on Evolution versus God. I was ecstatic, as if I got a passing grade, I was guaranteed to move to the next and final level in high school, and after that I would automatically be propelled as a freshman into college.

Again it was supposed to be a five thousand word written thesis (or twenty-five to thirty pages) on the origin of mankind—evolution or God. We could choose either and argue our points and then prove them to the best of our ability. I choose the latter—God—and was happy that it was ready to be handed in on the due date in class tomorrow.

I told mom I completed it. I checked on Brownie who was in her dog house around the back sleeping, so I left my hand written project in its folder on the front porch, and instead of practicing break dance that day; the Street Boys all hung out and had drinks and beer over Assad's house.

It was a bit of a windy day, as we sat on his front lawn and watched kids from our neighborhood fly their make shift kites. Some went soaring as far as your eyes could see, and others, well, even with the help of a relative, just couldn't go and stay airborne for long, until they finally got it right.

It was always fun for me to watch kids having fun, even if I was having a bad day.

Hours went by until we all decided to call it a day.

As I entered my driveway, small and big bits of chewed up paper blowing my way caught my attention. A bit blew and stopped at my feet. I took it up out of curiosity, as they were blowing everywhere. Before I could take a closer look at it, I looked up and saw Brownie dashing to and from the front porch, with her mouth full of paper as she playfully ripped them apart. She would usually bark for me when she woke up. This time, I heard nothing.

I smiled at her playful nature, but then my smile turned to a look of horror as I looked at the chewed up piece of paper I was holding in my hand. It was a piece of my thesis assignment!

What the what!

"Brownie!" I screamed her name as I dashed to the front porch.

When I got there, I almost fainted, as there were chewed-up paper everywhere. Brownie had playfully chewed on and ripped my final assignment to threads.

"What have you done? What have you done? Brownie! Come here. I said come here!" I screamed.

Brownie didn't budge, as she sensed my anger at her.

"Listen, young man, it's Sunday, so please stop the..." Mom started as she stormed outside.

She noticed chewed-up paper blowing everywhere.

"What's all this mess?" she asked.

I was silent as I scooped up handful of chewed-up paper.

"My thesis assignment, which is due tomorrow." I slumped as I took a handful of paper and threw it at Brownie in anger.

She whimpered and cowered with her tail tucked between her hind legs, as she could tell that I was mad at her.

"Brownie!" My mom simply exhaled as if to say, "Not again."

Yes, Brownie had ripped up my mom's news paper before, again, albeit playfully.

"Come here!" I ordered, but instead of obeying, she whimpered some more and then scampered off to her dog house around the back. That was her fortress to run to when she could tell she did something wrong.

"It's due tomorrow?" Mom asked as she started scooping up the chewed-up paper.

I just nodded yes.

Silence.

"Can you stay up all night, rewriting it?"

"No. I can write my part, but I need at least an evening or two after school to find my researched facts all over again." I sighed out of shock and disappointment. "I'll need at least two days."

Silence.

"Tell the teacher what happened. And if he has any doubts, tell him to call me. Tell him to call me, as some of these pages are just half ripped and clearly shows bits and pieces of your assignment."

She helped me to clean up the rest of the chewed-up paper blowing around.

Darkness fell, and I would usually go and say goodnight to Brownie, but this time, I didn't. I didn't even have dinner.

The Dog Ate My Homework

The next day in class I grew nervous, as after a while, the teacher started walking from desk to desk, collecting our thesis assignment.

I was at the back, and when he finally got to my desk and asked for it, I couldn't even look up to answer.

"Street, I don't have all day," he said with a frustrating out-stretched hand, waiting for it.

Silence.

"I…I don't have it, sir!" I finally exhaled.

"What do you mean you don't have it? You all knew today was the deadline." He sighed in disappointment. "Let me guess, you left it at home or on the bus, right?" he scoffed.

"No."

"So where is it then?"

Silence.

"Where is it?"

"My…my dog ate it."

"What!"

"I know you are not going to believe this, but my dog at it," I finally exhaled, which drew hushed laughter from my classmates.

"Silence!" my teacher snapped. "You think this is funny, Street?" he fumed. "I'll tell you what is funny. You don't hand in and pass this thesis today, you do not tally the points to move to sixth form and graduate to college. So since you don't have it, you are officially repeating this class for another year."

"What! I told you my dog ate it. I had it. She ate it yesterday. And I can prove it," I snapped.

"No need for that, Street. I have been a teacher for almost thirty years and have lost count from students who claimed that the dog ate their homework," he said, which drew laughter from the class.

Frustrated, I grabbed my bag and stormed out of the class with deafening ears from him calling me back to sit.

I sat there for a couple hours until break time when he finally entered his office. He was a bit surprised to see me sitting there but didn't say a word. Instead he just rest some folders and paperwork aside, took his glasses off, rested them aside, and sat. I could sense his uncaring disappointment.

Silence.

"I have some phone calls to make, in private, so if you will excuse me," he said.

Silence.

"Why don't you start with calling my mom?"

He looked at me with surprise.

Silence.

"Please. Call my mom. She was right there," I pleaded.

Silence.

"Street, listen…" He exhaled, scratching his forehead with both palms. "Street, in the past, you have asked me to do the same, thinking I wouldn't take your bluff. Sometimes, to save your ass, because I knew you were lying through your teeth, I didn't. And other times, when I did call her, well, let's just say it didn't end so well for you when you got home and faced the music with her."

I recalled, and he was right. But on this occasion, I knew she would corroborate my story.

Silence.

"Call her."

"Street, I'm trying to save you further trouble here."

"Please. Just call her."

Silence.

"Okay," he said after a heavy exhale, thought about it for a brief second, and then went through his contact list for us on his scroll pad.

He gave me one last chance for him not to, with a glance at me while he placed his finger on the dial pad.

I nodded.

He exhaled heavily again and then dialed.

No answer.

He was about to put the phone down, but I urged him to dial again. He did, and this time, she picked up.

He introduced himself, and they exchanged the usual "How are you?" and blah blah blah after he assured her that I was fine.

No parent wanted to get a call from their child's school out of the blue when they should be in class, going through a routine day. Because a parent's intuition would make you hold your breath for fear of bad news as you answer and say, "Hello."

He explained the final exam thesis assignment we were given two weeks ago to be handed in today, and then he paused looked me dead in the eyes and spoke.

"But, ma'am, while everyone else in class handed in their assignment this morning," he continued with a sad look on his face at my predicament when I get home, "Street... Well, let's just say Street didn't hand his in because, well... Well, because he claimed that he... he claims that his dog ate his assignment."

There was silence as he listened for a shock response, which never came. He instead got another, and as I guessed she was explaining and based on his facial expression, his whole demeanor changed.

"Okay. Okay. I understand," he replied as he listened. "Okay, sure. Let me...let me just think for a moment, as this situation is not customary."

Silence.

"Okay. Okay, only, and only for this extraordinary case, I will do as you request because I have to send these thesis off by Friday for them to score."

There was silence as he listened.

"And thank you as well, ma'am. Enjoy the rest of your day," he then said as he hung up and then just stared at the desk. Then he looked up and stared at me.

"What did she say?" I asked to break the silence.

He didn't reply but just took a fruit salad bowl from a side draw on his desk and slowly opened it as he then searched for a fork.

There was silence until he found the fork.

"What I'm about to say to you doesn't leave this room. You hear me?"

I nodded.

"You have two days, Street. I need your thesis on my desk first thing Thursday morning, or you can't say I didn't try to help you, son."

"I'll have it on your desk by first thing Wednesday morning, sir." I smiled with glee. "It's all still fresh up in my head. I just need to put it all back on paper."

"Okay. Now go. Break is almost over, and I have calls to make. Plus, I haven't eaten all morning."

I almost left the room. But I just stopped and said, "Thank you!" He had a mouth full of fruit salad, so he just nodded and waved for me to get out of his office.

"Thank you!" I also smiled as I whispered a soft prayer as I left.

I was met in the break room by concerned classmates of mine but just played it off that I was toying with him and that I just handed it in. They bought it, which was good, so as not to start a rumor mill about me repeating my class.

I spent the next two days at the library compiling facts again and sleepless nights preparing my thesis. True to my word, I met him at break time that Wednesday morning in his office and handed my thesis to him.

"Looks impressive," he said as he browsed through the twenty-five or so pages. "I'll speed-read through it after school and send it off with the rest tomorrow."

"Thank you, sir!" I smiled as I exited the room.

"Hey, Street!" he beckoned.

I reentered his office. He paused as he cleaned his glasses.

"For what it's worth, I'm sorry I doubted you. You should hear some of the crazy lame excuses that I've heard during my career from students who didn't show up for class with their homework or a due project. And 'My dog ate my homework' was the most lame and overused line." He laughed to himself. "Some of them didn't even have a dog. You thought me a valuable lesson—that sometimes, instead of being quick to judge, I should count to ten and give my students the benefit of the doubt until I prove them guilty, if in fact they are. Thank you! Now get outa here." He smiled.

I just smiled back and exited.

Several days passed, and Brownie and I were cool and chilling again with our usual routine. One evening after school and while going through my usual chill time with her, the butterflies came again. I smiled and told her to go get them, but she just looked up at them, barked, and then curled back up. I figured she wasn't feeling it that day, so I just stroked her. Suddenly, she rose, quietly jumped to the floor, and headed to the front lawn.

"Here we go, Brownie, get 'em!" I smiled.

But my smile soon changed to a look of concern, as Brownie totally ignored the butterflies but instead started sniffing through the lawn for a special kind of grass. She found some and started chewing on them.

Unlike now when we would take dogs to the vet, that was the norm for dogs back then when they weren't feeling well to administer their own medicine by chewing on a certain type of grass. Sometime after, and it could even be the next day, you would see it in their stool, or they would vomit it up, and before you knew it they were fine again.

This happened many weeks ago where she ate the grass, pooped out everything and by the next day she was happy and chasing butterflies again. No sign of grass poop or vomit this time around though, and although she had not eaten in days her tummy had grown quite puffy. And of late, she spent all the time in her dog house, even when I called her, she wouldn't budge, so I had to go sit and scratch her head and try to play with her. I got little or no reaction.

I told mom what was going on while we all had dinner, and mom decided that it was best that we take her to the vet the next day to get her checked out. As much as she was a stray pup I found wondering on the street, over time she became a part of our family. We all loved her.

The next day I was in a hurry to return home from school, as report cards were out. I was an A student with all the averages from different classes. And when I looked at the last thesis entry, remember the one on Evolution versus God? I got a B+. Still not bad for something I rewrote from scratch in just two days, right?

I also couldn't wait for us to take Brownie to the vet, but as I entered my gate, and still looking down at my reported card with a big grin on my face, I glanced up and surprisingly Mom was waiting for me at the front door.

"Mom, look! Look! Report cards are out!" I grinned as I walked briskly up the driveway.

It was only then when I got closer that I realized she was teary-eyed.

"Mom! What's wrong?"

I was met with silence.

"Mom! Are you okay? What's wrong? I asked again as I wiped a trail of tears from her eyes.

Still no answer.

"Mom, please! You're scaring me." I panicked until she finally spoke with one word.

"Brownie," she gasped as more tears rolled from her eye.

"What? What about her?" I asked as again, back in those days, dogs would disappear for several days and then suddenly turn up again.

Is she missing? I thought, thinking that she had ventured off property in search of more of that same grass.

"Mom! Mom! What about Brownie?" I asked as my body shook to the point where the report card fell from my hand.

"I went out to feed her. I…I thought she was sleeping, but…" she sadly said.

"But what? But what, Mom?" I screamed.

"Don't go back there," she sobbed.

"Mom! What happened to Brownie?" I asked frantically.

I immediately dropped my backpack and ran to the back yard, ignoring her calling my name to come back.

I went to Brownie's makeshift dog house, and there she was, all curled up and cozy in that old pillow and blanket I had used to make her bed.

I smiled.

I stooped and scratched the back of her neck as usual with a smile as she slept to wake her up as her front paw would move like she was scratching herself. But this time, she was unresponsive.

I kept on doing it. Still no response. I panicked. I gently took her up from the dog house. Her body was lifeless!

My teary-eyed mom slowly walked around and met me in the backyard and said the worst words I would never want to hear again.

"I'm sorry, Street. I don't know what happened, but she's dead."

"No, Mom. She's only sleeping. Probably she's in a deep sleep as she's not so well, remember?" I said as I tickled Brownie some more, but there was no response.

The silence was only filled with crying.

G and his girl eventually came outside. Everybody was all dressed and waiting for me to come home so we could all take her to the vet.

"I found her like this after breakfast this morning. I'm sorry, Street. She's in her eternal sleep until she wakes up in dog heaven." Mom consoled me.

I wept bitterly as I didn't just lose a dog; I lost a friend, a companion.

Mom, G, and his girlfriend consoled me while desperately try-ing to give various reasons as to why they thought Brownie could have died.

I wept continuously.

Mom and the rest of the guys eventually gave me space with parting hugs before they all sadly returned inside.

I stared at Brownie as I drowned myself in sorrow.

Have you ever been there, where the one thing or person or even a reason that kept you living day by day was now dead?

I wept some more, as although I was labeled as a break dancer, a bad boy, a street thug, and I could go on, I, however, had a soft spot. But now my soft spot was dead!

Call me stupid, but I went to the corner deli and got an empty carton box. I went back home. I dug a hole in the backyard so the box could fit. I placed Brownie in it and wept bitterly as I shoveled dirt over it.

I made a makeshift cross and put it over Brownie's grave. Mom just stood at the back door, hugging herself while watching me as she wept, but she didn't say a word as she felt my pain and my loss.

As strange as it might sound, while I sat on the ground, staring at the cross, while fond memories of Brownie flashed through my head, a single yellow butterfly from nowhere circled the cross and then gently perched on top of it. I started laughing and crying at the same time, as more happy memories of my beloved Brownie flashed across my mind.

My crying stopped after a few days, as I became a new man who had decided that I was now going to be my own lifeline.

There comes a time in life when the crying has to stop!

Because the only person or thing you can depend on to get you through a situation or even just to get you through day by day is yourself!

So that's my story about my beloved Brownie as I slowly snapped back into reality, standing by Bob's bedside. I discreetly wiped a tear from my eye. I was not sure if it was for my memories of Brownie, for Bob, or for both of them.

He was passed out, yet still I laid a hand on his forehead and whispered a prayer for him.

Stoke and Assad glanced at each other, as they both knew I was at a crossroad with my faith and my path, and they respected it. The subject about my Christian faith became a taboo topic among us Street Boys.

The nurse again came and politely asked us to leave, so we finally complied.

We all left the hospital in reflective vengeance mode. Us Street Boys vowed to have our revenge. And just like how they caught us off guard, we would catch them off guard!

For Bob

We met up with Michelle and her friends at the bus stop as we were leaving.

"So what are you not telling me about you and Willy now that you are all *ripe* for him?" I asked as I pulled her aside after group conversing for a bit.

She seemed stunned. "What? What are you talking about? There is nothing going on between us," she gasped.

I gave her a stare of unbelief.

"Street, please. There is nothing going on between us. He wants me and wants to be with me, but I don't care. You are the only person I want to be with. That man has never hugged me or kissed me or anything! I despise him. He even invited me to his birthday party this Saturday night at his house, and I said no!" she pleaded to convince me.

I just stared at her.

A bus pulled up, and her friends called her.

"Bob will be fine the doctor told us. I'm just not sure if you will be fine with all that's going on with you and Willy and his boys. I have to go. I'll come see you. I will be praying for you as always. Just believe me, as I want to believe in you." She sighed as she looked at me with worried, weary eyes, gave me a peck on the cheek, and entered the bus, which eventually drove off.

We caught the other bus for home.

My brother, his girl, and his whole bicycle crew of around thirty came over that evening when they got word of what happened. He and his crew were fuming and swore revenge when we told them the details of that night and the state of Bob in the hospital.

They all came over in fight mode to go visit Willy and beat the crap out of him and his boys, but I had a better idea. A beat-down with Willy and his brother and a couple of their thug friends sounded good, but what if we could have his entire gang of thugs "rounded up" together? That was when I told them about Willy's upcoming birthday party. They all liked the idea for us to wait until then.

I gathered everyone together and asked for a toast.

"For Bob!" we toasted. "Willy and his boys plan to party and celebrate with friends and family, with music, food and drinks and be merry and dance the night away this Saturday. While our friend, our brother, Bob, lay alone, in pain, heavily sedated and recovering in a hospital bed, from the wounds they inflicted on him, and for what?" I asked, getting a bit choked up. "What did we do wrong? What did Bob do wrong to deserve this? We just went to a break dance final. We danced. We won. We celebrated. We left! How did it all get to this? Because those sore losers caught us off guard. We never saw them coming, because it was not anticipated," I exhaled heavily, as I took a gulp from my beer and then a puff.

Silence.

"On Saturday, while they are celebrating Willy's birthday, they won't see us coming either. Payback! We will show them who we are, what we are, and humble them for picking a fight with the wrong crew. There will be blood! We will have our revenge for Bob," I continued. "I plan to crash a party this Saturday! And I want to make it swift and brutal, so by the time those fools regain consciousness, they won't even remember who hit them, or what hit them. We'll be going into the lion's den, and us Street Boys could use some reinforcement to make sure that none a those losers are left standing in the end," I said as I popped a beer from the cooler and handed it to G. He tossed the empty bottle he was holding onto for a while and took a few sips while stroking his goatee. That was always his giveaway that he was in deep thought.

There was silence until my brother put his cigarette out, took a gulp from his beer, and finally spoke as he lit a new one.

"They mess with you, bro, they mess with me. They mess with any a you guys, they mess with me. They mess with me, they mess with all of us. They mess with all of us, and we do what we do best—we fight back! We don't run away or cower and be bullied. We fight!" my brother finally barked, which prompted an uproar from his whole crew to get ready for fight night!

He looked at his girlfriend for approval.

As much as he was a tough guy, she was his lifeline; she was his *Brownie*.

Silence.

"We never asked for this. But sometimes you have to finish stuff in life that other people started that you never asked for," she simply said with a stone face.

"I'll have my girlfriend Clair on standby. And I will bring a couple extra first-aid kits just in case," she continued with a vexed tone as you could tell she expected an outcome in our favor but would still be at the ready to patch up any injuries. "Look at you all—my mighty army. Go kick some ass this Saturday! Let's end this! Let's end this!" she shouted to the cheers from everyone.

"Payback! Let's crash that shit of a birthday party—or Bob," Assad said.

"Let's do this and get it over with!" Stoke also said. "For Bob!"

"For Bob!" the rest of the crew all echoed in agreement as we toasted.

We all had a couple more drinks until I came up with a visual idea as we all gathered to map our plan of attack.

Our driveway was my chalkboard as I used one of my jumbo chalks to draw Willy's street and the two ways to enter and get to his house, and the fastest way to exit after our attack.

Yes, us Street Boys did that frequently with those jumbo colored chalks I used to draw on my driveway to mark an X exactly where we should each stand on stage during a dance contest and then draw long arrows with codes to coordinate and say who moves to which position and when.

But tonight's drawing on my driveway wasn't about a break dance rehearsal.

Party Night

We planned to get there when the party was in full swing so we wouldn't miss any late comers, so we got there close to midnight.

Not a big party, about thirty-five or forty people, mostly men, a few women and children, compared to over fifty of us all men. Yes, we weren't sure the size of the crowd although it was a house party so we recruited more reinforcement, including about a dozen of my promoter's thugs, who were just as eager for revenge, after what they heard these punks did to Bob.

Our plan was simple but lethal.

It was a street dance with music blasting, as they were all partying in the street, when we all rode up from opposite sides of the street, in bandanas covering our face.

I saw Willy dancing and laughing with Jess, the devil in the red dress.

They looked startled as if trying to figure out who we were, as all of us were wearing bandanas. I answered their question by calmly walking up to Willy through the gathering and, without warning, giving him a blindsided clobber with my elbow, which sent him crashing to the ground.

"Hey! Remember me?" I simply said as I knelt over him and clobbered him again and again and again.

He was half drunk, and his reaction time to fight back was way off, so I took advantage of it.

We learned a long time ago that it was better to forcefully hit someone with your clenched elbow for more damage because there was more muscle behind it from your upper arm and shoulder rather than to hit them with your fist, which had very little muscle in you lower arm.

He spewed blood from his nose and mouth as some of his boys ran to his rescue, hauled me off him, and started to give me a split-second beat-down before the rest of my crew charged in and instead gave them a beat-down.

The street brawl was on!

The ladies from his party all scattered in different directions, screaming. Willy and his boys should have done likewise, but instead, they stood their ground and fought back and got the beat down of their life, as they were outnumbered almost three to one. Guess they didn't believe in a fight-or-flee option.

My brother and I took turns trading vengeful blows at Willy. He gush blood from his nose and mouth, until my final vicious elbow to his chin left him unconscious.

"That was for Bob!" I said as I spat in his face and climbed off him.

The fight went on for almost a minute more until we all stood around, looking for someone else to attack. But who didn't limp off running was on the ground wailing, or unconscious.

In the end, a few of us were left bloodied and bruised, but I counted seventeen of Willy's gang, including himself, lying on the ground unconscious or bloodied and writhing in pain. The rest of them took off, running for their lives. I heard screams from inside Willy's house and from neighbors about the mayhem, but I didn't care. I walked over to his brother, who was lying unconscious on the ground, and still gave him a powerful stomp in the face, which knocked him out cold. I looked around to see who else I could finish off, as my adrenaline was still pumping, but they were all out for the count.

We heard the sounds of sirens approaching. Yep, someone called the cops.

"Shit! Let's go! Let's go! Let's go!" my brother shouted.

My promoter and his crew ran to their cars and sped off. G and his crew scampered for their bikes. Those including myself who didn't ride hopped on to the back of a few riders with bigger ten-speed bicycles, and we all rode off.

All the neighbors eventually came out in shock to look at the chaotic scene.

As we rode past Michelle's house, I saw her and her dad huddling at her gate as they looked on at what just unfolded. She didn't notice me as we all were wearing baseball caps and bandanas to cover our face so as to thwart a reprisal.

A few of us hid up the street as onlookers after the fifth police car arrived. We couldn't hear what was going on, but it was frantic. I had a vengeful smile of satisfaction at our retribution, as one minute I was in hiding in the dark shadows of the street looking at what they were doing to Bob, but on this night, I was also in hiding but instead looking at what we just did to them. Sweet revenge!

We discreetly left, and Stoke and Assad came back to chill at my place about an hour later. My brother and his crew didn't chill, but just went straight to their respective homes or back on campus to thwart any suspicion in case cops were circling the area looking for a hoard of bicycles.

As crazy as it sounds, most times us Street Boys never talk about a street brawl after it was over. There was no bragging, or mourning as most times we just put it behind us like it never even happened. It kept us calm instead of scared. That's why we never watched the news.

It was close to one in the morning and all three of us were drinking and watching a recording of a break dance battle on television. No talking. As always, we never talk about a beat down in the aftermath so as not to have any regrets for our actions.

I went to the kitchen to get another beer and heard a knock on the door. I looked at the clock, looked at my boys, and we all got into defensive mode.

I discreetly peeped through my window and saw the flickering lights of a police car at my gate.

It was the cops.

What the what!

I whispered to my boys, and they all changed their stance and pretended to be relaxing in chill mode.

Damn Snitch

I opened the door, and there were two police officers. And lo and behold, behind them was Jess, the devil in the red dress.

What the what!

I was caught off guard twice in seconds!

One of the officers told me Jess gave them reason to believe that we were behind the street brawl at the party earlier.

Damn snitch!

She looked at me somewhat scared as she nervously folded her arms, unsure of what was about to happen next.

The two cops, without even requesting my permission, tried to enter.

"Hey, I didn't give you po-pos permission to come in," I tried to stop them, but they just shoved me aside and entered anyway.

One of the cops looked angrier than the next. He took out his notepad and abruptly asked us our whereabouts that night.

"Here. Home. Chilling with my boys," I replied dryly.

"Isn't it too late to be chilling out with your boys?" the angry officer jumped in. "And what time did this *chilling* with your boys start?"

"Right after your daughter left. About an hour or two ago," Assad jumped in with an annoyed smirk as he gave Stoke the signal to play along. "Yeah, I've seen you and her both before at our break dance contests—in fact, just a few weeks ago at the finals."

"Oh yeah." Stoke smiled. "The promoter hired a couple of you off-duty cops as private security." He smirked.

"Nothing like a little extra cash on the side, eh?" Assad smirked.

The angrier cop seemed at a loss and was slowly fuming.

"They should have hired you at this party you're talking about instead of having this piece of trash I once had a one-night stand with haul you up into my crib this late at night." I glanced at Jess angrily.

The two cops both glanced at her, confused.

"What!" she said out of shock.

"Aw, she didn't tell you? Go ahead. Ask her!" I continued, trying to turn the tables. "After I kicked her out the next morning, she became history. Oh, and also a woman scorned literally. So now this?"

"How dare you! That's not true!" she screamed as she tried to attack me.

One of the officers restrained her, as the other angry officer looked at her with curious eyes.

"Hey! Hey! Miss, calm down!" the other officer said as he shielded her from me.

She got mad and stepped back to the door, gazing at me in a strange way that I couldn't surmise.

"Listen, I'm not here to investigate what went on between you two or his daughter," the calmer officer then shut the situation down by saying.

"Yeah, enough with your damn mind games," the angry officer barked.

"All I know is, we were told to respond to a birthday street party that turned into a brawl, leaving bloodied, beat-up bodies scattered all over the street. This young lady as you can see with blood all over her told us she knows where to find some of the suspects and led us here. So just want to ask you some questions."

I gave her a betrayed look, and she just bowed her head, now looking more scared than ever. Something wasn't making sense about her demeanor, and why was one cop so calm and the other so angry?

What the heck was going on here!

Her black dress had dried blood stains all over, as she must have rendered help to a few bloodied bodies, and a closer observation revealed that she had done a poor job washing or wiping blood stains from her arms.

"So if we were the culprits, how come we aren't as bloodied or bruised as she is?" I asked as the officers now scrutinized our attires and realized that we were all in clean clothing.

He looked at his angry partner for an answer. His partner just sighed, as if thinking.

"Why don't you three come down to the station with us?" the angry cop asked with a fake smile. "We just want to ask you a few more questions, so as to take you off our list of suspects."

The three of us looked at each other with shock, as we thought we were in the clear and knew that them taking us to the police station at that time of the night was going to lead to interrogation in separate rooms to see if we could all collaborate our alibi.

But then I got an even bigger shock.

"My son and his friends are not going anywhere, Officer! They have been home with me all night, and I can vouch for that."

I looked around, and it was my mom, standing at her bedroom door, huddling in her nightgown.

What the what!

Shit, she did it again by just turning up unexpectedly, as we didn't even know she was in her room.

"Excuse me, miss, but..." one of them started.

"No, *you* excuse me! Do you even have a warrant to enter my house?" she snapped with an outstretched hand, expecting the warrant.

There was none.

"Just as I expected. Now get out before I call Commissioner Frank in the morning and have you two disciplined for disturbance, home invasion, and harassment," she ordered as she grabbed a notepad from a corner table and started scribbling. "How dare you take advantage of these boys, trying to haul them off to the station, especially at this time of night because this damn devil accused them of a street brawl!" My mom angrily glared at Jess. "Stay away from my son, you ugly tramp," my mom ordered her with a warning stare. "And I said get out of my damn house!" she again ordered the cops.

Jess immediately exited. The two cops, now visibly embarrassed and upset, stared us down and started to exit.

"Oh, and, Officer Dainey and Officer Grant, I *am* going to file a formal complaint against you two with the commissioner in the morning. Maybe I can tell him I do not wish to pursue this complaint any further if I hear that this investigations against these boys were dropped. But if not, I will officially have this case flagged, especially if you two are thinking about any form of dirty cop reprisal, because I see the look on your face," she said, pointing to the angry cop. "And you damn well know all the consequences of what happens to an officer when you have a flagged complaint."

"Have a good night, ma'am," the angry cop said in a calm manner, realizing that they had breached protocol.

They could be heard debating inaudibly back and forth as they walked down our driveway. They stopped at the patrol car, and both of them spoke briefly with Jess. They all got in and then drove off.

"Hello, boys. I've had a very long day and was looking forward to some rest, but I got a call and have to be back in Cayman by tomorrow night." Mom exhaled heavily without a care of what the heck was going on. "I'm going back to bed. You two get going," she ordered Stoke and Assad. "And *you* have some explaining to do in the morning," she said with an angry point at me.

Moments passed, and I eventually lay in bed, knowing what was to come in the morning. As while we outsmarted the cops, I knew I couldn't outsmart Mom. We have had run-ins with cops before at a couple street brawls, outran them in many street chases, and were even roughed up at times, so that visit earlier didn't scare us.

We always tried to predict the inevitable should the cops get involved after a street brawl, so in case you're wondering what we did after the beat-down at Willy's birthday party to throw off the two cops? Well, simple. The three of us all eventually dashed back home, cleaned up, showered, changed into fresh and clean clothing, ditched our bloodied clothing in Assad's backyard, and then came back to my crib to chill as if we had been there all night.

Were we geniuses or badasses? Call it what you may.

My Father

The next morning, Mom, my brother, and I sat at the breakfast table eating. Only the sounds of cutlery filled the room as there was a nervous silence.

"So you either gonna eat or tell me what the hell is going on," Mom said as she took a sip from her orange juice and realized I hadn't even touched my plate.

"He messed up, but I got this…" my brother started on my behalf before she shut him down.

"I wasn't talking to you!" Mom snapped. "What the hell was last night about?"

I couldn't have a beer in her presence, so I chugged on my orange juice, slumped back in my chair, and started with, "Okay, so…" And then I just told her everything.

My brother backed me up the whole time until he excused himself to go smoke a cigarette outside.

Yes, I got an earful of reprimand from her until she cleared the table and headed to the kitchen to put the dirty dishes away, but then she stopped short, turned back, rested the dishes back down on the table in front of me, and sat.

She shoved the dirty dishes right up to my chest where I was sitting.

"I don't want this on my table!" she snapped, now visibly upset as she slammed a hand down.

There was a nervy silence as I tensed, expecting a bitch slap, as she had delivered before when I screwed up. It never came. And don't laugh, because even though my brother was much older, she would still bitch slap him too when he pissed her off.

"I raised you boys all on my own, since your drunken, wife-beating, deadbeat, poor excuse for a father made me pack you boys up one night, snuck out, and left. You were just eight years old, Adrian. Your brother, who was only eleven at the time, became the man of the house at this one-bedroom apartment I rented, and *you* became my reason to live on," she recalled with a sad stare at a photo on the wall of my brother and me with a happy pose when we were kids.

"You start college in a couple weeks. Focus and fix this nonsense squabble over a stupid break dance belt, Street! Or I will fix it!"

Oh no. Wait! She didn't just call my championship belt, which Willy and his boys cut up to make into wristbands, stupid, right? I thought to myself, but I dared not flinch.

She exhaled heavily and removed a ring from her finger. "The last woman your father was with, unlike me who didn't, called the cops after he hit her for the first time. They took him to jail, and as misfortune would have it, her brother, who was a street thug, was in the same cell with him. A couple days later, the brother got wind of the assault, and he and his other thugs in the holding cell beat your father to a pulp. He was pronounced dead on the way to the hospital," she said with a remorseless stare.

I was shaken.

"You never told me this before," I gasped. "You just always said you left and never saw or heard from him again."

"I didn't. Which mother would ever tell her young son a story like this?"

There was an uneasy silence as I was blown away with all that I just heard.

"You gave me this ring years ago when I took the job offer in Cayman," she started as she stared at it. "I still can't believe you spent your whole savings to buy it for me, but I will never forget you told me that morning I was leaving for the airport—that it was for protection, that you and your friends from church anointed it so that I would be safe as a single woman in a foreign land. It has kept me safe so far, thank God, but after what you just told me, I'd like you to have it to keep *you* safe," she said as she slowly removed it from her finger and reached for my hand. "Call it a mother's intuition, but I can sense evil lurking. Something terrible may or will happen to you, and I don't want to read about your demise in the newspapers," she said as a tear rolled from her eye.

"But, Ma..." I attempted once again to refuse it, but she shut me down and slowly searched for a finger that it fit and then slid it on.

"I have walked the good walk of faith. I have run my race. I have finished my course! I'm in a happy place, Adrian. So until the good Lord calls me home, I have nothing to live on for except to see you boys be all you can be and make me proud, make God proud! But if I was to lose you or your brother, I would have failed. Please don't make me fail," she said as she squeezed my hands.

We both shed a tear. I buried my chin in my chest in shame that I had given my mom reason to worry and be sad.

"Give me a reason to keep on living," she then simply said with a serious stare, as she gathered herself, took up the dirty dishes, and headed to the kitchen.

I just sat there for what seemed like forever, just reflecting and contemplating. I knew one of the Ten Commandments said, "Honor thy mother and thy father so that thy days may be longer," but I kind of felt like I was now entrusted to do so in order for *her years* to be longer.

My brother entered and broke my meditation.

The Swings

"Yo, bro, you got company!" my brother said as he reentered.

I looked up, and to my surprise, it was Michelle. She seemed off—with a plastic, nervous smile. I wasn't sure what her visit was about after all the fighting and bloodshed over the past few weeks, but she had a calm demeanor.

"Just thought I'd stop by," she said as she hugged her pocketbook and Bible and handed me a small potted plant. "I got this for us. Let's just call this our lucky plant." She smiled. "Ms. Brown wasn't home, so I have about an hour or so to spare while my other missionaries up the street wrap up their sessions."

Mom came from the kitchen to finish clearing the table. I introduced them.

"We'll be out back," I said as I led Michelle outside to the backyard. My brother followed behind me to have another cigarette but was halted in his track.

"G," Mom called him, "we need to talk."

He gave me a "See what you got me into" look, shook his head, stuck the unlit cigarette behind his ears, and went with her to the kitchen.

I felt bad as I knew she was in there giving him another lecture on keeping me safe and staying out of trouble at all costs. I knew he was going to fill me in and lay down some new ground rules later, but for now, my only focus was on Michelle.

We walked around to the backyard and sat on two side by side swings that my brother erected. That was he and his girlfriend's favorite outdoor spot for smokes and some fresh air.

"How are you doing?" she asked as she noticed my bruised hands with a couple of bandages on both knuckles, stemming from the fighting last night.

I stared at them. They have been through so many street fights that I'd lost count. Thank God, my mom stepped in when she did last night; if those cops had asked to see our hands or dragged us down to the station, we would have all been busted. The timing of her visit was no coincidence; maybe this was God slowly beginning to prove himself to me again!

Michelle put her stuff aside and slowly started to swing beside mine.

"So, again, how are you doing?"

"We won!" I smiled with uncertainty as I placed her potted plant, our lucky tree, on a column on our back porch and then joined her and pushed myself off to a slow synchronized swing. "It's nice. How often should I water it?"

"Once a week. No more than half a cup of water."

There was a moment of silence until she stopped swinging, took a deep breath, and spoke. "I'm worried for your safety, Street. I knew that was you and your brother's crew there last night, but I dared not say a word, not even to my father. Even Christians have secrets that they would rather not confess or tell. There's bound to be a reprisal."

"I know. And we're ready!"

"What's really going on with you and Willy?" She exhaled. "Did this really all start over a stupid break dance competition belt?"

Okay, I fumed quietly. *So if someone else ever disrespects my championship belt again by calling it stupid, I'm a be on COPS!*

"Because if that is the case, I apologize. I started all this," she said. "There would have been peace between you two if you never gave me that belt, if I never loaned it to his brother, if you and I had…if you and I had never met."

I stared into her worrying eyes after she made that last comment.

Have you ever regretted meeting someone?

Silence.

"You did nothing wrong. The devil was just roaming around that day like a hungry lion, seeking whom to devour, and he crossed our paths," I comforted.

"Wow. Listen to you, Mr. Preacher Man," she said with a sad smile. "You're no stranger to God, Street, but I worry for you and what I have caused." A tear rolled from her eye.

I stood up, gently stood her up from her swing, and hugged her.

She didn't hug me back.

"Don't worry," I again comforted. "All us Street Boys wanted to do was dance, but Willy and his thugs, who are sore losers, wanted to fight. We beat them on the dance floor until they retired from break dancing, and we're gonna beat them in the street, and just like how they stopped competing on the dance floor, the day will come when they will stop fighting, realizing that they will never win."

She didn't reply. I wiped another tear from her eye and hugged her even closer. Even with smudged eye shadow from her teary eyes, she was still as beautiful as ever. And then I did the unimaginable; I gently lifted her chin from her chest and kissed her.

The only response I got was a sniffle, as she used the knuckle from both thumbs to wipe her eyes.

Really!

I gently pressed harder against her lips, trying to pry them open with mine.

Epic fail.

"What are you doing?" she wearily asked, and yes, still not hugging me as she wiped another trail of tears.

I stopped.

"Look at me," I released my grip and whispered, as I raised her chin and realized her tear-filled eyes were closed. "You and I never met so that Willy and I could start a war over a stupid belt."

Oh, wait, did I just call my prized championship belt stupid?

What the what!

She exhaled heavily. "How is Bob?" she whispered with a heavy exhalation as she surprisingly more like hung her hands around my waist than hug me.

"He'll be out Saturday. We having a welcome home get-together for him, and I'd love if you'd be there."

"I can't. I'm leaving for England on Thursday. That's one of the things I came to tell you. I'll be gone for about a month—missionary work, which I am so excited about."

"So I won't see you for another month," I gasped, ignoring the purpose for her travel.

She just exhaled and this time finally hugged me around my waist and then awkwardly hugged me around my neck.

"I'll be back. Just please stay out of trouble until..." she said with a concerned gaze into my eyes. She never saw it coming, and I didn't just hug her again but this time kissed her.

Once again I tried to pry her lips open with mine, and this time, she complied.

"What are you doing?" she again gasped between kisses as our tongues met for the first time.

Her minty breath plus perfume put me in a trance.

"Just shut up and kiss me." I exhaled with a smile.

She gave a faint chuckle, sniffled, and complied.

We finally had our first kiss!

We slowly kissed for almost a minute until it grew passionate, and then—really!—my stupid brother interrupted.

"Bro, Mom wants you." He gave a "Your turn" sigh as he exited from the back door.

"Really, bro! The best moment of my life *ever*, and you had to interrupt! Really!"

He smirked as he lit his cigarette.

She chuckled, too, as she maintained her hug.

"What's her mood?" I questioned, preparing myself.

"She's good…now," he comforted. "I saved your ass again."

He asked Michelle if he could get her anything. She declined, and they chatted for a few as I went to get parting words from Mom.

Mom's ride came and waited, an unmarked police car; when you lived the street life, you knew the various unmarked cop cars. This convinced me and my brother that she wasn't bluffing last night when she threatened the two cops; she had connections or was now dating one of the big boys in the police force. But Mom never told, and we never asked.

Have you ever been in that situation where there is something that you are just itching for someone to tell you, but they never do, and you dare not ask?

We all exchanged long hugs, and she left with parting words for all of us before leaving for the hospital to visit Bob and then head to the airport.

We saw Assad by his gate as we waved her goodbye. He came over.

He dabbed my brother and me and tried to apologize to Michelle, but she wasn't having it.

"I should go," she said as she headed to my backyard to retrieve her stuff.

I went with her, and we hugged and kissed passionately for a while. I beckoned her to come inside the house, to take our kisses to the next level, but she declined.

"I can't believe I'm doing this," she said as she gently pried herself from my embrace and wiped her now smudged lips.

"So I guess this makes us official?" I smiled.

She just smiled, used her index finger to swipe my nose, retrieved her stuff, and gave me a smooch.

"We'll see." She smiled as she left.

"What time you leaving on Thursday?"

"I'm getting picked up around three."

"I'll be on The Main. Stop by for a hug and kiss." I smiled.

"Okay." She smiled as we headed to the gate.

One of her missionaries was there, talking to my brother and Assad. She was an elderly lady who noticed her smudged eye shadow from crying earlier, whipped it, and asked if everything was okay.

"Yes, I'm fine. Everything is okay," Michelle said as she did some facial grooming. "Everything will be okay, right?" she then turned to me and asked, which was about the ongoing feud between Willy and me.

"Yes." I sighed.

"So we cool?" Assad persisted to clear his conscience.

"Yes," she replied to him with a dry, forgiving stare. "I'll see you Thursday," she then said to me as they left.

"You struck gold, bro! Look at that body," my brother said as we watched them walk off.

"Shut up before I kick *your* ass too," I joked at him with a glance at Assad.

"I won't be around for you to do that." Assad smiled as he took a cigarette from my brother and lit it. "I got drafted!"

He showed us the letter from the army. Yep, Assad was going to be a soldier and had to report for enrollment in two weeks. Stoke was about to migrate to the US, and Bob was about to go off to university on the other side of the island. So sadly, the days of the Street Boys were numbered.

Thursday on the Main

My brother and I agreed that for now, I'd tell him my every move and timeframe, in case there's trouble so he knows where to find me. Mom also told me that she had arranged for frequent police patrols at our house and The Main to avert any future trouble with Willy and his boys. See, I knew she was dating that commissioner of police!

So that being said, there was a sense of calm; albeit a tense calm, as I knew retaliation from Willy was brewing.

My brother and his crew, Assad, Stoke, now donning the gold break dance championship belt, and I were all on The Main having drinks and smokes. I had my boom box going and the three of us started a cameo break dance contest. Everyone cheered on until a car pulled up that got our attention. It wasn't one of the police cars that we all noticed patrolling back and forth but ignored. It was Michelle in her friend's car on her way to the airport.

She got out of the passenger seat and walked over.

"Really!" she smiled and snapped as she yanked the cigarette from my mouth and stomped on it, to the amusement of everyone.

"Look at you!" I gasped at her attire as I tried to kiss her, but she stopped me as I leaned in, by placing her index finger on my lips.

"So, kissing a guy who smokes is like licking a dirty ash tray!" She smiled, as she handed me a piece of folded paper, and stuck the gum she was chewing in my mouth.

"I'm not sure of our schedule and how often I'll be in our hotel room but this is the number to reach me. How about we try for every Sunday at three o'clock?"

"Deal!" I smiled as I gulped on my beer to wash away the cigarette scent, and chewed on her gum as I looked at the telephone number she had written down on the piece of paper.

It was kind of weird that she didn't mind me drinking but hated the fact that I smoked. Go figure! Most of us didn't have cell phones or even a house phone back then, but there were public phone booths everywhere.

I walked her back to her car, for some privacy from my boys; we leaned on the trunk and chatted for a bit. I pulled her over to me, she stood between my legs, wrapped her arms around my neck and we kissed for a bit, before being interrupted by a screeching car that stopped across from us.

It was Willy and his boys.

Oh, boy, here we go again!

"What the hell! Come here, bitch!" Willy screamed at her as he got out of the car.

"No!" she screamed nervously, tightening her hug around my neck.

He didn't cross the street as my brother and his crew all sprung into alert fight mode and lined our side of the sidewalk, ready to jump him and his boys.

Michelle grew petrified as another car pulled up behind his. It was Willy's brother, with his face all bandaged up, and some of his thugs. They all got out of the cars, ready to fight. I knew a street brawl was about to ensue, and I didn't want her to witness.

"Michelle!" Willy again screamed at her.

She ignored him.

"Go! I'll call you on Sunday," I said as a now visibly shaken Michelle hopped back into her car, and they slowly drove off.

Fight!

In a rage, Willy, without warning, stormed over to me and took a swing, which I saw coming, so I ducked and met him with an uppercut that sent him staggering and crashing in the middle of the street.

The street brawl was on again, but this time, there was no clear winner or loser, as we were all halted within a minute by a cop car that screeched up with sirens and lights blaring. Yep, that same cop car we noticed patrolling earlier. Guess we were now under surveillance.

Some of Willy's boys took off running but were quickly halted by oncoming cop cars with cops that exited with guns drawn. Most of my brother's crew hopped on their bikes and scampered away too. Some got caught; some escaped. My brother could have taken off, too, but decided to stick with us to see the outcome.

Before I knew it, more and more cop cars with sirens blazing arrived.

Willy, his brother, and a few of his thugs were put in handcuffs.

And yep, so were my brother, Assad, Stoke, and me.

"They started it, Officer!" I said as I was cuffed.

"You have the right to remain silent," the frustrated officer who was the first on the scene snapped.

"And you have the right to tell the truth when we get downtown," I said worriedly, knowing that he saw how the whole brawl started.

"Just get in! Watch your head," he said as we walked over to his squad car, and he put me in the back seat.

Wow! One minute I was chilling with my boys and Michelle, and now here I am handcuffed in the backseat of a police car, thanks to that damn Willy and his bitch-ass thugs?

This has to end once and for all, I thought to myself, as this feud between us had been going on for several weeks and counting.

As we slowly drove off to the police station, I noticed the car that Michelle was in parked up half a block away. She never left. They pulled over and witnessed everything. Our eyes locked on each other as we slowly drove past her car. Her hands were covering her mouth as she gazed at me and sobbed uncontrollably.

Wow.

What a parting memory. I had let her down. I was disgusted with myself.

Jail

We were all processed at the police station, and it was there that I overheard one of the officers telling Willy that he violated his probation and as such would be sent to prison if we were to press charges, as one of the officers witnessed that he was the one who started the fight.

It was a crammed processing room, where we could over hear everything that was going on. We were later asked if we wanted to press charges. My brother said, yes, to finally get closure.

I heard Willy pant, "No!"

"My mom would never forgive me. Plus, me and Jess are expecting our first child," he said as he sat there still in handcuffs, bowing his head in his lap as he realized his fate.

What? Jess, the devil in the red dress, was pregnant?

Wow!

I also saw him cry for the first time.

What goes through your mind when you see someone you have known for the longest while, an antagonizer of yours, cry for the first time?

I had a split-second flashback of that one night stand I had with her after that night out at the club. I still had blurred memories, but I knew we had sex all night—without a condom stupidly, of course, because we were both drunk. And even to double-check, I recalled that there were no condom wrappers anywhere the next morning when I woke up and saw her sleeping naked next to me!

Could this be an episode for the Maury Show to determine who the father was?

Hush! I didn't say anything to blow my cover.

"And do you also want to press charges for assault?" the officer asked me.

I snapped back to reality by a nudge from my brother. I looked over at Willy. All I saw was an empty soul. I remembered what he did to Bob and what he wanted to do to Michelle and what he did to me.

"Yes!" I gasped as I buried my forehead in my handcuffed palms.

I heard an outburst from Willy as he broke down crying. Yep, he knew he was going to prison.

Don't ask me what I was thinking, as the officer walked off talking to another officer to take him away to another holding area for official processing, but I took a heavy exhale and blurted, "No!"

The officer stopped and turned around, looking a bit confused. Everyone in the holding area looked at me.

"What are you doing?" my brother, sitting beside me, asked.

"No! I…I mean we don't want to press charges," I said, to the shock of everyone.

My brother was in shock and at a loss but also confusingly and reluctantly finally nodded his consent.

"Young man, are you sure?" the officer confirmed.

I nudged my brother. He exhaled and stared at me with trusting eyes.

"Yes! We don't want to press charges. We just want to go home." He exhaled to the surprise of the room.

I would never forget the empty look of "Thank you" on Willy's face as he let out a heavy exhalation and wiped snort from his nostrils. Our processing was wrapped up, and we were all released.

Outside the police station, Willy and his crew just stared us down with an uncertainty of what would happen next. He walked over to where my crew and I were gathered.

"I didn't deserve what you just did. Thank you! I owe you one," he said dryly and then slowly walked off and left with his crew.

"This could have ended tonight!" my brother fumed. "What was that about?"

My mind was all over the place as we walked home.

"Kicking his ass, yes, but my conscience couldn't live with me sending him to prison, especially if he is about to be a father," I finally exhaled.

The silent response from my crew and my brother confirmed that they agreed. My mind ran to Michelle and what she must be going through after our earlier encounter.

The rest of the night went by quietly, with everyone on guard and on edge, as we knew that even though I let him off the hook, there was still a chance for reprisal with Willy's crazy brother hungry for revenge.

The Last Farewell

Saturday came, and yeah, Bob was discharged from the hospital.

Assad, Stoke, and I got some beers, jerk chicken, smokes and my boom box, and headed over to his house. But it wasn't a happy homecoming however, as when we got there that evening his parents met us at the gate, barred us from entering and gave us a earful, with a warning never to come around their son again, "or else…"

Wow!

We left all embarrassed and went back to crash at my place.

It was around 11:00 p.m. later that night. Stoke and Assad left and I was home alone slouched in the living room sofa having a beer.

The TV was on but muted, as I was listening to some break dance jams from my boom box.

There was a knock at the door that interrupted the thoughts that were going through my head.

I opened, and to my surprise, it was Bob!

"I snuck out. They're sleeping," he said as he took the beer from my hand and took a long gulp. "Hmm, that felt good."

He was wearing crutches and had two bandages on his head.

We bear hugged, as I was just grateful that he was back and recovering.

"I'm sorry," I said as we sat. I got emotional when I saw his condition.

"Don't be. I was stupid for not running the other way, as we always practiced." He laughed, wiping a tear from his eyes. "You guys didn't bail on me. I screwed up with our street brawl protocol."

"What were you thinking, man?" I chuckled.

"We just won the golden break dance championship belt, Street! I wasn't thinking." He smiled as he took my beer and had another gulp.

I went to the kitchen and brought out two more beers.

"I want you to have this back, bro," he said as he gave me back the silver necklace I had put around his neck in the hospital. "I was out. Didn't even know when you put it on my neck."

"Just to remind you that you're still Mr. Macho Man, even if you are all busted up lying in a hospital bed," I toasted.

"It's yours!" I said, giving it one last stare as I handed it back to him.

"No, this is a part of what makes you, Street."

"Made me." I chuckled, realizing that the days of the Street Boys were numbered. "Stoke has the golden championship belt as a reminder of who we were and how we kicked ass. This is your reminder of the Street Boys."

He sighed, smiled, and put it on.

"Bro, this is your last chance to take this back, because you know how much I love this damn chain man." He laughed as he adjusted it around his neck.

"And you better shut up and change the subject before I change my mind about giving it to you." I chuckled.

There was a moment of silence as we both stared at photos of us around the living room, and seemingly reflected on the fact that the Street Boys were about to be history.

Sigh.

He filled me in on what happens next re him and university and I filled him in on everything, since the incident that night.

He seemed a bit disappointed that I didn't press charges against Willy. He hesitated, but after a few more gulps from his beer can, he told me that this was goodbye, as he was moving in back with his parents before starting university in two weeks.

"Well, I'm glad you at least beat the crap out of him and his brother." He sighed. "Sounds like you two are trying to bury the hatchet, but the next time you cross paths with him, give him a knockout punch for me."

I promised.

I told him about Assad's enrollment, and then it hit us that with Stoke migrating anytime soon, the Street Boys were officially over.

"We had some good times," he reminisced with a big smile. "Remember that time when…"

And we continued talking about the fond memories, until he had to go. We agreed that he'd write to stay in touch and that I would tell the rest of the crew he said farewell.

There was another knock at the door.

It was his girlfriend.

"Hey, Street" she greeted. "Babe, okay, so, I did my best to cover for you, but your mom just woke up to check on you, and I told her you just made a quick run over here to return some stuff." She gave me a greeting hug and started to lead him outside.

"Shit, I gotta go," he said, and we hugged for the last time.

"Hey! You two take care of each other!" I halted them as they exited. "And if you break her heart, Bob, I'll come find you, and we gonna have a dance-off!" I ended with a sad smile.

"You hear that?" She nudged him with a smile. The three of us again hugged, and they left.

That was the last time I ever saw Bob.

Have you ever missed a friend that you wish you could see or hear from again but finally convinced yourself that you won't?

Sigh.

I slumped back in the sofa and, while reaching for the TV remote, gazed at a picture of us Street Boys on the center table, taken after our silver championship break dance victory.

Stoke had his wish with migrating to the United States. Bob had his wish with his scholarship. Assad had his wish with being enrolled in the army. Damn, even Mom and bro had their wish with me keeping out of trouble, for now at least. I was about to start college too. But I was the only one who didn't have my main wish come through—Michelle. But when it finally did, it came with unexpected consequences.

CHAPTER 6

THE PHONE BOOTH

I had a pocket full of quarters and went to my favorite phone booth up the street at around two to call Michelle.

Damn, I missed her!

One guy was on the phone talking, and another old lady was waiting.

I knew the guy, we dabbed, and I told him to make it quick. He did. The old lady got frustrated after not getting through with her call and left.

I had the phone booth all for myself.

I took out the paper with the phone number Michelle gave me and dialed.

It rang without answer.

It was about 2:30 p.m., so I didn't panic; I was early, so I just lingered around until three o'clock and dialed again.

Still, no one picked up.

After a few minutes, I dialed again. And finally someone from the front desk at the hotel answered.

I told them the name of the person I wanted to be connected to. She looked up the room number and transferred me.

"Hello!" a familiar voice from the room answered.

It was Michelle.

My heart melted. I smiled and sighed heavily at the beautiful sound of her voice.

"Hey," I simply said, remembering our last moment together.

There was a long silence from her end, followed by a heavy sigh.

"Michelle, it's me, Street."

The next thing I heard was quiet, restrained sobbing. But still, she didn't say a word.

"Michelle."

"Give me a moment, guys. I need to take this call," I heard her say to whoever was in the background.

"Are you okay?" she then gasped as a door closed, and it sounded like she went to another room.

"Yes! I'm fine," I asserted.

"Are you in jail?"

"No, silly rabbit. We got released the same evening. They even wanted *us* to press charges against Willy to send him to prison, but I didn't."

"You should have!" she gasped, giving me a moment of regret, as there seemed to be something she was not telling me. But what?

"How are things going so far with your mission?" I asked, trying to change the subject, as I knew she would just shut down if I pressed her for answers that she wasn't ready to relay.

I learned that especially in relationships, there are times you would be running your mouth with someone, asking for and insisting for them to speak up with answers, but they shut down. Silence while you rant on. And the more you press them to speak up, the longer their silence drags on. So instead of doing that, just simply have your say then shut your mouth and give them their time and breathing space. Eventually they will open up and have their say.

She just surprisingly again asked, "Are you okay?"

"Yes, babe. But are you?" I asked, sensing her mood.

She broke down crying.

"No! I have been worried sick since I saw you being hauled off in that police car. I wasn't sure what to think or what was happening," she sobbed.

"Hey. Hey...hey, I'm fine. I'm safe. I'm good. We're all good," I comforted.

Over the next few minutes, I filled her in on everything, including Stoke, Bob, and Assad, and she finally calmed that we were all okay.

She filled me in, too, as we spoke for almost half an hour.

Have you ever been in a situation where a missed loved one was nowhere next to you and even a far distance away but just by calling them and hearing their voice makes your day and places them at least mentally when you close your eyes right next to you?

I kept having to add quarters so as to not get disconnected but was slowly running out as we continued our conversation.

She dropped a bombshell telling me that now her trip may be extended to other countries in Europe, so she might be gone for at least two to three months.

I felt empty but what was I to say; she was a woman of God, doing God's work.

I grew silent.

"Street, Street. Street!" she whispered.

"I'm out of quarters. I have less than a minute left." I sighed at the realization that I won't be seeing her for a couple months.

"I'll be back. Just promise me you will stay away from those boys, and stay out of trouble until…" She sighed.

"I promise. I just got the beep, babe. We're about to get disconnected. I love you," I whispered out of the blue.

"We will never be disconnected." She chuckled as she blew me a kiss over the phone. "I…I can't believe I'm about to say this but I…"

And then we got disconnected, so she didn't finish what she wanted to say.

I stood in the phone booth for over a minute after that with the phone still at my ear as my mind was all over the place. I wasn't sure what to think or feel. I searched for more quarters to call her back but came up empty. Plus by now there were four other persons waiting and fuming at me for taking so long on my call.

Have you ever ended a call but still continued holding the phone at your ear for whatever reason, not to mention all the thoughts going through your mind after you finally put the phone down?

I finally hung up and left.

Next Sunday

Bob had taken off, Assad was enrolled in the military, and Stoke was busy with family getting his documents finalized to migrate to the United States.

The Street Boys were officially over!

Wow.

It was an empty feeling, because my brother never came by all week so I couldn't wait for Sunday to call the love of my life, Michelle.

Yes! Sunday finally came, but there was a hurricane out at sea that was giving us a torrential downpour of rain all day from its outer bands.

It was almost 2:30 p.m. when I decided to head to the phone booth.

I thought about taking my brother's BMX bicycle, but it didn't have splash guards over the wheels, so I grabbed my umbrella and made the fifteen-minute walk, armed with a pocket full of quarters to have a nice long chat with my boo.

The rain was pouring down; plus, it was windy, so windy that a gust flipped my freaking umbrella downside up, giving me a beat down from the torrential rain.

Has that ever happened to you with your umbrella out in public, especially when you're trying to look all neat and prissy and not trying to get wet?

But I made it to the phone booth just in time to shelter before I got a soaking, and locked myself in. And, luckily, because of the weather; there was no one else there.

I used my T-shirt and wiped myself dry, and after a few attempts to remedy it, I realized that my umbrella was ruined. But who cared? I was about to call Michelle on the prompt of the nearby church bell that chimed on the hour, every hour.

I did, and this time, she picked up after three rings.

"Hello!" that familiar, angel-like voice said.

"Hey, babe, it's me." I smiled, still trying to fix my ruined umbrella.

After a few exchanges, I realized that she sounded a bit distant. I put my umbrella down, leaning it on the ground in the corner of the phone booth.

"What's going on? Is everything okay?" I abruptly and curiously asked.

There was just heavy breathing on the phone from her end.

I popped in four more quarters for additional minutes.

"Babe, what's going on?" I begged her to talk to me, sensing something was wrong. "Michelle, Michelle!"

'Yes! I'm here," she finally sniffled as if she was discreetly crying.

"What's wrong, babe? You don't sound like your usual self. Talk to me," I pleaded.

There was another long bout of silence.

"Michelle!" I pleaded.

"Yes," she finally answered again. "How was your week?" she asked as a distraction from her mood.

"Fine! What's going on?"

I shut up and gave her a moment to exhale.

More silence until she finally spoke.

"Street, there is something I have to tell you."

My heart skipped a beat.

"I'm listening," I said, not sure what next to expect.

There was more silence and heavy breathing from her end.

"He's here," she gasped.

"He...he who?" I asked all confused, with my mind all over the place.

"Please don't be mad at me for not telling you," she quietly sobbed.

"Telling me what? He who?" I grew more and more concerned.

More silence and quiet sobbing.

"My boyfriend from church, my ex. He was a part of our group. He's here," she finally explained.

What the what!

"So?" I said, disconcerted. "You told me he was a jerk and you dumped him. So what's going on?"

More silence, and I inserted more quarters for extended talk time.

The familiar old lady walked up and stood meters from the phone booth, waiting to make a call. She was wet and fighting the wind with her umbrella also.

But I didn't care. I was sorry, but my head was in a spin.

"Talk to me!" I finally snapped, having enough of her sniffles and heavy breathing.

She finally explained, "I didn't know until that day I got to the airport and saw him, but I didn't say anything to upset you last Sunday. But my boyfriend...my ex was a part of our group. And for the past week, he has been begging for me to give him another chance, admitting that he screwed up."

I almost dropped the phone out of shock.

Now the tables had turned, and it was now me being silent with heavy breathing as she kept on talking, which eventually became blurred to me.

"I've told him about us, and he gave me a fine lecture about me and you being 'unequally yoked' and all that and just kept begging me to give him another chance."

"So what did you say?" I asked, having heard enough as my joints felt weak from the shock of what I was hearing.

No response.

"What did you say?"

More silence.

"Michelle!" I finally barked, feeling a hurt that I prayed no one else in love would ever feel.

She broke down crying. "Street, please try to understand. And don't be mad, but he was my first kiss, my first love."

"So?"

"So...so I...I...told him yes!"

What the what!

My whole body trembled, not from the cold rain outside, but from what I just heard. She kept on talking, but everything was blurred as I didn't want to hear anything else.

The old lady came and politely knocked on the door to ask me if I was almost done, as it was getting really bad out there with the rain and wind and all. I gave her an empty stare. Sensing my demeanor, she cowered and politely stepped back from the phone booth.

Michelle kept on talking and pleading her case. It fell on deaf ears as I didn't hear a word. The only thing I heard next was the automated voice telling me to add additional quarters as I had one minute left before we were disconnected.

I didn't.

The last thing I heard was Michelle pleading with me to forgive her and to try to understand her situation. And then I heard dial tone as we got disconnected. I stood there for a good minute with the phone still at my ear as I stared at the ground.

I exhaled heavily and looked up. There was the poor old lady still patiently waiting while fighting with her umbrella in the pouring rain. I hung up and opened the door to the phone booth.

She walked over, and we exchanged positions as I let her in and exited.

"Thank you. Are you done, sir?" she politely asked.

My mind ran on Michelle and what we had and what could have been. And what I just heard.

"Yes! I'm done!" I replied with those thoughts in mind as I emptied my pocket, still full of quarters, and gave them all to her. I fixed her umbrella, told her to have a good day, and slowly walked off in the pouring rain, leaving my broken umbrella behind.

I never looked back as I walked off and heard her say, "Thank you" and "God bless you, young man."

If this is God's blessing, I thought, *He can keep it. I don't want it. This is one of the saddest days of my life.*

Heartbreak

By the time I got home, I was drenched. I knocked, thinking my brother had stopped by as I hadn't seen him all week. No answer. So I went around the back to retrieve our hidden house key under the new hiding spot—Michelle's potted lucky tree for us. I got the key, stared at the plant for a bit, and then shattered it on the ground.

I was not sure how much time had passed after I entered the living room when I heard the front door opening. It was my brother and his girlfriend.

"What the hell! You okay, bro?" my brother asked when he saw my condition.

"Street! What happened?" His girlfriend rushed over to me.

I was sitting on the floor, still in soaking wet clothes. The cigarette in my hand was almost burned out without me even taking a puff, and the can of beer next to me was still unopened, although it had been sitting there for a while.

"Street!" my brother barked. "What's wrong, bro? Willy again?" he asked as he came over to me, getting all worked up.

"No. No, bro."

Silence.

"She dumped me," I whispered to calm his concern.

He calmed down, as he thought it was another run-in with Willy and his boys.

"What?" he said confused. "Michelle?"

I nodded.

"I saw you two making out 'round back before she left, and you two seemed like a match made in heaven. So what happened? What did you do to screw up this time?"

His girlfriend nudged him to shut up out of concern for my heartbreak.

"There was no heaven. Nothing. I called her, and she told me her ex was on the mission with her in England and that they are trying to patch things up."

"That bitch!" my brother snapped.

His girlfriend nudged him even harder again as he headed to my bedroom and returned shortly after with a face towel and one of my T-shirts.

"I dunno what to say, bro. For a moment there, I thought you had a run-in with Willy and his boys again. There're some situations I got your back with, Street, but in this lovey-dovey case, I...I don't know what to say," he continued, nudging his girlfriend for help. He tossed me the t-shirt and face towel. "Forget her and take that wet shit off before you catch a cold! Don't get sick on me, man. You start college in a week." He again nudged his girlfriend for intervention.

She always loved me as a little brother and was my biggest fan, cheering me on with her girls at all our break dance competitions. She slouched beside me on the floor, helped me to remove my wet T-shirt and put the new one, and mopped my hair with the towel.

"You didn't know she…?" she started.

"She told me he was a jerk and that it was over," I interrupted, just gazing into space, as I knew her question before she even finished asking it.

She exhaled heavily, opened my beer, took a sip, and handed it to me. "So let it be then," she suggested.

I sighed heavily at the thought that it was over with her, especially considering that we just exchanged our first kiss.

"Street. Street. Street!" she snapped as she held my chin and turned my face to hers after realizing I wasn't paying attention to whatever else she was saying. She had a look of concern in her eyes, as they got glossy from feeling my hurt. "Let it go. I have seen how many girls you have going crazy over you at your dance contests." She smiled.

"Not to mention how many girls he brings home from the clubs every now and then," my brother added, as he reentered with two beers, handed one to his girlfriend, slumped in the sofa, and gave me a vigorous "You got this" scratch in my head.

They opened their beers, and as was customary, we knocked cans together to make a toast. But this time, no one said a word, as there was nothing to toast to.

"You two made me finally stop saying 'To hell with love and relationship' when I met her. I prayed that I would find love again and have a relationship like yours. I thought I did. But look where it got me," I gasped as I chugged on my beer.

"Bitch!" my brother again fumed.

My girlfriend nudged him to shut up.

"You'll be all right. Just leave her alone and focus on college, making your mom, your brother, me, and the Street Boys proud. Just leave her alone," she pleaded as she gave me a bear hug, kissed me on the forehead, and beckoned me to go shower and change into dry clothing, as my jeans were soaking wet.

I eventually complied, and once again, I just stood in the shower with the water beating down on me as I tried to accept the fact that it was over between Michelle and me. As my brother's girlfriend suggested, I should just leave her alone, as after that last phone call, we were now disconnected in more ways than one.

Easier said than done!

CHAPTER 7

CLAIR

The week went by fast. I didn't hang out on The Main. There was no sign of Willy and his boys. My brother hardly stopped by. Stoke only stopped by once or twice. Bob started university way out of town; Assad was at a military base, training.

Before I knew it, Sunday came again.

I was a confused soul; as two o'clock came, which was the time I would start getting ready to go call Michelle. But I just sat there on the backyard swing in silence, reminiscing on our first kiss. And then don't ask me what I was thinking, but I got up, stopped at the corner deli, got some quarters, and headed to the phone booth.

It was a nice sunny day, and to my surprise, no one was there.

I was at a loss as to what to say or what more I wanted to hear from her now that she broke my heart, yet still, on the stroke of three o'clock, which I could tell from the nearby church bells chiming on the hour, I popped my quarters in and dialed.

The phone picked up on the first ring, and it was her.

"Street!" she answered instead of the usual "Hello" as if she was anticipating my call.

I didn't reply. She kept on talking, all this time begging me to say something and saying how sorry she was for everything. I still didn't say anything.

"Street, please, I can hear your breathing. I'm sorry I hurt you."

There was brief silence.

"But I've made up my mind."

A tear rolled from my eye at those words. The automated voice prompted me to add more quarters or I would be disconnected. I didn't.

"My ex and I had a long conversation Friday night at dinner. Since then I thought long and hard and prayed about it, which made me decide that it's definitely over between us…"

Those were the last words I heard from her as we got disconnected. The "teenager in love" me kept holding the phone at my ear as I listened to the dial tone. I reached for my pocket to retrieve more quarters to call her back. I slowly dropped four quarters in, one at a time, but when I got the prompt to dial, I didn't.

I slowly hung up and left for home.

Here I am going through torment and heartbreak, thanks to you, yet you two are over there, having romantic dinners, I thought to myself, fuming as I walked home.

When I arrived, my brother and his crew had just arrived. So was Stoke. They had the house stereo blasting, and everyone was just drinking and chilling on the front lawn. I lied about where I was as I dabbed my brother, my crew, and some of his crew members. I was offered a beer, and we all chatted for a bit. Yes, I didn't want to look stupid and admit that I just went to call her after being instructed to leave her alone.

And yes, it was my brother and his girlfriend's idea to have a social get-together for me to cheer me up as I started college the next morning. His girlfriend, somewhat tipsy, walked over and playfully yanked me away.

"So what do you think?" she said as she gestured at one of her girlfriends talking with another girl.

"What!"

"Hey! I'm trying to play matchmaker here. She and I had a chat about you in the week. She owes me a big favor and she said yes to going on a date with you." She grinned. "I put in a good word for you. Go talk to her!"

"Really? No! I'm not her type." I smiled, knowing that familiar face and her reputation and with thoughts of Michelle still running through my head.

"Okay, fine!" she said as she hugged my arm and yanked me over to her where she introduced us.

It was Clair.

I had seen her many times at my break dance competitions, but she was what was labeled as an "off-limits high-end girl," who, as college kids, we just couldn't afford to maintain. Although she was a beautiful teenager, word was, she also only dated older men—yep, sugar daddies.

We spoke for a bit, as my brother's girlfriend gave us our space, and I had a "What the heck" moment and just asked her out to the club the following Saturday.

She looked over at my brother's girlfriend, who was keeping an eye on us the whole time, winked, and simply said, "Cool. I know you don't have a car, so I'll come pick you up around noon on Saturday. But look at these nails, I have to get them done and also get a special hairstyle for you. Oh, and then we have to go to the mall so you can get me a nice, sexy dress," she went on. "What's that look about?" she asked when she noticed my "I so can't afford you" stare. "Street, you know I'm a high-maintenance girl. I wanna look hot and sexy for you! You'll be the most popular guy in the club, and I just wanna be the hottest girl!" she continued as she stepped closer to me and started to slow-dance although break-dance music was playing.

"Sounds like a plan," I lied. "Hey! I'll be right back," I said as I noticed Assad in the crowd, in his camouflage uniform, talking with Stoke.

I walked over, and we bear-hugged.

"What the hell, man! Look at you!" I said with pride as we exchanged a few greetings.

"Yeah, this brutal training is driving me nuts, bro. They gave us the rest of the day off, because tomorrow they taking my platoon out to sea and told us to expect the worst."

Me and Stoke dabbed and laughed, but Assad didn't find it funny, as he swam like a brick in water; let's just say, he couldn't swim.

"You got this, soldier!" I smiled as we hugged again.

"I know. I can't let my dad down nor you guys. I got this," he asserted, almost to himself.

"Oh, I'm glad you're here for this final negotiation, Street," Stoke then said. "So is this officially mine? I leave on Friday," he asked, tugging at the golden break dance championship belt he was wearing.

Assad looked at me to concur.

"Yes!" I smiled.

"Yes! Yes! Yes!" Stoke said with a glee punching the air, as he took out a wad of cash, counted out a portion, and handed it to Assad, who was equally delighted.

"Whoop whoop!" Assad smiled as he counted it, then stopped after counting it a second time. "Hey, are you high, bro? This is more than we bargained for, Stoke"

"I know. And I know you like fast cars, so put in that super fast turbo engine you keep drooling about. Upgrade!" Stoke smiled as he held my hand and handed me the rest of the coiled up cash. "And you, sir, take Michelle shopping and then on the date of a lifetime." He smiled. "My parents closed our accounts and gave me my cut. We have no further use for Jamaican dollars, as we are all migrating together."

Haven't we all been there where the money we travelled with to another country is now labeled as foreign currency and is rendered practically useless because of the rate of exchange between both countries?

I didn't say anything to update them on what was going on between Michelle and me.

We chatted some more, had a few drinks, updated them on Bob and Willy, said our goodbyes, and everyone slowly started leaving.

"So are we on for next Saturday?" Clair asked, playing on her cell phone as I entered the living room heading for my room.

She was one of the fortunate ones who could afford to have a cell phone in those days—no doubt thanks to one of her sugar daddies. She was sitting next to my brother's girlfriend; both were in the sofa, chatting and watching TV.

I squeezed my pocket to feel the wad of cash Stoke gave me and realized I could now afford to take up her offer. But seeing right through her, all she had to offer me was a good night out and wild sex. It sounded like a plan, but although she was even hotter that my brother's girl and was every guy's dream girl on campus, you could call me weird, but there was just a certain vibe about her that didn't click with me.

"How about I let you know by Friday. Just wanna see how I feel after this first week in college, where I know they might literally throw the book at us."

She agreed, with my brother's girlfriend as our messenger to confirm the date.

College

My heart was shredded at the thoughts of what Michelle and her ex were intimately doing over there to patch things up, besides having romantic dinners. My crew was no more. My brother knew what was going on and started spending more nights at home to be my "caregiver."

Still, I was a lonely man.

The next morning finally came for me to make my mom proud as a mechanical engineer.

First day of college, and we did the usual blah, blah, blah introductions in my class. Surprisingly, most of them knew me from break dancing as one of the Street Boys. There were twenty-four of us in my class. There were only two girls; the rest were boys. And we were told that there would be another student that would be added in a few weeks due to "some complications."

I hit it off with everyone in my class. As I said, most of them knew me from them attending our break dance competitions.

As the week flew by, we quickly became friends—hanging out at breaks, having lunch together, and most times, walking to the bus stop together.

One of the girls from our class was on her way to school Thursday morning, walking the ten or so blocks from where the bus station was, when she was assaulted by three teenage thugs who were hanging out at this open lot that was popular for petty drug trades. Thankfully, she wasn't sexually assaulted, as we were told of rape cases in that vicinity before because it was a wooded area that you could easily haul someone off into, but they stole her pocketbook and a gold chain she was wearing.

Our principal notified her parents and reported the incident to the police, but I had other ideas.

Most of us in class decided on a payback to meet her at her bus station, walk with her, and if we see the thugs, beat the crap out of them. Yep, as one of the Street Boys, I opted for street justice instead of running to the police, and surprisingly, a few of the guys in my class were badasses themselves, who agreed.

The next morning, we did see the three of them as she identified, and one of them was wearing her gold chain.

It was about thirteen of us versus these thieves, so without warning we caught them off guard, attacked and beat the crap out of them. Yep, another mini street brawl with my new crew, just before class. She yanked her chain from the thug's neck and kicked and stomped him a few times as he lay on the ground bloodied and writhing in pain. We searched them all but she never did find her pocketbook. We beat them up some more and afterwards, told them the reason for the beat down; almost like when you shoot, then ask questions after. We then all left them with a stern warning to leave her, and us alone, or else.

We kind of braced for a reprisal so always walked in large groups back and forth to the bus station, but in the end, for weeks later as we walked with her as escort to and from school, we never saw them again. Most of the guys in my class and I, from that day formed an alliance; 'One for all, all for one!"

Okay, so rewind back to that Friday, on the first week of school; it was hard work as they threw us off in the deep. One minute we were in class taking tons of notes, and the next minute, we were in our overalls, tool belts, and all, in the gigantic mechanic shop, learning all the crafts of being a mechanical engineer.

But we accomplished week one. Phew! Then came the weekend, and all was quiet.

Stoke

I got home, and Stoke, who had migrated to the United States that afternoon, left a farewell note in an envelope taped to my front door with instructions. The envelope also contained cash. When I went around the back, still reading where it instructed me to search, I opened our backyard shed, and tucked away under a bottom shelf was our golden break dance championship belt.

What the what!

I was confused, but at the end, the note then simply read, "I'm off. Here's some extra left over cash, bro. Don't be mad, but I took your boom box as a souvenir, and I'm just lending this belt to you, in memory of our crew. They stole the bronze belt, cut up the silver belt. I couldn't leave you empty-handed by taking this golden belt. You made us Street Boys famous. All the girls wanted us, and all the guys wanted to be like us. But we made a deal, so I'm just lending it to you. I'll be back for it one of these years. Thanks, bro, for some of the best memories of my life ever. Street Boys for life!"

Wow! I got a bit choked up.

I just slouched to the ground staring at the belt as I had flashbacks of all those great nights us Street Boys had—winning break dance championships, the street brawls, the highs and lows of our friendship, our brotherhood—and just maintained a sad smile on my face.

And yes, I had loaned him my boom box Thursday night for the private send off party his family threw for him. I wasn't invited, as they also knew about the Bob incident and thought, I was trouble. I didn't mind him taking it, as the cash he gave me could easily afford me to purchase that spanking new boom box I wanted. And yes, divided we now were, scattered even between countries and living our separate lives, but we all vowed to remain Street Boys for life!

I Don't Know What to Think

I was heading back from the backyard several minutes later to my gate, as I had forgotten to check the mailbox, when I saw a lady standing there. It was one of Michelle's missionary friends.

"Not today," I said as I retrieved the mail and started to walk away.

"Wait, Street, she said that's your name. Please can I just have a moment? It's about Michelle..." the elderly lady said, which halted me in my tracks.

"What about her?" I exhaled as I turned around.

"She said you two had a falling out, and she wants you to call her on Sunday. Street, I am worried about her." She sighed. "I dunno, but that morning before she left, we were all over her house, and that boy Willy came to visit. She left with him and went over to his house."

"What!" I said out of shock.

"They were gone for almost half an hour. When she finally came back, she looked visibly upset and shaken. I hauled her in the bathroom and asked her what happened, as she claimed she was just going over there to have a talk with him to finally leave her alone."

"And? And!" I fumed.

"And...and all she said was that it didn't go as planned and that she didn't want to talk about it as it didn't...it didn't end well," she said.

What the what!

My body jolted as I couldn't believe what I was hearing.

"What did she say happened?"

"She didn't. She just kept saying she didn't want to talk about it. And then she just kept saying she needed to see you. And then our ride came, and the next thing I knew, there was a street brawl, and we saw you being driven off in handcuffs in the back seat of a police car."

My mind was in a spin. Did Willy force himself on her, as Assad tried, and did he finally have his way with her now that she was ripe?

"I have to go." I sighed as I headed to my front door in a state of discombobulation.

"Just call her on Sunday, please, as there's stuff going on with her over there in England too. She hasn't said, but I know her. I can tell. She begged me to have you call her," she pleaded as I walked away.

I wanted to kill Willy, if my thoughts on him raping her were accurate.

But then I actually turned on her and questioned who the real "devil in the red dress" was. Was it not Jess but, in fact, Michelle, who downplayed the whole incident with Willy that departure day? Was she playing him, yet over there having romantic dinners and kissing and making up with her ex from church and playing me also, all at the same time?

My brother's words came back to me: "Bitch!"

Still, I needed confirmation. I needed to hear from the horse's mouth. What the hell was really going on?

The next night, my brother, his girlfriend, and Clair, who wanted us to go clubbing, came over. His girlfriend was pushing me for the hookup to clear my head. It was an okay evening, as I didn't disclose to anyone what was going on.

We put some music on, had some jerk chicken, beers, smokes, and then my brother and his girlfriend went to his bedroom.

I Lost My Mojo

Hours passed. Clair was constantly on her cell phone, one minute giggling, and the next minute frowning as she was seemingly communicating via text messages to multiple people. The music channel was on showing nonstop music videos. I got us another round of beer plus a vodka mix for her and we started giggling to the sounds of my brother and his girlfriend making love. I turned up the music to drown out their corny moans and groans.

I looked at Clair who was now, way tipsy, as she took a long gulp from her glass, tossed her phone aside and then surprised me by leaning over and first smooched me before we started to kiss passionately.

She put her glass down, knelt between my legs, and started to unbutton my jeans.

Oh ooh, here we go!

On any other given night, I would have let things get down and dirty from there, but something just didn't feel right; maybe I still couldn't get Michelle out of my head. I dunno, but I just wasn't feeling her.

She attempted to pull my boxers down, when I held her hand and whispered for her to stop. She let out a drunken giggle and persisted, until I stood up and told her I couldn't.

"What's wrong with you? I'm *Clair*! Nobody has every refused this!" she said as she started to remove her skimpy summer dress and gyrated on me.

What the what!

That body was a ten out of ten, because unlike Willy's girl, Clair both had the body and the beauty. However, although my body was ready to jump her, my mind, strangely, was just in shutdown mode.

I stopped her from undressing any further, we kissed some more. I told her not tonight as I was all messed up in the head.

She told me my brother's girlfriend told her what was going on and that she was sorry for my hurt and understood. We kissed some more. She went to the kitchen to refill her glass with her vodka mix and then asked which bedroom was mine as she needed to lie down a bit. I pointed to the door, and she entered.

Michelle had my mind in a vacuum. One mind was locked in on her and was torn about my guesses about what went down with Willy, and what was going down with her ex; and another mind told me to get over it, and go make magic with that beautiful half drunk, damsel in my bedroom.

A few minutes later, Clair upped the ante by coming to my bedroom door clad in just one of my tank tops and her thongs.

"Street. Are you sure my Beemer is safe in your driveway?" the spoilt, uptown girl asked with a drunken burp as she hugged the bedroom door.

"Really!" I smiled in assurance.

"I know you said not tonight, but if you change your mind you know where to find me," she said with a tease, as she slowly sucked on her index finger, stroked her hair, and winked.

Then to my amusement, she used her heel to angrily kick my brother's room door next to mine twice.

"Are you horny goats done already!" she shouted and giggled as she folded her arms and just gazed at me before coming over to sit next to me and burst out laughing.

She started kissing me all over before my brother's room door opened.

"Really," his girlfriend yawned.

"It's about time! Did you have your fill? Because my tank is still on E," Clair said, tossing a cushion at her, hinting that we didn't have sex.

My brother's girlfriend gave me a half-asleep confused look as she returned from the kitchen with a beer.

"It's past midnight, and you two need to go to bed!" she then ordered.

"I tried everything to get him between the sheets," Clair slurred, now also half asleep as she caressed me.

My brother's girl dragged her up and helped her to my bedroom. They both crashed to the bed, and I heard them chatting for a bit until I heard silence.

My brother's girlfriend eventually exited, turned my bedroom light off, pushed up the door, and sat beside me.

"She's passed out. So much for me trying to play matchmaker. I guess she wasn't your type?" she asked as she nudged me.

"Oh, trust me. Clair is everybody's type!"

"So?"

"I dunno. It's Sunday, and I now have reason to believe that something went down between Michelle and Willy. I just can't wait to call her."

"Really, Street! Don't! If what you think or feel is true, then just leave this girl alone! I've known you for years, and I've seen many women come and go in your life, but this…Michelle has become your poison, your kryptonite. Forget her! Go to bed!"

She hugged me around the neck and gave me a long smooch on the cheek, took a gulp from her beer and handed me the bottle to finish it, hugged me even tighter, and gave me another kiss on the forehead. Then she went back to bed as she smiled, pointed to my room, and winked as if to say, "Go get her!"

My mind was all over the place. I sat there for a bit and was half drunk, too, so I didn't even know when I fell asleep.

The next morning, I woke up in bed.

After wiping the sleep from my eyes and rolling over, I realized that Clair was curled up snoring fast asleep next to me.

I lifted the sheets to check, and she was still dressed in tank top and thongs, and I was just in my boxers.

I gently turned her over and gazed at her for a bit.

She looked beautiful!

Maybe I should give her a chance now that Michelle is history, I thought to myself, as she looked so beautiful, even as she slept. I tried to get myself worked up to make love to her, but again, my body was strangely just in shut down mode; nothing was rising to the occasion.

"Rise and shine!" my brother grinned as he softly knocked and entered my bedroom, sipping on his tea.

My brother and I started talking with gestures so Clair couldn't hear as he gave me a "So did you finally hit it" gesture. I gave him the no. He gave me an "I so want to strangle you right now" gesture. I held back the laughter. I gave him an "I dunno what's going on. Maybe I lost my mojo for real" gesture. He gestured with his hands as if about to roll dice to say, "Do you want me to hook you up with some a those pills?" I gestured no. He then gestured, "So what's wrong with you? Look who's beside you, man."

As a tease, I slowly pulled the sheet off her to expose her sexy half-naked body, curled up asleep.

I held back the laughter as he gazed and almost dropped his tea cup, as he gave me a "You lucky bastard" look.

Our muted conversation was interrupted by his girlfriend calling him.

"Yes, babe, I'm coming," he replied as he gave me a "Make sure you hit it before she leaves" gesture and left.

He came back to my room about a minute later and handed me one of the pills, which was a sexual male enhancement drug.

"One of these pills will have her tapping out before you know it. Take it! I've seen you kick yourself before, at a missed opportunity. Don't let Clair be the one that got away! Don't let her be the one that got away!"

I'll never forget him saying that, as I pulled the covers back over her, and just stared at her face as she slept. I wanted to take her so bad but still felt nothing and figured I'll just call it a day and invite her over again tonight.

Have you ever been in the mood for love and wanted to, but the person you were with just didn't, or couldn't arouse you?

I told him, and he insisted that I take the pill.

"By the way, I replanted you guy's lucky tree in the back garden, man. Think it blew off and got all busted up in that freak storm the other day."

"Thought it was dead, but it's alive and well," he continued as I stood up and started getting dressed.

I didn't make him any wiser that I had smashed it.

His girlfriend wobbled out, still sleepy, slouched in my bed, and started using the tip of Clair's long hair to tickle her own nose until she frustratingly woke up.

She looked around, realized where she was, used a pillow to beat her as we had a brief pillow fight before Clair told us to leave her alone, then used the pillow to cover her head and dozed off again.

The three of us left and headed to the kitchen to start breakfast.

"Really, bro! I can't believe you didn't tap that last night!" my brother gasped as he poured some juice.

His girl slapped him on his shoulder to shut up.

I finally told them more details about what I heard might have gone down between Michelle and Willy.

"Bitch!" my brother gasped.

But surprisingly, instead of his girl hitting him again, she too slammed her plate down and echoed the same.

"That bitch!" she fumed. "Leave her alone Street! Promise me you won't call her today."

"I won't!"

"Really, Street! I just saw that. I know you. I know your eyes, and they speak more than your mouth sometimes. And yes, I just saw that look! I said promise me!" she snapped.

I stopped making my plate and slowly gasped, "Okay."

"You win some. You lose some, bro. But go take a look at the consolation prize sleeping in your bed," my brother said as his girlfriend nudged him to shut up.

Clair eventually woke. She got dressed only in another of my t-shirt as she came to the kitchen with a hangover and helped us with breakfast. My brother and I looked at her, then at each other, then back at her from behind as she bent over way low; searching the pantry's bottom shelf for one of the cans of sausage she said she would prefer to have for breakfast.

"Take that damn pill!" he whispered, as he angrily nudged me shoulder to shoulder.

What the hell is wrong with me? I thought as I stared at her beautiful body. My mind was ready to take her right there, but my body still strangely wasn't being responsive physically. I blamed it on Michelle, as she broke my heart.

Have you ever been intimate with your new love but during the whole time of that heated moment of passion, you just laid there, closed your eyes, and let him or her just take you because your mind was on your ex or someone else whom you still weren't over with?

Don't ever confess that!

We all had breakfast. My brother and I hung out a bit, and then they all left to run a few errands.

The Last Sunday

It was Sunday at around 2:00 p.m. I had just finished my homework for class the next morning and was pondering what to do with the rest of my day as I had a beer and smoke in the backyard swing.

Then 2:30 p.m. came, and I couldn't resist the temptation. I dressed, stopped at the corner deli for some quarters, and headed to the phone booth.

There was a guy on the phone. The old lady who I helped with her umbrella and gave my remaining quarters was next in line.

She and I greeted each other as the guy hung up and she went to make her call.

It was quick, but still ended after 3:00 p.m. She hung up, said goodbye, and left.

But the minute I was about to enter the phone booth, I heard a voice behind me simply say, "You promised!"

I turned around, and it was my brother's girlfriend.

Busted!

"Yes, I followed you!' she then admitted as she stretched out her hands, demanding that I hand over the quarters.

I refused. She held her ground out of frustration and disappointment and insisted with body gestures from her outstretched hand to hand them over.

There was a brief standoff over my quarters.

I finally did.

"Get in the car!' she ordered. "I said get in the car!"

I looked across the street, and it was Clair in her Beemer and my brother.

Sigh.

I got in, we drove off, and I could tell by the silence while driving that everyone, including Clair, was disappointed at me.

Have you ever been in that situation?

"There's an old saying that you can lead a horse to water, but you can't force it to drink!" My brother sighed.

"But I love her! I love her," I said almost to myself.

The car came to a screeching halt.

"Get out!" Clair screamed. "I said get the shit out of my car! I like you and all, Street, but it's obvious your mind is somewhere else with this bitch Marcel or whatever her name is. Last night you made me drink to the point of getting drunk because no man has ever rejected my advances before," she said. "You embarrassed me by saying no! Nobody has ever said no to Clair! Forget later for me to stay the night again. Unlike you, I don't live my love life looking in the rearview mirror. Get out!"

Silence.

I slowly got out. I was sitting in the backseat with my brother's girlfriend, and as I was getting out, I saw him turn around and give her a wink, as if to say he was getting out with me.

He did. His girlfriend hopped in the front passenger seat.

"I'll see you guys back at the house." His girlfriend then sadly smiled as the car sped off, as we watched hand gestures from both of them as if they were arguing.

I was at a crossroads; as here was everybody's beautiful dream girl, Clair, chasing me while I was chasing…Michelle, who was trying to patch things up with her ex and, for all I cared, slept with Willy.

"What's going on, bro?" he asked as we took turns kicking an empty beer can down the street together as we walked home.

I didn't reply.

"This is Clair! One of the hottest girls on campus, bro! She spent all night in your bed, something most guys can only pray or pay for, and you didn't hit it? Is everything okay down there 'cuz I got the hookup with them pills?"

Silence.

"I'm fine down there, just not up here," I said as I used my palm to slap my forehead.

He admitted that he fooled around with her around the same time that he started dating his girlfriend and gave me an earful on love and relationship and the secrets as to why he and his girl's love life were enviable, giving just cause to leave Michelle alone.

When we got home, his girlfriend was on the front porch, having a smoke. She clearly looked disappointed at me after stating that Clair was in my bedroom.

The Love Bush

"Can I have a minute?" she said to my brother, instructing him to give us some privacy.

"You promised me, Street!" she said angrily as I sat beside her. She grabbed my chin and snapped my face around to hers. We were inches apart as she gazed into my eyes. "What am I gonna do with you? I hooked you up with Clair as a distraction from this Michelle, yet this is your thank-you?" she gasped out of frustration, handing me her cigarette for a puff.

"You're drowning in love, Street, and when you sink to deeper depths, you will be drowning in hurt and hate, and that's where all hell can break lose, leaving you to waking up in a hospital bed or jail, asking yourself, 'My God! What have I done?' Go figure why we have murder suicides in marriages and relationships!" she warned as she released her grip.

"I dunno why this is happening to me, sis." I sighed. And yes, sis was my pet name for her. "My motto became, 'To hell with love and relationship' after Mitzie threw away our three-year relationship and cheated on me last summer, and with, of all persons, one of our break dance rivals just because they beat us that night. Yep, she was a hype girl who simply told me that she didn't date losers. Yet now here I am in love all over again with a cheater who claims to be a devoted Christian."

"Your brother cheated on me once at our internship fraternity party. I fought him, but he never fought back. I was finally restrained after I busted his nose. He said he told you he got the injury from football practice. I left, and although our dorms were walking distance apart on campus, I avoided him for several weeks because I was just done. Everyone, including Clair, persisted and finally convinced me that he, that they were both drunk that night and it just happened. Yes, the girl he cheated on me with was Clair!"

What the what!

"She admitted that she led him on. She begged my forgiveness and begged me to forgive him. Instead I kicked her ass, too, in case you are wondering where she got that scar on her cheek from."

Sis still looked visibly upset as she took up a can of beer next to her feet and took a sip. Then she offered me a chug also and took her cigarette and beer back.

"She has since convinced me that while she hustles men, she would never cross that line with my brother again, out of respect for me. She hasn't faltered yet!"

"So how did you two finally end up back together?" I asked, wondering if Michelle and I would ever end up back together.

She smiled, recollecting.

Silence.

"One cold rainy night, me and my girls pulled up at a gas station after study, to get some snacks for our beach trip the next day," she finally continued, "The four of us were all laughing and racing for the entrance as it was pouring, when I realized that there were bicycles parked up everywhere. I stopped as my girls ran inside. I knew it was your brother and his boys. I knew those flamboyant bicycles. Before I could decide my next move I saw him saying hi to my girls and then walked outside as one of them pointed to me. His shoulders dropped as he just stared at me." She smiled.

"Almost twenty other cyclists followed and went to their bicycles. I was dripping wet. He walked over after signaling for them to take off. He then took his hoodie off and placed it around my shoulders. We just stared at each other for a while. He started the blah blah blah apology again and begged me to forgive him," she continued. "I slapped his face. He smiled. I slapped it again. He smiled again as if to say 'I deserve this.' And I'll never forget he simply said, 'I messed up. Never again. Forgive me.' I was about to slap him again until he asked, 'Will you?' I didn't answer but just stared at him. He leaned in to kiss me, and and let's just say I hesitated at first by wearily thumping him in his chest, but eventually, I didn't stop him. Guess there's my answer."

"Wow. That sounds like a scene from a romance movie." I smiled.

She nudged me with a smile to shut up.

"We took things slow after that night, and yes, I made him beg for days and forced him to get a tattoo on his wrist with my name on it, as proof of his love for me—and me only thereafter. He did! We eventually made up, and here we are, three years and counting." Sis smiled as she put out her cigarette and raised her right hand, exposing her wrist, showing a tattoo of his name also, with a half heart. "When we hold our wrists together, it forms a full heart of love with both our names."

Wow.

I was at a loss for words as I gazed at it. She noticed my state of mind, stood, took my hand, and led me to our front lawn by the neighboring hedge.

"What reason has this Michelle given you to maintain respect for her and still believe in her? Because from how I see it, you now have more doubt than love for her."

"None!" I sighed.

"Your brother gave me this Swiss knife for protection," she said with a devilish grin as she reached in her pocket and pulled it out. "See that scar on his arm? Ask him how he got it from me. I know how you settle your differences, Street—you fight! Don't ever get into a physically violent confrontation with this girl or anybody associated with her over love because I can sense where this is heading. Walk away and count it as *her* loss. Leave her alone! Don't disappoint me again!"

There was silence, as she reached to the hedge and cut a stem that had love bush growing on it.

Jamaican love bush was a yellow parasitic plant that looked like extra long spaghetti. It could consume a whole hedge in weeks, killing it. Our Jamaican myth was that if you loved someone, you should take a piece of love bush, spit on it, call that person's name and then throw it on a fresh hedge. If it locks in and grows, that person will one day be yours, but if it dies, oh well, go figure.

"The landscapers in charge of our dorm section on campus were going nuts, as G claimed, this is how he knew we were going to eventually get back together." She smiled as she handed the piece of love bush to me.

I walked over to a section of the hedge that had no love bush, performed the ritual, and tucked it into the hedge.

"And now we wait," she said as she came over and hugged my arm. "If it lives, you will be with her. But if it dies…"

Sigh.

There was silence, as I knew it would be the opposite.

"But until then, Clair is in your room." She nudged for me to go and talk to her.

I went in and saw Clair standing in front of my dresser, picking at some scabs on her stomach. She was visibly upset and quickly pulled her T-shirt down as I entered.

"Hey. Are you okay?" I asked.

"I'm fine, it's just hives," she said as she sat on the edge of the bed.

"What's wrong with me, Street? Why you not attracted?"

Silence.

"I'm sorry," I said about the earlier phone booth incident. She accepted my apology, and we just held hands as I sat beside her.

I was ready to make love to her as we kissed passionately for a while, but once again, I felt no sexual urge from my body to take her.

"I should go. I don't feel so good," she said as we parted lips and hugged me with a worried smile.

"Okay. Please go see a doctor about those hives."

"I will."

She spoke with my brother's girlfriend a bit, who showed equal concern as she showed her the hives as they spoke, and then left.

Weeks passed, and I never called Michelle again. I never saw Clair again. But one Monday morning as we were all getting settled in class, there came a familiar face that was about to put a whole new spin on my life.

CHAPTER 8

WILLY!

Surprise

It was a typical morning in class. The teacher excused himself and later returned with that delayed student that he said would join our class eventually. I was chatting with one of my classmates, and when the teacher shut us all up to get our attention, I looked up, and it was Willy!

What the what!

Really! What were the odds?

He introduced him and told him that because he had to play catch-up, he was going to let him sit and understudy with one of the top student in the class.

"Why don't you go sit with Street back there?" the teacher then urged.

Willy looked at me as if he saw a ghost, and to be honest, I looked back at him the same way, too, because, really, what were the odds of us meeting up again like this?

He reluctantly walked over to my desk, put his back pack down, and pulled up a chair next to me to copy my notes. We didn't exchange a word as the teacher started the class.

"Okay, so let's pick up where we left off on Friday," the teacher said as he drew an image on the chalkboard. "Who can remind me what the catalytic converter is?"

My hand was the first to be raised.

He pointed at me to answer.

"It's a device built into the exhaust system of a motor vehicle, containing a mechanism for converting pollutant gases into less harmful ones," I answered. "Just like beating the crap out of some pollutant people to make them, less harmful."

"Correct! Except for the last part," the teacher said, not realizing my pun at Willy, as the rest of the class chuckled.

"Hey, guys. What are the odds? This is the Willy I've been telling you about!" I then whispered to some of my classmates sitting nearby around me as the teacher kept on talking.

They all stared him down with hatred in all-for-one mode.

He obviously realized at that point that he entered a whole new battlefield with new faces, but our fight was far from over.

"Welcome to the lion's den!" the girl who was robbed by the three guys weeks ago and was sitting across from me said to him with hate as I also told her what he might have had done to Michelle.

That did it. He immediately got up and headed for the exit.

"Excuse me!" the teacher said as he noticed.

"I'm sorry," a now visibly shaken Willy said. "Where is the restroom?"

The teacher directed him, and he left.

Break time came, and he still hadn't returned. Don't know! Don't care! But after break he again showed up in the auto mechanic shop, where we were going to do an arc welding session.

He, the principal, and the teacher spoke briefly, and then he came over to my workstation. I seized the opportunity when the teacher left us alone to practice welding.

We all had our goggles on and were welding scrapped muffler pipes together. I was showing him, and when it was his turn, I thought he was just enraged at the occasion. So I deliberately turned, and in reaching for a rod, he used the blow torch to burn my wrist. I still have the scar to prove it.

"Yo! What was that?" I snapped as I was getting all pumped up.

It was just a matter of time before I was about to attack him, but I wanted some answers first.

He just grinned.

"And what happed between you and Michelle that day she was leaving?" I said as I removed my gloves and welding goggles.

"Fresh meat Michelle?" he went on with a nasty attitude. "Let's just say she was ripe and ready to be picked."

"Did you?"

"Ask her!" he replied with a devilish grin. I snapped. He didn't even see the right elbow coming, which caught him on the chin, sending him crashing into a workstation.

I didn't know what was up with him that day, but he fought back like a little girl, as my other classmates formed a circle, joined in, and gave him a beat-down that he would never forget.

His face was all busted up as the teacher hearing the commotion stormed in and broke us up, pulling me off him. I was facing suspension or even expulsion, as that college had a zero tolerance policy for fighting.

Willy and I were dragged to the principal's office, and slowly, one by one, everyone else who was present also entered.

One of the other girls in my class, entered last with a vengeful stare at me as she slowly leaned against the wall and maintained her gaze. I hardly even ever spoke to her because she claimed to be a holy of holy church girl, and hated me and my street thug lifestyle as she tried to pull off another Michelle missionary at school. I always shut her down, and instead of just leaving me alone, she was consumed with hatred. She then told her exaggerated account of what happened.

Bitch!

It's funny how some people, including people that you don't even know, will dislike you for no reason.

Have you ever been there? If so, don't even waste your time trying to figure out why. Just ignore these demons and keep on living your life.

All my other classmates pleaded the Fifth Amendment when questioned.

They were all eventually dismissed, and Willy and I were about to give our own account. He was ordered to go first. I was nervous, as all he had to say was "Yes." I did attack him first, which would lead to my immediate suspension, pending investigation that could see me even being expelled.

"So based on what that young lady said, that he attacked you first; is this true?" the uncaring frustrated superintendent who seemingly just wanted to get this over with and finish his bowl of chicken salad, asked Willy.

There was an eerie silence as he used tissue to wipe more blood from his lip.

I held my breath.

"Street and I go way back. This is my first day here, and we have our crazy initiations. We weren't fighting. I was just being initiated," Willy then said, to my surprise.

I looked at him, but he didn't look back at me.

"So you are saying you don't want to file a formal complaint?" the superintendent asked.

"No. We're cool. It was just horse play that got a bit rough, sir," he said, finally glancing at me. "We're cool!"

"Okay. Okay. I'm not sure what's going on here between you two, but fine! No more initiations or horse play, or I will have both of you suspended. Am I clear?"

We both agreed and left the room.

"That was my thank-you for you not sending my ass to prison," he said as we walked down the hallway.

I just sighed, as I knew my mom would kill me if I had gotten expelled from school.

"So are we even? Because I was pressured by that girl and the principal to say yes to get you expelled," he stopped and asked.

"Yeah, we cool." I sighed with uncertainty. "What happened with you and Michelle that day?"

"What? Really, Street? Ask her!" he simply said with a heavy sigh as he wobbled off.

He was reassigned thereafter to understudy with another student in another class, and the rest of the day and week went by quietly.

Please Let Clair Be the One that Got Away—Swear

Another week passed, and yes, I still hadn't called Michelle, although it was Sunday after three in the afternoon. I was on the front porch, doing homework, when my brother and his girlfriend visited.

They looked visibly upset. I thought they were having a fight, but then they both turned their attention to me.

"Hey, bro, you got a minute? We need to talk!" he ordered with a look of worry and concern as they both sat across from me.

"Yeah, what's going on?" I stopped and put my homework aside sensing their demeanor.

"Clair!" he simply said.

"What about her?"

"Did you?"

"Did I what?"

"Did you two sleep together?" his girlfriend jumped in, cutting to the chase.

"She slept in my bed that one night, but…" I started.

"You know what she means, Street! This is serious! Did you two have sex?" my brother interrupted.

"What?" I laughed, now totally at a loss at the reason for their interrogation.

"Don't lie to me, Street, because I would never forgive myself if you did," his girlfriend broke down crying.

"What?" I gasped, at a loss. "Hey, what is this? Wait a minute. Okay, you two are totally freaking me out right now. What's going on? What's this about?"

"Did you use a condom if you slept with her, bro? Just tell me the truth!" my brother persisted.

"No, I didn't!" I insisted.

"You didn't use a condom?" His girlfriend broke down crying even more.

My brother consoled her.

"No…" I started before again being interrupted by my brother.

"How could you not use a condom when you know her reputation? Oh my god, this is bad. Mom's gonna kill me," he gasped.

Next thing I knew was, it was his girlfriend consoling him.

What the what!

"Wait! Wait, okay!" I then said as I got up scratching my head and pacing the porch as I tried to make sense of what was going on. They both looked petrified, consoling each other.

"Are you guys even listening to me? I didn't say no, meaning I didn't use a condom. I said no, meaning we never had sex!"

"I know you, Street, and your eyes can't lie!" his girlfriend gasped as she kept wiping tears from her eyes, got up, angrily held my chin close to her face, and stared at me. "Swear to me that you never slept with her!"

"What? You always told me never to swear because..." I started.

"Swear to me, goddamn it!" she snapped as my brother restrained her from slapping me.

Yes, she had slapped my face before when I screwed up big time, and I just took it like a man, because I knew it was out of love, care, and concern.

Have you ever been roughed up or slapped in the face by someone who was cussing and screaming at you but you didn't retaliate because you knew you deserved it?

"Okay, okay! Geez! I...I swear! I swear to God, we never had sex... We...we just kissed," I said, and I panicked and slumped into a chair. "Now can one of you tell me what the hell is going on because you are both freaking me out."

There was a moment of silence, only interrupted by my brother's girlfriend's sniffling.

"She's in the hospital," she finally spoke.

"Never saw this coming, although we should have, based on her lifestyle," my brother added.

"Was it that bad?" I asked, clueless.

"She told you?" his girlfriend asked.

"Yeah! That last time she was here, she told me that she had hives, and I even suggested she go see a doctor instead of using across-the-counter meds."

There was more silence as they gazed at each other until my brother spoke.

"She did. And it wasn't hives, bro."

His girlfriend started crying again.

"Okay, and? So what was it?" I questioned.

"The doctors couldn't figure out what was going on with her condition, so they ran multiple tests," his girlfriend sobbed, "one of which came back as HIV positive. Clair has AIDS!"

What the what!

I couldn't believe what I was hearing.

"We just came from the hospice where they admitted her. She suspects it was one of her sugar daddies that she went on that week-long cruise with before one of her final exams last semester. She said he was very controlling and forced her into multiple orgies without protection during the whole cruise with random women," she continued. "But she complied, with the promise of the car she is now driving and anything else that she asked for as a condition to be his sex slave."

"She got what she wanted, and more." My brother sighed in sadness.

"I still want you to be tested." she exhaled. "Just to be safe, as I would never forgive myself if I were to lose you, either of you, because I introduced you both to her."

I was at a loss for words.

"I hope she learned her lesson and stop being a high-end call girl. So how long before she gets out and all is well again?" I asked.

No response.

"Guys!"

Still no response, until his girlfriend finally spoke, breaking down crying again.

"The doctor on Wednesday, who was her primary surgeon, gave her four months to live," she sobbed. "I insisted on a second opinion and pleaded to have another doctor evaluate her. They complied, but the other doctor that did his own independent evaluation only gave her three months."

What the what!

She huddled in my brother's arm as she sobbed. I was just shaking in shock, as the seemingly beautiful and healthy-looking girl that was sleeping in my bed just a few weeks ago was now dying of AIDS and only had a few weeks to live.

The rest of the evening was filled with crying. I had no thoughts of further homework or Michelle, just thoughts of Clair and her looming death.

How Could You Know?

That Monday after school the three of us went to visit her. When we got to her room, the nurse was changing her, so being a fellow female, only my brother's girlfriend was allowed in.

I could see them talking for a bit until a couple minutes later we were both allowed to join them.

It had been weeks since I saw her, and by now the "hives" had even spread to her face.

She was in the middle of saying something to my brother's girlfriend when she turned her head, saw me, broke down in tears, and turned her head away from me to the wall to hide her face.

My brother gently pulled his girlfriend a few steps back from her bed to the room curtain to give us a moment.

I was just shuddering with shock at how quickly her body had deteriorated.

"Hey." I smiled as I held her hand.

She pulled it away and sobbed even more.

A tear rolled from my eye as I looked back at my brother and his girlfriend. They were beside themselves.

With all the street brawls I'd had and even compared to Bob's incident, this was easily the saddest, most empty day of my life because I was looking at someone, my beautiful Clair, who was about to die in weeks.

I reached out and held her hand again. This time she allowed me to, and even reached over and held our hands with her other hand.

Have you ever been there, where you held the hand of someone that you knew was going to die, knowing that, that moment will be the last time you ever felt their touch?

Sigh.

Silence.

"So do you still think I'm beautiful?" She sighed.

"Yes!" I replied, as another tear rolled from my eye.

"Liar." She laughed and sobbed at the same time.

I gently turned her face back to me. It had broken out in hives.

And yes, I still chose to call it hives, because I refused to believe and accept her actual condition. And call me crazy, but I leaned over and gave her a soft pecker on her lips and then wiped tears from her eyes.

She broke down crying again.

"How did you know?" she asked, still crying.

"How did I know what?" I replied, confused.

"I remember a class trip to this massive zoo in Manchester last semester," she started. "The guide told us that in the wild, animals can detect when there was a sick or infected one in their herd and thus avoided them, eventually kicking them out so others in the herd won't be infected. I didn't know that. I didn't know. So how did you know I was infected?"

There was silence.

Once again, it crossed my mind that this must have been divine intervention, as I learned long ago in my church days that at times when we, as believers, found ourselves in certain situations and couldn't help but pursue our worldly desires, God would put us on a leash, as in "shutdown mode," to prevent us from the ill fate that we were blindly pursuing.

"I didn't know," I consoled.

"Street, I'm Clair. Every guy wants me in their bed. I spent a whole night in yours, and you never made an advance. Your body and mind clearly sensed something was wrong with me and just shut down," she sobbed. "How did you know, and why didn't my body sense the same and say no at that moment to that person that infected me?" She wept bitterly.

I had no answer.

Silence.

I kept holding her hand as we maintained a soft stare at each other, and all I saw in her eyes was an empty soul filled with regret at her chosen lifestyle.

"I don't wanna die!" she sobbed. "Please, Street, I've heard stories about you back in the days when you were a church boy. Pray for me. Please."

She caught me off guard at that request, as let's just say God and I were not on speaking terms. Yes, I was in malice mode with Him after that earlier incident I told you about that caused me to lose my faith.

"Please pray for me, Street. For the past few years, random men paid me to do whatever they wanted to do with my body sexually, in return for me telling them what I wanted in return. They complied. It was a win-win, and this is my reward," she sobbed. "I lost! So if all this talk about God and Heaven is true, I want it. Forgive me, Street. Forgive me, Lord, for I have sinned." She sobbed even harder.

"Don't call it dying," I hushed as she broke down, "If you are a believer in Christ, when your time comes, you don't die. You just fall into an eternal sleep from this world. And when you wake up, it will be in paradise."

She smiled as she wiped her eyes.

"Wow. You are no stranger to God. I see your heart. Go make your peace with Him. My life was short and sweet, but it's over, Street. And you will go down in history as the only guy who ever rejected Clair." She tearfully smiled as she squeezed my hand, and I gave her another peck on the lips.

"Did you get me the gummy bears?" she asked my brother's girlfriend, changing the subject. She was listening and also crying and beside herself.

"Yes," she said as she walked over took a pack of gummy bears, Clair's favorite snack, from her handbag, opened it, and fed her.

"Please," Clair said to me as she squeezed my hand, "pray that I will be well again."

I was beside myself as I just stood there until my brother's girl-friend nudged me to pray. We all held hands. There was a deafening silence. And then I reverted to my test game.

Remember it?

"Satan!" I whispered. "Once again you have proven yourself. So, God, how about you do likewise once more and heal Clair? Please. Heal her, in the name of Jesus," I prayed, somewhat with doubt, as answers to my prayers had left me disappointed so many times.

After that, I searched for more words to test or prove God, but my prayer was eventually turned into a whisper in "tongues," meaning praying in the Holy Spirit. Yes, I did receive the baptism of the Holy Spirit years back while being a devoted Christian in church and was told that it was something you never lost regardless of the journey you chose to take in life thereafter.

They barely heard my whispered prayer. The only thing I think they heard in the end was me saying, "Thy will be done. Amen."

"Forgive me. Thy will be done, Lord," Clair cried as she tightly squeezed my hand. "Amen."

I reached for my wallet and took out a one dollar bill, which I always kept as my lucky dollar. I knew Clair liked to chase money, so as a loving gesture, I handed it to her.

"This is yours—my lucky dollar." I smiled. "If you ever make it out of this, I'm gonna want it back." I smiled as we hugged and I kissed her. "But if not, come visit me in a dream and tell me how much this money is worth in Heaven."

Wow.

She started crying again, as she squeezed hard on the dollar bill until we all hushed and consoled her.

It was a life-changing moment, as here was Clair counting down the days until she died, but that moment made me feel like a born-again Christian.

We crashed that night with her, trying to cheer her up and inspire her. Eventually, she fell asleep. The last thing I remembered was hugging her with words of inspiration and kissing her on her forehead before we all left.

The next day, after class, my brother, his girlfriend, and I all met up again and got more gummy bears, flowers, and a teddy bear as we headed to visit Clair again. But to our disappointment, when we got there, we were told that her parents had issued a strict order for no other visitations from anyone else but them. They apparently were embarrassed about her condition and, from now on, wanted to keep it as family visitations only.

Wow.

Weeks later after being barred from ever seeing her again, we eventually got the sad news that Clair passed away.

Clair was dead.

I wept.

I remembered sitting in our backyard swing when I heard the news. I wasn't crying as my brother and his girlfriend went back inside to give me some alone time after were all out back chilling together. Tears, however, just flowed from my eyes, as I was both saddened at her passing and yet grateful that God had put my body in shutdown mode that night because we were both drunk, horny, and ready to have sex, although, as was with the case with Jess that night, I was still out of condoms. I could have easily been infected too.

"Thank you," I whispered in prayer. "Your will be done."

From that day, I took a pledge to renew my faith and to avoid fighting and to try to be a better person.

That was, however, easier said than done.

CHAPTER 9

PROMISE ME

It was an empty few weeks after that; at Clair's sad passing. Her funeral was kept way out of town on the other side of the country so we didn't attend. No more Street Boys, Willy and I agreeing to a fragile peace treaty, and no Michelle.

One night I was home alone after school, and just beside myself, as I was mentally drained and tried to move on from the life that I knew over the last few months.

I was on my last beer and wanted more. So I decided to eventually walk to the corner deli up the street and make a purchase, before it was cut off time for them to sell alcohol.

I was heading to the cash register to pay for my six-pack of beers when I saw Jess at the counter paying for some stuff.

She at first nervously ignored me and didn't say a word, until I paid for my beers, exited the deli and, there she was outside waiting for me.

I brushed her aside and walked off.

"Street! Street!" she yelled.

I kept walking until I almost got to the back of the deli to take a short cut to my street.

"Street!" she again yelled.

I continued walking, until she ran and caught up with me, grabbed my arm and spun me around.

"What? You damn snitch!" I yelled.

"What? I'm no snitch. Please, I need to talk to you," she pleaded.

"I don't wanna hear shit," I scoffed as I walked off.

170

She grabbed my arm, preventing me.

"Please," she begged.

"You brought freaking cops to my crib to try to get me arrested!"

"Willy's brother threatened me to do so. Willy was still semi-conscious, so he didn't know. But I had to, or he would tell Willy I refused, who would in turn beat the crap out of me for siding with you guys if I didn't comply. So the officer urged that I accompany them to your house instead of his brother to avoid another brawl."

"So you came, pointed us out, and snitched."

"Because I feared for my life!" she started sobbing. "You don't know my life."

I looked at her confused.

"Officer Grant is a relative of theirs. Yeah, the one that was all mad at you all that night, while the other one kept calm. He wanted revenge, so I had to role-play because I know he was going to go back and tell them about the whole encounter. Not sure if you picked up on it, but that's why I was acting so weird," she explained, sobbing. "I had to play along Street. Willy has constantly been accusing me of cheating on him since he got out of jail. He beats me for the slightest reason. I am a battered and bruised girl, Street. I'm tired."

"You did a really good job 'role playing' when you charged at me that night."

"That wasn't role playing," she said as she abruptly and angrily thumped me in the chest.

I didn't retaliate.

"You know I'm Willy's girl, you know he would beat the crap out of me if he knew I slept with you. Yet you told the whole world that night," she continued angrily. "How could you? Who's the real snitch?"

She had a point, as that morning she was leaving my house, she told me she was seeing someone who was incarcerated; I just didn't connect the dots. And she didn't expect Willy to get out so soon. But he did, and when I found out that she was his woman, I should have kept it our secret.

"You made me sound like a slut. I'm no devil. Yes, I have been attracted to you for years, but you never noticed me when I came to your dance competitions, always cheering you on. Maybe I wasn't pretty enough for you. Maybe you just wanted my body. But against all odds, you noticed me that night at the club and invited me back to your place. How could I say no as I have always stupidly fantasized about that intimate moment with you. You are the only man I slept with besides Willy in years. And I don't care whether you believe me or not."

This was too much for me; more dirty dishes to add to my table, as mom put it. I just stood there waiting for her to finish so I could be on my way.

"Okay. Guess we both owe each other an apology. Are you done?" I said.

"Almost. I'm glad you guys pulled that line about that cop's daughter being over your house, which he didn't buy, because he doesn't have a daughter." She smiled while crying. "That line saved my ass because I convinced them that you were lying too about us sleeping together, or I'd be a dead woman."

Silence.

"What would Willy do if he found out we were sleeping together?" I dryly asked.

"He would kill me," she dryly replied.

We chatted some more, but suddenly, remembering the beat-down I got from Willy and his boys, plus what they did to Bob, I suddenly dropped my beers, took her hand, and led her to a hidden corner at the back of the deli, turned her back toward me, pinned her face to the wall, and took her.

"What are you doing?" she groaned in shock, as it was forced, furious, and painful for her, but she never once resisted or stopped me. All she kept begging was for me to go easy as she covered her mouth with one hand to muffle her loud grunts and moans and clawed the wall with the other as a show that it was hurting.

She endured, as I ignored her pleas to go easy and continued forcefully on purpose as a payback.

I was not sure how long we went on for, but we were both out of breath and almost sweaty when it was finally over. I had my pleasure in what I just did, but I felt no pleasure at the end. I felt nothing.

She was crying from the agony, as she turned around and adjusted her mini dress as I also fixed my clothing.

Have you ever had intercourse and, after it was all over, felt no pleasure, no nothing?

"What was that about?" she sobbed quietly and almost breathless as she thumped my chest, then covered her face with her palms until we just stood there staring at each other for a bit.

Silence.

"I'm pregnant!" She suddenly broke down.

"What?" I said in shock. I was at a loss for words.

"I may be wrong, but Willy was out of jail a couple days after you, and I had sex that night, but based on the time frame the doctors told me about my conception, it is a possibility that I may be pregnant with your child, Street."

What the what!

She started crying some more. She wiped her tears and hugged me. I didn't hug her back and still hadn't spoken a word.

"Promise me that you won't say a word to anyone! I don't care who the father is. I don't care! Regardless of this mess, you two can go to hell for all I care. I just want to live a quiet life and be a good mom to my child!"

I exhaled heavily as I now saw a different side of this devil in the red dress.

"Promise me!"

Silence.

"I promise." I finally spoke with a heavy exhalation. "You should do a DNA test."

"No!" she asserted. "He knows my every move. If he found out I did that, he would know there was another man, and he'll beat me to death! I am at peace with myself, Street. Make peace with Willy and yourself, and let's just get on with our lives. Please, Street, let this be our secret. Don't tell anyone!" she begged as she squeezed my arm.

"I promise," I gasped, realizing the magnitude of this situation and that I certainly can't break *this* promise.

I hugged her. It was a long caring hug.

"Let me go, Street. You can have me whenever you want, wherever you want," she said as she hugged me tightly. "But although I am in love with you, I belong to someone else. I can't go on living like this. I can't walk away from you, so please, walk away from me and let me find myself again. Please, walk away, and set me free." She sobbed as we hugged.

I consoled her.

Have you ever been there where instead of because of being in love, you instead found yourself trapped in a relationship for whatever reason besides love?

We eventually released our embrace and kissed a bit as she adjusted her attire again, gave me a soft kiss, and hurriedly walked off to the front of the deli on her way for home.

I just stood there with my mind in a daze.

I had made my peace with her. Damn! Was I about to be a father? But then I remembered my promise to her and just leaned against a light post, lit my last cigarette from the old pack, crushed the box, and wearily tossed it aside.

As strange as it sounded, I felt her that night; I felt her heart and her soul and her sincerity. It was almost as if I was falling for her, but I had to stop myself, and fast, as she was Willy's girl.

Have you ever found yourself falling for someone who belonged to someone else or, worse, falling for someone although you belong to someone else?

Sigh.

I popped a can of beer and chugged it down until it was empty. My mind was in a spin; Jess, Clair, Michelle—these three girls in my inner circle had so far taken me on three totally different journeys. My teeth grinded in hate, as I remembered Mom's story about Dad. And now Jess was telling me how Willy constantly beat her. They grinded even more at the loss of Clair and then, yep, Michelle. All these situations were happening so fast, so soon. My drained teenage mind couldn't handle it. I grabbed my beers, and instead of going home to an empty house, I decided to take a bus ride for some fresh air to clear my head.

Don't you do that sometimes for whatever reason—just want-ing to go for a run, a walk, or even a drive to nowhere?

That was how I passed time away sometimes back then, when bored or if I had too much on my mind, I would take a bus ride to nowhere.

DON'T LET ME COUNT TO THREE

The bus route I chose to board was short; so an hour or so after you boarded at the terminal, it made its route and was back dropping you off. After a few drop-offs and pickups, and halfway into my ride, just gazing through the window reflecting, this smelly hoodlum came over from his seat and sat beside me.

More than half the seats were empty, so what is this? I thought.

The next thing I knew was, he pulled a knife out and stuck it in my side.

What the what!

"Gimme your wallet!" he then abruptly ordered.

Really! Is this my life right now? You damn thief! I thought.

I didn't budge. He jammed the knife harder until I felt it pierce my T-shirt and skin. Soon, some blood started to appear on my T-shirt.

"I said give me your wallet, asshole!" he again whispered with the smell of alcohol on his breath so as not to alert other passengers.

I didn't comply as my mind seemingly drifted off into a different world. Although there was blood, I didn't feel a thing. He stuck the knife harder, causing me to finally raise my head and look at him straight in the eyes. It was as if this smelly, frail-looking junkie had met his match.

"I'm going to count to three!" I finally said with a heavy exhalation and a sad chuckle, out of being weary and fed up. "Or just like David used Goliath's own sword to chop his head off, I am going to use your own knife to end your misery."

He looked confused for a moment, stuck the knife harder into my side, and just said, "What?"

"Don't let me count to three!" I said. I was so angry and enraged.

We stared each other down for a bit until I took a sad, angry, heavy exhalation and started to count. "One…"

He didn't flinch, but I could feel the blade that pierced my skin starting to tremble as if his hands were trembling. He did a poor job of disguising that he was growing nervous and confused.

"Two!" I said with empty eyes as I shoved the knife away and fully faced him. "For in just a little while, my wrath will be spent, and my anger will turn to their destruction," I found myself quoting from the book of Isaiah as I got even more pumped up and stood with fists clenched. "Please don't let me say three!"

He froze and was like a deer caught in the headlights of an oncoming car. He stared at me as if he saw a ghost, panicked, and literally fell off the bus seat, got up, and rang the buss bell.

"What…are you? Who are you?" he asked nervously as he walked backward to the front exit.

"I'm just a nobody from nowhere," I replied.

The bus stopped he gave me a questionable, confused glance and was about to exit.

"Hey!" I stopped him and beckoned him to come back as I sat. He reluctantly did but was now visibly shaken. I handed him the rest of my six-pack, plus a twenty I took from my wallet.

He looked so lost and confused. But weren't we all sometimes like that in this world called life? He reluctantly took it and was about to exit when I again called him back. He nervously complied. I pointed at the spot of blood on my T-shirt and beckoned for him to give me the knife.

He refused.

I beckoned again. He still refused.

"As you wish," I exhaled heavily as I walked toward him.

"Hey! What's going on back there? Who's getting off? Can you guys make this quick?" the bus driver ordered.

"I will!" I replied.

"Three!" I then snapped, and I charged at him to give him our famous elbow punch.

"Okay, okay, okay! Geez," he replied as he held up one hand to ward me off and frantically dug in his pocket for the knife with the other. He found it, threw it on the ground, and ran from the bus.

He stood by the sidewalk and maintained a confused stare at me through the window as the bus drove off.

I checked myself, and it was just a slight flesh wound. I stared at the knife for a while; it had a blade around six inches long. I contemplated how many crimes that thug must have used it to commit, as it was old and rusty. I took it up, sat down, stepped on the blade with one foot, and used my hand to pull hard on the handle until it snapped from the blade.

I broke it. I broke his cycle of robbing passengers on busses with this knife.

Sometimes that's the only thing you can do in life to someone or something that is a threat or causing you harm—break it off!

Not sure why I didn't just toss it out the window; maybe I wanted to show it to my brother and tell him about my bizarre encounter.

I continued sipping on my beer for several minutes later until we hit a delay, which was caused by a car accident. After several minutes of just sitting there, I also went outside to check what was going on, as by now traffic was stopped from both sides.

The Calling

It was a little boy, about twelve or thirteen, who was hit by a motorcyclist as he exited a bus ahead of ours and ran across the street for church. There was a bit of commotion, as I just stood there confused, watching concerned folks check his vitals while administering CPR.

He was in great pain but seemed like he was going to be okay.

What is this? I found myself questioning and talking to myself. *All he wanted to do was come to church and worship You, but look what*

You allowed to happen instead. Is it even safe to simply attend church anymore? I questioned myself.

My ways are not your ways. Lean not on your own understanding, acknowledge me in all your ways, and I will direct you path, a voice suddenly echoed in my head.

There was silence mentally until I snapped back to reality when an ambulance arrived and took him away. The cops also cleared the scene.

And then I thought, *Was I just talking to myself, or was that God talking to me?*

Have you ever had a tough decision to make so you prayed about it? And when the time finally came for you to decide, you decided but still weren't sure if it was your choice or God's choice?

As the road cleared, I gazed at the church across the street and, against all odds, finished my beer, crossed over, slowly walked to the back, and entered the congregation. It was my first time back in church in years, thanks to the war with Willy, being heartbroken by Michelle, Clair's death, or this thief just now.

I was always told that church was the one place you should run to when you became a lost soul trying to find your way back. And that I was—a lost soul.

I sat in the empty back row, the pastor was preaching, but I didn't hear a word he was saying, as my mind was in a different world. The choir sang, and the next thing I knew was a nice old lady gently tapped me on my shoulder; yep, I might have dozed off for a bit.

I remembered her from the phone booth, but she seemingly didn't recognize me, as I had my hoodie on with my head bowed. But as I looked up, she did and said hello.

I didn't reply.

She had a basket in her hand.

"Sir, we are collecting offering. Is there anything you would like to offer to Christ our Lord?" she asked with the sweetest, softest smile.

I sat up, collected myself, and searched my jeans jacket for cash. I had none, as I had spent the last of what I had on beer. The only thing I felt was the broken knife from that thief. She patiently waited, but I removed the broken knife from my pocket and slowly placed it in her collection basket.

She started at it and gave me a confused, forced smile, and walked to the next bench. I then left without still not hearing or focusing on what the pastor was preaching about.

Have you ever been in church, sitting all cute and seemingly attentive as the sermon went on, but you were not attentive because you were playing on your phone or your mind was simply somewhere else?

Don't ever admit that to your pastor.

A Promise Kept

A couple of evenings after that, Willy and I stopped at the corner deli on the way home from school. We bought some beers and were just having a drink before we went our separate ways. Yes, we were slowly burying the hatchet. He noticed Jess and his brother walking past on the other side of the street and called them over. She was clearly concerned that she saw us two talking together, as she wondered if I had told on her.

"Hey," she said with a forced smile and gave him a kiss as they approached.

His brother looked like he wanted to charge at me and started running his mouth until Willy shut him down.

"It's two against one, bro. Let's take this fool out," his brother said, itching for a fight.

"I said stand down! It's over!" Willy shut him down.

"Over? What you mean over? So you just gonna let things slide after what these punks did to us? You really going to let these punks win—again?" he fumed.

There was a tense calm.

"Remember what we did to them too. Nobody won, bro! Let's just call it a draw!' Willy tried to calm as he removed a beer from his back pack, popped the cap off, and handed it to him.

His brother was so mad he angrily slapped the bottle away. It shattered on the ground.

"So what is this?" he fumed at the sight of us two chilling and having a drink. "You a Street Boy now. bro? You damn sellout!"

That made Willy so furious he gave him a straight right, which sent him flying across the parking lot. He then splashed the rest of the beer from his glass beer bottle and was about to smash it over his head, but I restrained him and pried the bottle from his hand.

"Yo, chill! Chill!" I tried to calm him down as I forcefully restrained Willy.

What were the odds? There I was parting a fight between enemies against enemies.

"Don't you ever talk to me like that! We'll settle this at home," he barked. "Now get the hell outa here!"

His bloodied-nosed brother, visibly scared as hell, about round 2 later, got up and tried to apologize. "Hey, I'm sorry, bro," he said as he wiped blood from his nose.

"You ain't sorry yet!" Willy snapped. "Get the hell outa my face. I'll see you at home!"

Jess further tried to calm him.

"So what's wrong with being a Street Boy?" I smirked to Willy as his brother wobbled off.

He just shook his head and chuckled as he lit a cigarette and retrieved his backpack from the ground.

"Okay, so now that we're all gathered here, I need to get to the bottom of something once and for all," he said as his whole demeanor changed. "Did she tell you she was pregnant?"

"She who? Michelle? Cuz I've been hearing some talk about you two," I said as my demeanor also changed.

"Excuse me! What is he talking about Willy?" a now confused and upset Jess said.

He tried to diffuse the situation with a weary chuckle, as he didn't see that one coming.

"Hey, J, can you give us a minute to talk, man to man?" he said as he nudged me away to follow him.

"Did you sleep with her, Willy? Tell me the truth!" she said, now clearly upset.

"Not here, Jess! We will talk on the way home. Please, just give us a minute."

He then took out some cash and handed it to her.

"Hey, its movie night, remember? Go get some snacks and your usual favorites as usual for later."

"Did you sleep with that bitch Michelle?" she said, counting her words as she got more furious.

He gave her a quick slap on the chin.

"What did I tell you about disrespecting me? Especially in public!" he stared her down with a now clenched fist. "No! Now go get some snacks and let's go home. You're carrying our baby. Don't want you to get all worked up."

She did a poor job of holding back the tears as he gave her a peck and wiped tears from her eyes. She gave me a "Remember your promise" glance and entered the deli.

He was beside himself. He searched his bag and came up empty.

"I need to get more beer, man." He exhaled heavily.

I gave him a can from my backpack.

"She's having our baby, Street. That's a life-changing moment for me. I'm hanging up my gloves, man. No more fighting. I'm about to become a daddy."

"Cheers!" I said as we knocked cans. "Congrats, man, and you right about what you said earlier. Let's just call this a draw!"

"My brother thinks you and Jess were fooling around while I was in jail," he said as he slouched. "She and her girlfriend came over my house the day before I was released to get my room in order. She has a key, so she let herself in. He was asleep, so they thought they were home alone, but he woke up to them laughing and talking about you—yes, *you*! And what he said sounded like a sexual encounter between you two."

"What!" I scoffed. "That fool must have been sleepwalking or dreaming!" I lied.

"Just tell me the truth, Street… Just tell me the truth," he started as Jess walked out and approached us. "Did you sleep with Jess?"

She froze, and her bag of snacks almost fell from her hands. I was scared for her, so I didn't even make eye contact.

"Look at me!" I said to him.

He didn't.

"Willy!"

He slowly raised his head, turned, and gazed into my eyes, in fight mode.

"The closest encounter I ever had with your snitch girlfriend was that night she brought those po-po's to my house," I lied. "No!"

She broke down crying in sweet relief.

He turned around and saw her. "Babe, what's wrong?" he asked as he walked over and hugged her.

"I don't feel too good. What are you two talking about?"

Uneasy silence.

"I just wanted closure, Mommy. And now I have it," he said as he kissed her.

Her body was still shaking, petrified at her fate at the hands of Willy's fists had I had said yes, so her eyes smiled a weary and relieved "Thank you" at me.

"Hey, Jess, can you give us a sec?" I said as I nudged Willy a few meters away.

"So what's going on with you and Michelle?"

"What? Nothing!" He glared at me.

I tried to compose myself as I held my fist to my forehead and punched it a few times.

"Did you... Did you..." I tried to just let it out. "Did you rape her?"

"What!"

"Did you rape her?"

He laughed almost embarrassingly as he chugged on his beer.

"Give us a minute, babe," he said to Jess as he pulled me even further away so she couldn't hear our conversation.

"She and I have never even kissed," he then said as he gazed into my eyes.

"But she's *ripe* for you now," I threw in his face.

He laughed.

"She is! But I guess I'm just not the type of guy she wants to pick that cherry."

"What happened that day she came over your house before leaving for the airport?"

"What? Nothing!"

"She was clearly upset and said it didn't go well."

"Nothing happened!"

"So why were you so upset that day you saw me and her kissing?"

Brief silence.

"'Cuz I was jealous at seeing her all cuddled in your arms and kissing *you.*"

"Are you lying to me?"

His demeanor changed as he started to get upset. "There's only one way to find out, Street. Ask her! I waited my whole life for that moment with her that I saw you two having on The Main, bro. Yes, I got my baby mama, but I was still jealous. Michelle was the fantasy love of my life, but to her, I was just another face in the crowd. You can have her. Nothing happened. Ask her!" he said as he walked off to Jess.

"Hey!" I said as he walked off.

I gave him our gangster street fingers signal as confirmation if everything was now cool between us, and he just nodded, took a beer from the grocery bag Jess was carrying, popped it open, and playfully hugged her as they walked off.

They left, and I left for home, feeling a bit in limbo. I had no remorse about lying to his face about Jess and me; based on what she told me that night, if I had said yes, he would have beaten the crap out of her and probably killed her and her baby. And in violating his probation with such a crime would easily have him end up serving life in prison or receiving even the death penalty. Plus, he would have declared war on me all over again.

Have you ever been there where you have had to tell a lie to save someone's ass? It's never a good thing to lie. But imagine the even worst feelings you would have had from the consequences if you had told the truth.

Sigh.

I didn't want that blood on my conscience; so for all you self-righteous folks who are reading this screaming, "Shame on you!" for lying to that young man to his face, my simple question is, "If, fearful for her life, Jess had put you in the same situation she had put me in, to not say yes, what would you have said?"

"Let ye who is without sin cast the first stone!"

I got home, and as I walked down my driveway to the house, checking my mail, I glanced over at the seven-foot-high hedge, and the love bush I inserted weeks ago still hadn't budged.

Oh well, I thought. Something about Willy's demeanor didn't quite add up. Did he in fact sleep with Michelle, and as I did to him with Jess, he stared me in the face and lied that he didn't?

Karma?

CHAPTER 11

DOMESTIC VIOLENCE

"Husbands, love your wives, and do not be harsh with them"—a verse from Colossians.

I was around the backyard on the swing, having a beer and just enjoying the evening, when Jess suddenly appeared from the side gate, crying and moaning. She was bloodied from head to toe as it looked like she got quite a beating; one of her eyes was gouged out, her left arm was limp as if broken, and she could barely walk as she dragged her fractured legs to get closer to me. And then to my shock, she had a dead fetus in her hand. She opened her mouth to speak, as black blood drained from it.

I was so terrified my beer fell from my hand and I fell off the swing as she got closer.

"Look what you did, Street! Look what you made him do to me!" she bawled as she got closer and closer to me.

I was still sitting on the ground, so I used my arms and feet in a panic to crawl back so as to get further away from her.

"It doesn't matter whose baby it is anymore. Look what you made him do to me," she said, limping closer and closer each time, showing the bloody fetus. I backed into our side fence but could not move any farther.

"Wait, Jess, wait…What…what happened?" My voice trembled.

"You promised me! You promised me!"

"But I didn't. I didn't say anything! Wha-what happened?" I pleaded as my body shook in fear.

"Look what you made him do to me, Street. Look what you made him do to me!" she screamed as she violently lunged at me.

I sprung up screaming, terrified, trembling, and sweating. I looked around and slowly calmed myself, thanking God that I was in bed and it was only a nightmare.

Phew.

I lay back down for a moment and just stared at the ceiling. *Was that just a dream or a premonition?* I thought to myself.

"I will never tell nor confess for your sake, Jess," I whispered, with thoughts of her fate in mind if I was to do so. She was no longer a sex object for me, as I now found myself caring about her.

Later that morning, I met up with Willy at the bus stop, and we just casually chatted. There was no conversation about Jess, Michelle, or my dream as we rode to our connecting bus terminal.

We met up with other schoolmates there, boarded, and eventually disembarked. About fifteen of us were walking the rest of the journey to school when the girl that was robbed several weeks ago suddenly, in fear, stopped dead in her tracks, shifted over, and squeezed my hand. We followed her stare to the open lot, where she gazed at the three thugs who had robbed her loitering and having a smoke.

Yep, after over a month of not seeing them, they were back!

I warned them never to come back, but here we go again. I gave one of my boys my backpack and slowly walked over.

"I warned you punks never to show your face here again," I said as I approached them.

"Listen, man, we don't want any trouble. We just want to hustle and put food on our table later," one of them said nervously as he pulled a ratchet knife.

"Are these the guys you were telling me about?" Willy said as he walked over, itching for some action.

I nodded.

"You don't remember me, do you?" he said to one of them. "Your father was once my supplier. He duped me."

The other guys in my group dropped their backpacks, in fight mode.

"Please. I'm sorry, man. I'm sorry about the other day, okay? And what went down with you and pop, but go settle that with him. We sell weed as a hustle. Not sure what I was thinking that morning."

"Don't apologize to me," I said as I beckoned the girl who got robbed over.

She held my hand as she stood up to them. The guy who robbed her apologized.

"Every time you see any of us passing, just look the other way, okay? Do your hustle, and just ignore us," I said as I beckoned for him to give me the ratchet.

The thief hesitated. Willy dropped his backpack and clenched his fist. The thief, realizing they were outnumbered almost five to one, complied.

"We not here looking for trouble, bro. Just wanna hustle," he then said as he reached out to dab me. "So we cool?"

I didn't.

"Is this the knife he used?" I asked her as I took it from him with an "I dare you to resist me taking it from you" stare.

He saw the gaze in my eyes and did a quick glance at the rest of us in attack mode, ready to give them a beat-down. So he complied.

"It looks like it," she said, still a bit shaken.

I handed it to her.

"What you wanna do with it?"

"Cut him!" one of my boys shouted.

She paused as she maintained an angry stare at the thief and put it in her jeans pocket, and we all walked off.

"So we cool?" one of them again shouted.

"We'll see!" I shouted back.

"To be continued," Willy, however, warned.

The Great Debate on Domestic Violence

We arrived at school and were all in our locker rooms at various sections, changing into our overhauls for arc welding class.

"Hey, Street! I never did say it, but thanks for standing up to those thugs for me again," the girl who got robbed, who was a few lockers away, said as she changed.

And yes, it was a unisex locker room, as we simply slipped our baggy overhauls on over our school dress code, which was jeans and T-shirt.

"One for all, all for one." I smiled.

"Come here," she said. She smiled, walked over, and gave me a hug and a long kiss on the corner of my lips. "Thank you, my bodyguard!"

"Anytime." I smiled as I hugged her back and exchanged a kiss on her cheek.

Willy was standing at the other side of the locker room, changing. He just smiled, as he could see and hear what was going on.

"Oh, ohh, what's going on here?" one of the boys from our class, whom she had just started dating, said as he walked in to change. "You trying to hit on my girl, Street?" he joked. He pried her away from me, and they kissed. "Don't ever let me smack your lights out for cheating on me." He smiled as he hugged her tighter. Her demeanor suddenly changed, and she shoved him away.

"What?" he asked confused.

"Don't ever talk to me like that," she snapped.

"Like what? I was only joking." He defended himself.

"Yeah, that's what my ex used to say until he started beating me for real, until I finally said enough and dumped his sorry ass," she said, recollecting.

"What? You never told me that," he said.

She chuckled sarcastically. "And which girl would be quick to walk around, telling everyone that she gets the crap beat out of her man for random shit?"

He was visibly taken off guard at how quickly the mood changed. "I was only joking, sweetie," he said as he pulled her aside. "Listen, my parents raised me well. Those bastards that robbed you, I will beat the crap out of them again if I have to. I will fight if I have to, but I have never and will never put my hands on a woman!"

189

"You better not or at least not me, because I will fight too," she consoled herself. "I was physically abused by my ex many times, sometimes for the stupidest of reasons, like not vacuuming, not doing the dishes, being late with making dinner, and even for one time at the store for returning a hello to another customer who simply smiled at me and said hi," she continued, getting a bit emotional. "I stupidly accepted it as the norm until I finally told someone about it—my mom.

"Sweetie, I would never put my hands on you," he pleaded.

She was beside herself. "Mom had my dad and some of his friends pay him a visit and beat the crap out of him that last night he hit me after we had an argument over whose turn it was to have the television remote. He served time in jail too, as she also pressed charges."

There was a brief uneasy moment of silence until she broke it with an unsettling question.

"Sometimes I hear my neighbor being beat up by her husband. I'd just put my headset on. He's a truck driver, so he's gone for weeks at a time, and I have seen the many men she's had come over. She's very loud during sex, so we all knew they were more than just her male friends coming over to visit. He's caught her a couple times, and she says she simply takes her ass whooping but she is never leaving him. And then always she smiles and says that he has no intentions of leaving her either. Sick! Why do you men beat on the woman you claim you love? Is it a show of power?" she questioned.

Silence.

"It's a lame-ass show of authority, because men who do so are all pussies," I said, glancing at Willy, remembering my dad.

"You ever hit a woman, Street?" She sighed.

"I've slapped that ass a few times when we getting down and dirty in bed," I said, acting out my performance, which brought some cheers from the guys. "But, no, I've never, and I would never stoop that low," I simply answered, as I put on my tool belt.

"What about you, Willy?" she shouted to him.

More silence.

"Women need to know their place." He then exhaled as he continued putting on his gears.

"Wooh!" She laughed sarcastically. "So you do beat on your bitches?"

He didn't reply.

"So tell me something, Willy. What if your mom or your sister or whichever female relative told you that their man was beating the crap out of them?" she baited as she walked over to him.

No response until he finally spoke.

"I'd kill him!" he said, strapping his tool belt on.

"Yet you beat your girl?"

"Who said I did?"

"You with your reply!" she said as they continued back and forth.

"Hey, listen, are we here for class, or is this the great debate?" he asked out of frustration.

"Both!" she replied.

"Okay, okay, so let's debate then," he said as he closed his locker and leaned back against it. There was a brief silence as he gathered his thoughts, took a deep breath, and then spoke. "Why does the world find it so funny when a woman beats the crap out of her man?" he asked.

She and her boyfriend burst out laughing.

"'Cuz…" She laughed.

"'Cuz what?" a stone-faced Willy pressed. "You find it so funny," he said, turning to her boyfriend. "Would you find it funny if that was happening to you or a male relative or a friend? Why the hell does the world find it so funny? But when a man hits a woman, the laughing turns to rage and cops and court and prison."

The boyfriend looked visibly embarrassed and stopped laughing.

There was dead silence as everyone searched for words.

I broke the silence by telling them the story my mom told me about my father's demise. "You have a beautiful girl right here that you just started dating, bro," I continued at my classmate to bait the waters in disgust at domestic violence. "Would you ever hit her?"

"Hell no," he said as they hugged while she jokingly removed the thief's ratchet knife I gave her from her tool belt and held it at his crotch as a warning.

"You have a baby on the way, Willy." I turned my attention to him. "Would you ever hit the mother of your child?"

His body shook at the direct question. He started me right in the face.

Silence.

"Only if she gave me a reason to. And if he gives you a reason to," he said, turning to the girl, "use that knife to defend yourself."

Silence.

"What *justifiable* reason would that be, though, Willy, to hit your woman or man? To end up talking with our fists or this knife instead of just reasoning or even arguing out the issue?" she questioned.

There was no answer.

The bell rang for class to start, so the conversation, to the relief of some of us, ended there as we all left.

The rest of the day went quietly.

Several days passed by quietly with no drama, no fighting, and no surprises.

Against All Odds

I got home from school one evening the following week, and as I entered my front yard, I saw my brother and our grumpy next-door neighbor having an animated chat about our hedge. The neighbor, an elderly man, was clearly upset about something.

I just said hello to them both and kept it moving.

His girlfriend was in the kitchen, packing away groceries. I greeted her, and we exchanged a hug and pecker, and we chatted a bit.

My brother eventually entered a few minutes later, scoffing that the neighbor was ranting about a new batch of love bush that was growing out of control and eating away his hedge. His girlfriend and

I glanced at each other, and she gave me a smile and a wink, saying that the love bush I had planted was blooming, albeit strangely, just on one side of the hedge. Still, based on our folklore, it was a sign that "She loves me" rather than "She loves me not." But then, Michelle was now still history.

Sigh.

"You're all set with groceries for the next couple a weeks," he said as he munched on a bag of chips, took out his wallet, counted out some cash, and handed it to me. "This should keep you for school, beers, and smokes until we hear from mom next week."

"They didn't have the ice cream you wanted, so I got my grape nut favorite, ha ha! Remember that deal we made? And they didn't have crunchy peanut butter, so we got creamy," his girlfriend said as she continued packing away.

"We finally were called by her mom and were able to locate Clair's tombstone. We visited with flowers and paid our respects a bit in case you were wondering why we were a no-show with dinner yesterday." His girlfriend sighed sadly. "Whenever you are mentally ready, we can take a ride there to her grave site for you to show your respects also."

There was a sad, silent moment.

I nodded.

"I need a drink!" She then exhaled heavily as she poured one. She was sad at the loss of her friend and, worse, a friend that she introduced me to.

"Besides that, you should be all set with everything else," my brother dabbed, trying to change the subject.

"We staying the night, just going out for dinner, and yes, we will order yours for takeout," his girl said.

Silence.

"Chinese?" I finally asked, trying to change the subject myself.

"Hibachi," she said.

"Even better! Roast duck with—" I started to order.

"Yes, I know, I know." She smiled as she hugged and kissed me on the forehead.

"Oh, and a stop at the liquor store for me to restock my dorm's supply of beers and smoke," G continued. "We had a li'l party in my room for one of my boys last night."

"I told you to tell everyone to bring a bottle," she said.

"It's all good. Those are my peoples, my bicycle crew," he said as they kissed.

"And I'm your brother, so grab both for me also," I requested.

He nodded and beckoned for me to give him back some of the cash he just gave me.

I gave him a mean little brother's look of "Nuh-uh!" There was a playful tussle for him to retrieve back some of the cash I put in my front pants pocket.

"Will you two cut it out?" His girlfriend laughed as she noticed and playfully parted us. "I got you, Street. My treat, plus dinner. See why you should do like me and get a part-time job on campus, babe. Nothing beats a little extra cash," she said to him. "Can you put away these bags, Street, and do those dishes, please? You know overnight dishes in the sink is a no-no rule in this house." She playfully bumped me with her hip over to the sink and was about to exit when there was a knock at the door.

"Oh, hell no!" my brother gasped, thinking it was our grumpy neighbor coming to give him another earful about us maintaining our side of the hedge to prevent the spread of the love bush. He peered through the window next to the door and paused in surprise.

"Who is it?" I asked.

He didn't reply.

"Who is it G?" his girlfriend asked and, out of curiosity, went to look for herself.

"Oh, hell no!" she also gasped. She turned to a stone face, and after a few glances at my brother, she abruptly opened the door with an attitude.

"Hello, I'm here to see—" the voice started.

"He's not here!" my brother's girlfriend snapped as she held up her index finger to say "shush" to the visitor!

"Who's that?" I asked as I exited the kitchen, munching on the rest of my brother's chips as I popped open a beer.

"I hear him," the voice said.

"Well, he…he doesn't want to see you," my brother's girlfriend stood in defense.

"Who is it?" I again asked.

"It's me, Street!" the voice said.

My brother, having enough of the standoff, beckoned for his girlfriend to let the visitor in. There was a brief standoff until she reluctantly complied by just letting her in the doorway.

My beer almost fell from my hands. To my surprise, it was Michelle!

What the what!

The Interrogation

"Hey," she meekly greeted as she slowly entered, clutching a gift bag—no pocketbook, no Bible, and for the first time ever, she was not in a dress but instead was in stretch jeans, a T-shirt, and a denim jacket.

She was looking hot as hell! But strangely, I was more sad than happy to see her.

"What are you doing here?" my brother's girlfriend abruptly asked.

Michelle seemed a bit confused that she was unwelcomed.

"I…I literally just came from the airport, dropped my stuff off at home, and came to see Street, hoping that he would be here because—"

"Because what?" his girlfriend snapped, now with folded arms, still using her body to bar her from fully entering.

"Yeah… Because?" my brother pressed her.

Michelle seemed even more confused, as all this time I was at a loss for words.

"Well, because he…he used to call me every Sunday while I was away. But then he stopped. I haven't heard from him in weeks," she said. "Please, I am not sure what this vibe is all about, but I…I just came to talk."

"Talk? Talk!" my brother's girlfriend said with an attitude. "Okay, let's have a talk then." She ushered her inside.

She offered her a seat in the sofa and sat closely on one side of her. My brother sat even closer on the other side to sandwich her.

"Hey, Street," Michelle greeted in a awkward, confused tone.

I didn't respond as I wasn't sure how to feel or react as I sat in the smaller sofa across from them.

"Chips?" My brother's girlfriend offered her as she leaned over and took the bag of potato chips from me.

"No, thank you," she politely refused, but my brother's girlfriend scooped a handful from the family-sized bag and angrily chewed on it while maintaining her stare.

I wanted to laugh, as she was tipsy and clearly toying with her after all that I told her. She was angry with Michelle for hurting me and taunting her to react so she could fight her and kick her out. She was a badass. Yes, I'd seen sis in cat fights before, she's was one hot-headed dame you never wanted to cross the line with, especially when she had been drinking.

"Beer?" my brother then offered as he took my beer and had a gulp, then passed it to his girl. She finished it.

"I don't drink," an uneasy Michelle replied.

There was a moment of silence.

"Okay, so what is this? What's going on here? Street!" she then gasped.

"You tell us!" his girlfriend snapped.

"We just took his chips and beer away from him, which he was clearly enjoying," G started.

"And he was so enjoying you," his girlfriend jumped in. "So likewise, who took your li'l ass from Street, your ex at church or Willy? Why you dumped him?"

"Now that's a very good question," my brother added. "You said you wanted to talk, so let's talk. Forget your dirty li'l secrets. What's going on with you and Street?"

"What! What do you mean?" a now totally lost Michelle said. She was clearly getting unsettled.

"You know exactly what he means! What's going on between you two? Why are you playing Street for a fool?" She stood up, ready to smack her.

G held her hand and calmed her. She sat back down, still fuming.

"What!" Michelle gasped in confusion.

"Hey, enough with your games," my brother's girlfriend continued and finally cut to the chase. "You damn church girls! Playing Street for a fool with your holier-than-thou self while patching things up with your beloved ex in London over romantic dinners. Oh! And word on the street is, you also slept with Willy. Sooo?"

"What!" a now visibly confused and upset Michelle snapped. "What are you talking about?"

"Tell her, Street, because if she says 'What!' one more time…" she fumed, clenching a fist. "Here's your chance to finally get your answers and closure from this church slut!"

"Excuse me!" Michelle snapped as she stood up and headed for the door. "Okay, so I don't have a clue what's going on here, but you guys are freaking me out," she said as she gave me a confused glance and opened the door to leave. "I should go."

"Yeah, get out of here, player! Next stop on your return visit is Willy's house!" my brother's girlfriend shouted.

"Don't forget your gift bag, bitch!" my brother barked as he tossed the bag to her.

"What? Excuse me!" Michelle then snapped, exited, and slammed the door.

There was an awkward silence as my brother and his girl gazed at me for a reaction. I was still trying to process what just happened and thinking she never had a chance to explain herself. But then there was another knock at the door. This time, the person didn't wait. They opened it, and it was Michelle again.

She was clearly unsettled.

"Okay, so please, can somebody please, please tell me what's going on here? Because I am no player or…or a bitch or a slut!" she yelled, gazing at my brother. "What is this, Street? I prayed for this day to see you again, but I never expected this welcome. What's going on?" She started getting emotional.

"That's all we want to know. What's going on?" my brother's girlfriend replied with folded arms and an uncaring stare. "Why don't you just tell us the truth?"

Michelle was at a loss for words. "May I sit?" she finally spoke.

My brother and his girlfriend drifted farther apart from each other in the sofa for her to sit, but she instead slowly walked over and sat beside me.

My brother took out a cigarette and lit it, gave his girl one, and passed the pack to me. I lit one and took a puff. Strangely, she never complained about me smoking in her presence this time around.

"The floor is yours, bro," my brother said as he and his girl sat back as jurors, waiting for the conversation to unfold.

Silence.

"You told me on the phone the last time we spoke that you thought long and hard about it and that you made up your mind and that it was over between us," I finally spoke as I sighed heavily. "So why are you here? Oh, to bring me my consolation prize now that you and your ex are back together?" I continued as I glanced at her gift bag.

"Street, what are you talking about?"

"You told me it was over between us!" I snapped as I sat up from my slouch. "So why are you here?"

"I never said it was over between us—as in me and you! I said I thought about it, and it was over—between me and him; my ex! We got disconnected from that call, and you never called back for me to explain."

I looked at my brother and his girl, who were now looking at each other confused.

"Okay, blah blah blah! So you broke up with your ex. So what's the story with you and Street?" his girlfriend was now at a loss and a bit tipsy and also wanted to clarify.

Michelle sighed heavily. "I'm in love with this silly guy sitting beside me," she said as a tear rolled from her eye. "I knew I was in love with you, Street, that day on the main when you were break dancing with no music in front of all those passersby to impress me, which more like embarrassed me." She laughed and cried at the same time as she wiped a tear from her eye. "And then you gave me your prized championship belt."

"You never told me you *gave* it to her," my brother whispered.

His girlfriend nudged him to shut up.

"So when you said it was over…" I started.

"I meant it was over between my ex and me. Yes, we went to dinner, and yes, I told him all about us. And yes, he didn't take it very well, but yes, he's history!" she finished. I was at a loss for words until she upped the stakes even higher. "I love you, Street, to the point where you distracted me from my missionary service. Every Sunday at 3:00 p.m., I was always late or absent from our evening prayers and supper at the hotel because I would wait for your call. Every Sunday! I waited and waited, but you never called again. I have lost count how many times I'd just lock myself in the bathroom and…" She sobbed.

The atmosphere in the room suddenly changed.

"Okay, I need a beer!" my brother said as he glanced at his girlfriend, who raised her hand for one also, as he recomposed himself and headed to the kitchen.

"Okay, Street, so shame on you for not calling," my brother's girlfriend now rolled her eyes at me and said with a confused stare at me.

I stared back at her in shock and wanted to clobber her with the cushion next to me, as it was her insistent command for me not to call her back.

"Babe, I think Street could use a beer, too, as this is getting kinda awkward," she shouted to my brother as she lit her cigarette.

There was awkward silence, which was only serenaded by sniffles from Michelle.

"Okay, we got that part settled," my brother reentered with beers and sat by his girl. "So what's going on with you and Willy?" he abruptly asked.

More silence.

"Yeah. What happened that day you went over to his house before you left for the airport?" I asked. "I heard it 'didn't end well.'"

Even more silence.

"Okay. So we have to go in a bit because we made reservations for dinner, and I don't want them to cancel our table, thinking we are no-shows. So enough with the silence and sounds of crickets already!" His girlfriend exhaled out of frustration at Michelle's delayed answers as she took a gulp from her beer.

"Yeah. One of your missionaries told Street that the visit didn't end well. So?" my brother jabbed as he sat and passed me a beer.

We all maintained a stare at her as she took a napkin from her jacket pocket and wiped her eyes and nose. Michelle finally spoke. "So he insisted that I come by his house to see him for a minute as he had a send-off gift for me. I hesitated, but he wasn't home alone, so I went," she started. "We chatted a bit, and he tried to give me a watch, claiming that he was going to count down the time before I got back. I refused it. He was clearly embarrassed and somewhat upset. He asked for a hug, so I hesitantly gave him a 'church hug,' and he tried to kiss me." She stopped.

Silence.

"And?" I questioned.

More silence as she started sobbing.

"Michelle," I consoled as I became overwhelmed with vengeance. "And?"

"He closed his gate behind me and tried to kiss me again. I refused. He then tried to pull me to his front porch, but I wrestled from his grip," she continued. "He started ranting about how much he loved me and had been waiting all these years for me, and I simply told him to stop waiting in vain because he will only have me over my dead body!"

Silence.

"He had a defeated look in his eyes as his unaware mom came out to the front porch and beckoned to him about some undone errand before she had to go. Willy just looked at me with empty eyes and a sad smile and then walked off up his driveway."

"So you're saying nothing happened?" My brother exhaled.

"Just a church hug." Michelle sighed.

"Okay, so let's get this straight. You officially broke up with your ex?" his girlfriend started.

"And nothing happened between you and Willy?" my brother jumped in.

A now drained Michelle just simply nodded in tears.

My brother's girlfriend clobbered me with a cushion. "Okay, I think we're done here," she then said as she stood up a bit wobbly and threw another cushion at me. "Really, Street? I was about to give this poor innocent girl's face a makeover with my fist, all because of a misunderstanding." She then burped. "Let's go, babe. We'll be back in a few, guys. I've heard enough."

I looked at sis and tossed a cushion back at her.

"Nail this!" she burped as they left.

The two of us just sat there in silence for what seemed like an eternity.

"Why didn't you ever call back?" Michelle finally spoke.

Silence.

"Street."

"Because I thought it was over between us." I sighed. "I misunderstood."

More silence.

"Let's go get some fresh air," I suggested when I saw her fanning cigarette smoke from her face.

She complied, and we went to the backyard and sat in the swings.

"You have no idea what you've put me through," I said as I took a puff. "*Hurt* is an understatement."

"Why didn't you just call back, Street?" she sighed. "It's just sad that human nature sometimes causes us to, instead of seeking clarification, we act on our misconstrued assumptions in certain situations. It's like picking at a wound caused by someone that really hurt you instead of giving the person the opportunity to explain and heal that hurt if it wasn't intentional. Not because we sometimes think 'That's what's going on' in retrospect means 'That's what's going on.'"

Silence.

"I'm sorry." I sighed, now growing weary of the situation. I leaned over to her swing to kiss her, but she stopped me by holding my cheeks. She then brushed something from my lips, took my cigarette, and tossed it away.

"You hurt me too," she whispered.

"So I guess we're even then." I sighed.

"Kissing someone who smokes is like licking a nasty astray." She smiled, took a lip gloss from her pocket, and applied it to her lips and popped a gum in. "So after that reaction from your brother and his girl, I guess I am now the bad guy?"

"No, I am," I said as I rinsed the cigarette taste from my mouth with a gulp from my beer, kissed her gum from her mouth, and chewed on it. "Kiss me." I leaned in to meet her halfway.

She squeezed my cheeks even harder. "What am I gonna do with you, Street?"

"I want to believe you," I said, changing the subject.

"What do you mean? What's stopping you?"

"You just sound too good to be true!" I exhaled.

Silence.

"Okay, that's it. I'm leaving," she said as she rose and started to walk off. "It was nice seeing you again."

"Oh, leaving me for real this time?" I scoffed.

"Really, Street! What's this? What's wrong with you?" she said as she angrily spun around.

I went after her, grabbed her by the waist, dragged her as close as she could be pressing against my body, and kissed her. She never saw it coming, and still a bit mad, she thumped me on the shoulder a couple times. Then she dropped the gift bag, hugged me around the neck, and kissed me passionately for a bit.

"Come," I then ordered as I led her back inside the house.

"Where are we going?" she asked, all worked up, as she followed me, unlike the last time when she refused to.

I just glanced back at her and winked with a smile as we entered from the kitchen and I led her to my bedroom.

So Place Your Bets—What Do You Think Happened Next?

"Oh, wait!" she said as she ran back outside to retrieve the gift bag, reentered my bedroom, placed it on the dresser, walked over, hugged and kissed me. "I see you planted our lucky tree in the garden. It's beautiful." She smiled. "What did you do with the vase?"

I swallowed hard at a response and then remembered what G had said.

"It, umm, it was blown over in a freak storm we had, and broke."

"I've got something for you," she then whispered in between kisses.

"I've got something for you too." I exhaled heavily at the moment finally arriving and not caring what she meant.

She allowed me to remove the jeans jacket but hesitated as I slowly slipped her T-shirt over her head, exposing just her bra. We kissed even more passionately as I tried to unbutton her jeans. She squeezed my hand to stop.

"What are you doing, Street? What are you doing? You know we can't," she started with a heavy exhalation.

I interrupted her with a deep kiss and pushed her on the bed then removed my T-shirt. She kept on pleading for me to stop as we kissed and wrestled and rolled about on the bed; one minute, I was on top of her, the next minute, she was on top of me. Then we rolled and clumsily fell to the floor. We both burst out laughing. I was on top of her again as we paused for a moment.

"Ouch! Street, please stop. I see right through you. You're not that guy to force himself on me, on anyone," she said as she used the back of her fingers to stroke my face. "You will only have me when I'm ready, but I'm not right now. Not like this, not yet."

I eased off her and was in a trance as I stared at her beautiful topless body covered only in a lace bra. I was in heat, and I passionately kissed her some more before I tried to unbutton her jeans again, only to be met with a firm jab from her knees into my groin.

"Ow, ow, ouch!" I groaned as I rolled off, her clutching it. "Really! Was that, like, totally necessary?" I moaned.

There was heavy panting from her side until she burst out laughing again and rolled over to sit on top of me. "I prayed for you, Street, when I sensed I was falling for a street thug," she said as she exhaled heavily and sat up on my thighs.

She was right; I had no fight in me toward her as I gazed at her because I had never and would never fight or force a woman to do anything against her will.

"See? You don't even have a boner." She smiled, gazing at my groin.

And then it hit me. *Oh, boy, here we go again*, as I remembered how my body was in shutdown mode with Clair for all the right reasons, but now again, for what reason? My mood suddenly changed, as I thought to myself that this was no Clair; this was my dream girl. I couldn't recall what else she was saying, but I realized that her bra had front instead of back hooks, and I quickly popped them open, exposing her breasts.

OMG!

She was caught off guard and used both hands to cover them. I rolled her over and was back on top. This time, I was the one sitting up on her thighs and unbuckling her belt. She used one hand to try to stop me because the other was covering her breasts. Epic fail. I was now unzipping her jeans until she stopped me with a bitch slap across the face.

"Stop! Get off me! I said get off me!" she ordered between heavy panting as tears streamed from her eyes. "You are no better than all those bastards that tried to lure me in their bed. You disappoint me, Street. It's over between us," she cried.

I snapped back to reality.

What have I done? I thought to myself, as this was not me. I stood up and apologized. She wasn't having it. She hurriedly got dressed and left. I called for her to stop and come back a few times but to no avail.

This was easily the most embarrassing moment of my life. I sat on the floor for what seemed like an eternity and as was the case earlier, prayed for that knock at the door again from her, but it never came. I was so angry with myself because I wanted to beat the crap out of Willy and Assad for what they tried to do to her, yet here I was, trying to do the same—forcing myself onto her also.

I didn't know if I was praying or if I was whispering to her, but the only two words that came out of my mouth were "Forgive me."

The Gift Bag

Night came, and I eventually ended up in the shower. As usual, I just stood there in deep thought, disgusted with myself for what I did earlier, as the water sprayed over me. My thoughts were interrupted by a knock on the bathroom door and a female voice. I hurriedly turned the shower off so I could hear better, thinking it was Michelle, but it was my brother's girlfriend.

"Street! Are you almost done? I need to pee so badly." She knocked again.

They were back.

"Aah, yeah. Gimme a second," I said as I partially dried off, wrapped myself in a towel, and exited. She rushed in.

I stood by my dresser to get dressed for bed and realized that Michelle had left her gift bag. I was tempted to look inside it but was too humiliated to because of what happened earlier. And then eureka; this was the moment to see her again before the night was over—by returning it.

I quickly got dressed.

"Guess it didn't end so well?" G said as he entered my room and saw my mood.

I just shook my head and exhaled heavily to confirm. "She left her bag. I'll be back in a bit."

"We can take you," he suggested.

"Nah. I could use the walk and some fresh air."

"Is everything okay, boys?" his girlfriend asked as she also entered my bedroom and sensed the mood.

"Everything is fine," I lied as I smooched her on the cheek, dabbed my brother, grabbed a beer and a smoke from the refills he bought, and started to leave.

"I got your six, just in case," he said with a coded wink.

That meant he would probably summon his crew or follow behind me in case there was any trouble, as visiting Michelle at her house was still high-risk considering Willy's brother wanted to continue our feud.

I got to her house several minutes later. There were lights on, which I prayed meant she was home, but even better for me was the fact that there was no one hanging out at Willy's house.

I called her name a few times. No answer. Then she finally came out on her front porch.

"Who is it?" she shouted, as it was a bit hard to identify me under the cover of darkness.

"It's me. Street."

She stood there for a moment, just gazing at me.

"I… You left your bag, so…so I…I just came to return it," I said.

"You can have it!" she said. "Everything in there is for you."

"Thanks, but you have to officially hand it to me, right?" I said. "Hey, I apologize again! You know me. You know me! I would never force myself on you. I'm not that guy. It was just horseplay that went too far. Heck, think about it. I never even had a boner. I never even had a boner because—" I shouted until she interrupted.

"Will you keep your voice down? Our neighbors can hear you," she snapped out of embarrassment.

Brief silence.

"Of course, I wanted to, but as you said, not this way, not like this," I said. "I prayed for you, too, Michelle, and by God's grace, I promise you I am not going to screw this up. Yes, I was acting like a jerk earlier, and I'm sorry. I'm so sorry. See my heart, not my stupid actions earlier. I'm no Willy or Assad, boo. I'm Street, and yes, I screwed up because one minute you were telling me you love me and the next minute you were telling me it was over because I took things a bit too far," I pleaded.

I couldn't make out the expression on her face, but she just stood there with arms folded.

"Please. I never had a boner! I never even had a boner!" I then shouted, which annoyed her to the point that she stormed down her driveway to the gate and told me to hush!

"My neighbors can hear you!" she whispered angrily.

"I never had a boner." I sighed as she pinched on my lips for me to shut up.

"My father is not here. That's why you are still here after all this commotion." She sighed.

"What time is he coming back?"

"In a few days," she said.

"Are you okay being home alone?" I questioned, sensing her anxiety as I saw her glance at Willy's house.

"Okay, that's it. I'm staying with you until he gets back!"

"Are you serious? You can't! He would kill me when my nosy neighbors tell him that I had a boy sleeping over."

"Well, go pack your shit and come crash with me then! You have five minutes. I'll wait for you."

"Really!" she scoffed. "After what you tried to do to me earlier?"

I exhaled heavily in guilt, took her hand, and used it to slap me across the face again. "I deserved that! But I don't deserve you putting me in the category of past men who tried to force themselves onto you, because I am not that guy. I didn't even have a boner!"

"If you say that one more time..." she fumed as she pinched hard on my lips again.

Our moment was interrupted by a car that pulled up to Willy's gate. It was his brother and a few of his thugs, and yes, they saw us.

She grew tense.

"I'll give you my room and take the couch," I said. "My brother and his girl are staying over for the next couple of days, so you won't have to worry about me and you being home alone. And even if we were, I promise that—"

She pinched my lips again for me to shut up. "I forgive you." She then smiled to my relief. "Yes, you really upset me, but I know enough about you to know that it was just a moment of heated passion. You're not that guy! I hope."

We just stared at each other for a moment.

I heard Willy's brother shout something to us but ignored him. As if this punk was ever to try me tonight, I was going to end up in jail, and he was going to end up in the ER.

"Street…" She sighed wearily.

"Yes, boo."

"Can I trust you?"

I sighed out of frustration as I knew I was guilty of creating her doubt. "Yes!" I finally said, as another car pulled up a little distance from the car parked by Willy's house.

She grew even more tense.

"Go pack your sleepover bag, and let's go, boo. I don't like this," I pleaded.

We watched as Willy and two of his thugs came from the house to meet his brother at the gate. He recognized me as they had an animated conversation while popping beers, lighting smokes, and pointing at us.

Michelle then abruptly just hugged herself and headed back up the driveway to her house.

"Michelle!" I called but didn't get a response.

She didn't say a word but just went inside her house and closed the door. More lights were turning on in her house instead of off, as if she wasn't quite ready for bed or just needed additional lights on as a sense of security.

Ten minutes went by and then fifteen.

I didn't know why I waited, but I just waited, knowing that Willy and I were now cool, so to hell with his brother. I was also wondering if Michelle was ever going to come back out. I had then given up and was about to sadly walk off when I noticed that the other car that had parked a few houses from Willy's flashed their headlights and slowly pulled up at Michelle's house. It was tinted, so I couldn't see the passengers.

I remembered what happened to Bob that night and immediately went into fight-or-flight mode, but I exhaled a sigh of relief as my brother and his girlfriend exited. Two of my brother's bicycle crew also exited from the back seat and held a gaze in fight mode at Willy and his crew.

"You good?" my brother simply asked.

"I dunno, G. I dunno." I slumped.

"Let's go home, Street," his girlfriend said as she hugged me and led me to the car.

But just as we were about to enter and drive off, we heard a shout: "Hey! I thought you said you'd wait for me!"

It was Michelle. She locked the door and headed down the driveway with her overnight bag. It was a beautiful moment as we hugged. She refused to kiss me as we all hopped in. I was the last to do so, and I made somewhat of an eye contact with Willy. We gazed at each other for a bit until I hopped in and we drove off.

I was not sure what was going through his mind, and frankly speaking, I didn't care. In my book, I sided with his brother that this feud between us was not over. But for now, Michelle and I had kissed and made up; well, we didn't actually kiss, but here she was on her way to spend the night at my house, in my bed.

Talk about a priceless moment.

"Hey, guys, can you make a quick right here?" I requested to my brother's girlfriend from the back seat. "And then a left on Torrington, then up the hill?"

Sis complied and gave me a smile and wink through the rear-view mirror as she knew exactly where I wanted her to take us.

We soon arrived at a cul-de-sac where there was just a freshly cut meadow and a sole phone booth that glistened under the streetlight.

"Just give them their moment," I heard my brother's girl said as I exited and led Michelle with me.

"What is this?" she asked.

"The little things that are priceless," I replied as I led her to the phone booth.

She seemed confused.

"This is the phone booth I called you from every Sunday. And that is the church tower that would chime three o'clock for me to call you." I pointed in the distance. "I just wanted to show you, because I always created a visual of you in the room at the hotel, getting ready for bed, waiting for my call."

"Wow!" she exhaled heavily. "I always pictured you asking people the time because I knew you never wore a watch." She smiled. "I visualized where you were calling me from too. Somehow I thought it was downtown where we have numerous phone booths to choose from, especially by the shore strip."

Silence.

"So what was so special about this one?' she asked as she hugged my arm and rested her head on my shoulder.

Silence.

"Because… Well, because it was walking distance to here, so I didn't have to take the bus to downtown." I laughed, which was greeted by a playful thump on my arm as she just gazed at the phone booth.

She took some quarters from her pocketbook, entered the phone booth, and dialed her hotel number and playfully asked for herself and to be connected to her room. She listened as the front desk clerk told her they had all checked out and left. She then hung up with a smile and yet somewhat of a sad gaze into nowhere.

"Everything okay?" I questioned as I hugged her.

"Yes. Just some flashbacks. It wasn't the perfect trip, but I don't want to talk about it," she said as she hugged me. "Let's just go home."

I wanted to press her for more answers, but I left it at that.

"Okay, guys, let's go 'cuz I feel like I wanna pee again. Damn, is it this chilly fall weather? Why can't I hold my pee anymore?" my brother's girlfriend said to our amusement.

My brother and his crew, who exited the car and were chatting, put their cigarettes out and reentered. So did Michele and I.

They took us home, lingered for a bit, and then left to drop his friends off. Michelle was in my room, changing, and I was in the living room sofa, relaxed and watching TV.

Mace

"So you like it?" I heard a voice ask.

I looked at my bedroom entrance, and there was Michelle in pajama shorts and a black T-shirt with the words "Golden Belt Break Dance Champions" printed in gold on the front. She then turned around and used both her thumbs to point at my name printed big and bold on the back, also in gold.

"Wow! Awesome! Where did you get this?" I said as I sat up.

"I got it specially made for you back in London." She smiled. "Just thought it would look cool with your golden championship belt and your gold sneakers."

I went over and hugged her. And this time, she allowed me to kiss her.

"But because you were a bad boy earlier, I get to wear it first," she said as she took my hand and led me inside my room.

She then went to the gift bag and took out a bottle of cologne, a beer mug, and some other stuff and then presented me with them.

"Wow! Thank you." I blushed.

I sprayed some of the cologne on my wrist and then on her T-shirt—well, my T-shirt.

"Nice!" I sniffed.

We conversed for a bit as we patched things up until my brother and his girl returned gave the code knock on my door to confirm their presence and went straight to bed.

Minutes later, Michelle used a few of my nine pillows to form a barrier between both half of the bed and told me I could come join her when I was finished with my movie. And yes! I said nine pillows! So forget you if you have a problem with me sleeping with nine pillows!

"Turn the lights off, please," she then politely asked as she sighed. "I can't believe I'm doing this."

I assured her with a smile as I turned the lights off and was about to exit.

"Hey!" She halted me.

I stopped and turned the lights back on.

"I'm a very light sleeper, Street, so please don't give me a reason to use this." She sat up and then pointed a bottle of mace at me before again cuddling with it.

I smiled, turned the lights off, and exited. I barely watched the rest of the movie, as I had another beer and slowly dozed off. I was thankful to God that the woman of my dreams had forgiven me and was in my bed, curled up and sleeping. I eventually snuck into my room with the lights still off to change into my pajamas.

"Don't even try it!" I heard she whisper half asleep.

"Boo, stop, I'm just changing into my pajamas."

"So turn the lights on then so I can see what you are doing," she ordered as she rolled on her back and just watched me undress down to my boxers only.

I put my sleep top on and then crawled into bed beside her.

"I thought you were taking the couch," she whispered.

"I was gonna until I noticed these barriers," I said, looking at the line of pillows she had to separate my side from hers in the bed.

I leaned over, she met me halfway, and we kissed passionately for a while. I then tried to climb over to her half of the bed before she abruptly halted me.

"Street. Street!" She exhaled heavily and wearisomely. "Not again! I've had a very long flight and a very long day in more ways than one. Can we just get some sleep, please? Or I'll just get dressed and leave."

"Okay. Okay." I exhaled heavily, now that my mojo was back.

She noticed my boner, giggled, and just used a pillow to cover it. I complied by getting up to turn the lights off and then snuggled in my half of the bed and just lay there, dozing off, listening to her peaceful breathing, which soon turned to soft snoring.

She was on her side, face turned to me, sleeping. Here was my own "sleeping beauty" in all her glory. I smiled to myself—well, except for her clutching that bottle of mace as she slept.

I didn't even know when I fell asleep, but I was awakened by my brother knocking at my bedroom door.

"Yo, Street, you seen my beeper anywhere?" he asked as he opened my room door. "I gotta go meet up with my—" He then stopped as he noticed Michelle still fast asleep in my bed. He covered his mouth to hold back his surprise.

"No, bro, it probably fell out of your pocket in the car, again!" I yawned.

"Is that?" he started out of curiosity.

I put a finger on my lips to say, "Hush."

"So…so did you?" he asked as I pulled the covers halfway off her to identify that it was in fact, Michelle.

I pulled the covers even farther down and realized that we were still dressed as the way we fell asleep, so I gestured no.

My brother looked so disappointed. "Okay, that's it!" he said as he quietly stormed off.

I got up to go to the restroom, but he soon returned, met me at the door, blocked my exit from my room, and shoved a full bottle of pills in my hand. Yep, it was his blue pills.

"So I dunno what's wrong with you, bro, and with all due respect to Clair, that there lying in your bed is a once-in-a-lifetime opportunity! Look at her, bro. Look at that body. So just take the whole damn bottle!" he screamed in a whisper as he tried to lock me in my bedroom.

We had an animated moment until his girlfriend exited his bedroom.

"You found your beeper, babe? Did they confirm what time to meet up?" She yawned before noticing that Michelle was asleep in my bed.

"You li'l bugger." She playfully slapped me. "So did you two…?" she started to ask before my brother nudged me to hide his bottle of blue pills.

"No, they didn't!" He then angrily sighed.

"So I was asking if they kissed and made up for good, but you were answering like a totally different question. Can you just take your mind out of the bedroom for once?"

My brother gave her a gesture as if to say, "How can I when I'm in his bedroom?"

We just all chuckled and gazed at Michelle for a moment, who was still fast asleep.

"So do you believe her, Street? You believe that nothing happened between her and Willy and that she dumped her ex, all for you?"

To our surprise, Michelle answered half asleep. "I did." She yawned before she changed her snuggle position. "I told you I was a light sleeper, Street, so can you guys just give me a moment? I was in the middle of a really good dream. It's like I was down by the river, baptizing people, but instead of me leading them from land into the river to baptize them, I was constantly rescuing a line of drowning people, baptizing them, and then leading them to the shore."

We had a moment of contemplative silence.

I felt so contented in that moment that I ran over and jumped on the bed and tried to kiss her, but she stopped me.

"What?" I questioned her rejection.

She yawned and stretched both arms wide, with one showing her still clutching the can of mace.

My brother and his girl noticed and failed to withhold their laughter.

"New age 'chastity belt?'" His girl chuckled.

"Like it's even real! Prove it!" I dared as I playfully tickled her and tried to pry the can of mace from her hand.

"Street, stop!" She shoved me away, still half asleep.

G and his girl were cracking up as I persisted until Michelle, having enough, sat up and gave me a quick squirt from the mace in my face.

It burnt like hell as I screamed. I ran to the bathroom to flush my face with water. Surprisingly, instead of helping me, all three of them were cracking up.

"Really, Michelle!" I said as I eventually reentered my bedroom with a damped face towel, soothing my eyes.

My brother and his girlfriend, still laughing, hugged me and led me to the bed, where Michelle cuddled and nursed my eyes.

"I'm sorry, honey, but you told me to prove it! Give it another minute or two to wear off," she comforted as she dabbed my eyes with the damp towel. "It was just a quick squirt, not a full spray. I'm sorry, but you asked for it."

"So much for your sense of humor," I scoffed, feeling better.

"Don't blame me." She sighed with a half yawn as she continued to nurse me. "You told me to prove that this mace was real," she said as I heard her rest the can on the bedside table. "I complied. So what else do you want me to prove to you?"

The laughter stopped.

My brother and his girl excused themselves and went to check for his beeper in her car and found it.

I was feeling better. We all had breakfast, and after we ate, they both left for some group project on campus, confirmed by a message on his beeper.

Michelle also left to do some housework at her home and came back to spend a second night with me.

This night, however, was our worst moment ever spent together, and strangely enough, it was not because of anything she or I did.

The Broken Tooth

My brother and his girlfriend made oxtail with rice and beans for dinner.

It was Michelle's favorite, so she took a second serving, and while chewing on a bone as we chatted over dinner, she suddenly let out a scream, spat blood in her napkin, and rushed to the bathroom.

Moments later, she returned, clearly in pain, and told us she had broken one of her wisdom teeth. But she said she would be fine after my brother's girlfriend gave her some painkillers.

She went to lie down in my room. The three of us finished dinner and had a couple beers and smokes as we watched a movie. But we were constantly alerted by painful moans and crying from Michelle.

I went to check on her, and to my shock, her jaw was now swollen, and the face towel wrapped with ice she had on her mouth was now saturated with blood.

She was also close to passing out.

I screamed for my brother and his girlfriend.

"Please, please, take me to the hospital," she sobbed. "I can't bear this pain any longer."

We were all in panic mode. My brother was on his beeper, and his girlfriend was on her phone, trying to make contact with a dentist. But it was Sunday, so no one was responding. We all freaked out as she continued to cry uncontrollably from the pain. Then my brother suggested that we drive to the nearest dentist. She could barely even walk because of the pain as we got her to his girlfriend's car and took off.

The dental office was closed. We drove all over town to other dental offices, and they were all closed. No surprise because, even though this was around after four in the evening, it was Sunday! Michelle was lying in my lap in the back seat, exhaling soft moans as she drifted into a light sleep, only to scream out in pain again when it woke her up.

We drove around for hours. The many hospitals we stopped at turned into a cursing spat at the front desk, as they all turned us back, insisting that she will have to ride it out and wait until the morning to see a dentist. We drove around some more. No luck!

We finally got back home after midnight. She was in my lap in the back seat, sleeping but still moaning in her sleep from the pain. We woke her, and the crying started again as we took her to my room.

My brother and his girlfriend continued to console her some more with the promise that they would skip school and we would all take her to the nearest dentist first thing in the morning. They eventually retired to bed.

I was sitting up in bed with Michelle lying in my lap, still groaning and crying from the pain as she drifted in and out of sleep. I had never felt so helpless in my life, as I softly brushed the hair from her face and gazed into nowhere.

Time went by, and by now, it was almost 3:00 a.m. I was dozing off but was kept alert because of her sporadic crying and twists and turns from the immense pain to the point where tears were streaming from my eyes, too, because I felt so helpless.

The Test Game

I was worn out, and in my mindset as I comforted her without luck, I suddenly remembered Ephesians 6:13: "Having done all, stand."

That was one of our signature scriptures back in my church days, which simply meant that when you find yourself in a situation that you want to get out of but can't, just give it your best shot, and after you have done all and still with no positive results, just stand, and leave the rest to God.

We did all that night by driving all around and even out of town for over eight hours to every medical facility we could find but without luck, I thought to myself as she started crying again.

Against all odds, it then dawned on me that, in this case and in so many other cases where we find ourselves in a bad situation, when it comes to us having done all, we shouldn't just stand, but we should also pray! But I was still in malice mode with God, so I refused to.

Her crying got so loud that it woke G and his girlfriend, who came back to check on her. They sat and comforted her for a bit but then eventually went back to bed after I assured them that I would be staying up to monitor her all night.

I finally decided to put my malice with God aside. I prayed for His forgiveness, and yep, I then played my silly test game again: "So, devil, once again *you* have proven how evil you are, that Michelle couldn't even enjoy something as simple as having Sunday dinner. So, God, can you prove yourself once again for a change by letting the pain go away?"

Her crying from the pain intensified. I was left with no other option. As Ephesians 6:13 said to stand or, in this case, pray.

"Hey," I started, as I was a radical who never believed in praying to God with all those mushy, self-righteous words but instead just talked to Him, our Heavenly Father, as you would talk to your earthly parent or guardian. So I talked to Him, and I also prayed in tongues, for her pain to go away until we could get her to a dentist in the morning.

This went on for a couple minutes. Nothing happened, and her crying continued. I gently got up and went to use the restroom. I washed my hands and stood there staring at the mirror with a look of disappointment at a wasted prayer—or so I thought.

I slowly composed myself after a few minutes and went back to my room. To my surprise, Michelle was lying in an opposite position, all covered and snuggled with pillows. I walked over, changed for bed, and gave her a hug as I lay behind her. She was breathing heavily at intervals, but no more tears were streaming down her cheeks.

We lay there for several minutes, and I started to doze off until she spoke.

"Street."

I remained silent as I knew she was going to again beg me to take her to the hospital.

"Babe," she continued for me to respond.

I was at a loss for words at what to tell her as most dental offices didn't open until 9:00 a.m., so she still had several hours to ride out before she could get treatment.

"Street!" she groaned softly, as it was clear she had no energy left in her.

I exhaled heavily and finally replied. "Yes, babe?"

No reply.

"Babe," I whispered as I rose up and tucked her in.

She uttered something, as she dozed off, but I didn't hear her clearly.

"Say that again, babe," I whispered as I kissed her cheek.

She exhaled heavily a few times again and then spoke. "The pain is gone."

"What?" I said in shock.

"The pain is gone." She sighed. "I don't know what happened, but strangely, it doesn't hurt anymore."

I sat there in shock. Was this the power of prayer or…? And I couldn't find an alternative to finish that question.

"You didn't eat the rest of my oxtail, did you?" she surprisingly asked.

"No," I said as I laughed and cried at the same time.

"Good, 'cuz I want it for breakfast."

I snuggled with her and kissed the back of her neck.

"Let's get some sleep, babe. I feel like I just ran a marathon," she said as she used her elbow to raise her upper body, reached for the can of mace on the bedside table to my amusement, turned around, kissed me, cuddled in my arms, and in no time, started snoring.

Wow.

I lay in bed with a big smile as tears streamed down my face. God had once again proven Himself to me. *Now we're on a roll*, I thought to myself. *Jesus walks with me!*

But was He trying to keep up with my pace, or was I following in His footsteps as terrible events that unfolded after that night once again tested my faith?

CHAPTER 12

CHURCH BOY HATE

Damn These Bus Rides

Monday finally came. My brother's girlfriend skipped her first class and took Michelle, who was feeling much better, to the dentist. Michelle also invited us to her church's annual weekend retreat for teens starting on Friday, to which we all gave her a lame promise to attend. I did however promise her that I will attend night service with her on Wednesday, where she and her youth fellowship team would be making final preparations.

I met up with Willy at the bus stop and frankly just told him everything about me and Michele and what she told me about their uneasy encounters as we boarded and settled.

"Hey, I've gangbanged many girls in my life, but I'm no rapist, bro," he explained as we rode the bus together. "Michelle is every guy's dream girl, but I guess she was just not into me. You are one lucky bastard!"

"Just leave her alone, man. You in college and you got a baby on the way, so focus!" I sighed, for closure.

"But I waited all these years for her." He exhaled. "I was gonna take her by any means necessary."

"Forget her, bro. She's mine," I warned, "'cause if you do try to take her by any means necessary, we will both be on the seven o'clock news." I smiled seriously.

Silence.

"Let's just, for you, label her as the one that got away." I sighed. "The Gospel of Matthew said that on one occasion, Jesus, while hungry and walking with his disciples, came across a fig tree with no fruit, no ripe fruit. He cursed it and kept on moving. She might be ripe now for your picking, but there is no… There is no picking that will happen for you, or this will end very, very bad between us. And I won't watch the news!"

He gave me a confused stare.

"That was the coolest threat I ever got." He chuckled.

"That wasn't a threat, bro. That was a promise." I sighed in somber rage as we were about to arrive at our terminal. "Just leave her alone."

He halted me with a grin, took out a dollar coin, flipped it in the air, and covered it on the back of his hand with the other hand as it landed.

"Okay, dude. So you really wanna go there with me? Deal! We flipped a coin for years all the time to see who would go *first* when we used to compete in break dance competitions." He smirked. "So let's stick to the rules. You say she's still a virgin, so call it! Who's gonna have her first?" He grinned.

"What?" I gasped, trying to make sense of his proposal.

"Call it! Head. Yep, she will surely be giving me that before I take her for the first time. Hopefully, she will just get weary and give in! One night with her, home alone with me at my place, that's it! And tail, I will leave her alone, and she's all yours. Winner takes all!" He exhaled.

We tried to stare each other down with his sick proposal, but nobody flinched.

Frustrated silence.

"Deal! Winner takes all," I finally spoke. "So if I call it and lose, I will let you have your wish with Michelle," I lied. "But if I win, you leave Michelle alone. Plus, I get one night with Jess by my place, and the next morning, I don't care if you smack the crap out of her. I will let her swear to not tell," I dared with assurance that she still hadn't told him that she spent a night at my place before.

"You disrespecting my baby mama?" he asked, a bit apprehensive.

"You disrespecting Michelle, my girl, because she is the one that got away." I stared him down.

We had a stand-off until he finally let out a surrendering chuckle.

"Fine!" he said as he put the coin back in his pocket. "You win again, Street!"

"No. I didn't. I lost at trying to win you over as a friend," I said.

"No, I lost trying to wait for and finally win Michele over as my girl." He sighed.

There was a long moment of silence. He couldn't resist the temptation, so he took the coin back out of his pocket.

"Let's just do this for fun." He grinned. "Heads, I would have won. Tail, you would have won."

He then flipped it and paused for a moment as he stared at me. Then he slowly removed his hand.

It was tails.

He got so mad he tossed the coin through the window.

"So what time should I come get Jess later?" I smiled with a tease as we horse played for a bit.

"Don't even try it!" he said as we arrived at the terminal and got up to disembark.

"At least you got Jess all to yourself, no competition." I smiled sadly, looking back at him, as I knew of the physical abuse she was going through. He didn't reply but just held a blank gaze as we slowly made our exit through the crowded isle.

There was a tight rush to get off the bus from other passengers trying to catch a connecting bus. This dude forced his way between Willy and me. It was the norm for passengers to try to rush before you, so I didn't make a big deal of it, and instead just gave him a serious glance.

He looked like a junkie crackhead with his blond-dyed Mohawk hairstyle. I reached back to pry him away as I was stepping off the bus because I felt his hands on my ass. I was about to confront him when we finally got off, but Willy held me back. The guy then apologized and quickly disappeared into the crowded terminal.

"Pervert!" I said to Willy, as we crossed the street to meet up with our other schoolmates.

Willy was cracking up.

"C'mon, Street, I saw how close he was bumping into your backside, but I figured he was just some freaking gay dude messing with you." He continued chuckling.

A few of our classmates were getting coffee and other breakfast snacks from our regular street vendor at his booth, so a few of us just waited for them as we chatted. One of my classmates was ordering extra stuff and asked me to loan him five bucks.

"Really, dude?" I laughed as I reached for my wallet in my back pocket. "That's gonna be ten dollars you owe me now, and I want interest." I laughed. But then my laughter suddenly stopped.

"Where's my wallet?" I frantically searched.

I held a gaze at Willy as I tried to process how it went missing.

"Shit!" I then snapped. "That damn dude behind me on the bus was no pervert. He picked my wallet!"

"Wait here!" Willy said to the others as he hurriedly followed behind me in pursuit of the thief. But after a few moments of frantically scanning the crowded terminal, we knew he was long gone.

Several minutes later, as we neared school, Willy was still chuckling at the incident. "I'm sorry, Street. The whole thing looked so comical with you and that guy that I never imagined that he was picking your pocket. I'm sorry, bro. I got you for lunch later. Heck, I got you for the rest of the week."

"That was one month's allowance that damn thief took from me," I said.

Even though I told them that my brother would replenish my funds, my other schoolmates also vouched to cover lunch, bus fare, etc.

The rest of the day went by quietly. I told my brother what happened, and the next morning, as I rode the bus with Willy to the terminal, we were both in fight mode and on high alert as we scanned for the pick pocket to beat the crap out of him.

Nothing.

The next day, while still looking through the crowd, I noticed about twenty or so familiar faces sitting on bicycles scattered in various parts of the terminal as we got off the bus. It was my brother and his crew. They were all dressed for classes but wanted to start the morning with a beat-down.

"See him?" my brother, also in fight mode, asked as he rode up to us.

"No." I sighed as I scanned the crowd.

Yep, my brother and his crew were also there to give this pickpocket the beat-down of his life also. This thief thought he was lucky to have stolen my wallet, but instead, he was lucky to have not ridden the bus that day.

It was at that moment that I learned that your "lucky day" could actually stem from missing the bus or calling out from school or work or cancelling an errand or taking a different route to your destination or even just being early or late instead of right on time. Sometimes, the simplest of things you decide not to do or what just happens to your frustration in a typical day can actually make that day the luckiest day of your life!

"These damn pickpockets that ride the buses are like sewer rats that take the same bus or route every day, looking for an unsuspecting victim. We will catch him. Don't be late for class, and I don't wanna be either. See you later, bro," he dabbed, as he signaled to his other friends, and they all met up and rode off.

Another quiet day went by until Wednesday when I was supposed to meet up with Michelle later that night to accompany her to church. I hadn't seen her since Monday morning, but she did leave a written reminder in my mailbox Tuesday night.

My brother and his crew again met us at the bus terminal that morning, and again there was no sign of the pickpocket. The classmate that was, however, robbed by those street thugs told us that she saw someone that matched the description on her bus just now and that he headed off in the direction that we walked to school.

That put us on high alert, and G and his boys again took off as we walked to school. We got to that familiar corner where those thugs that robbed my classmate hung out, and lo and behold, there was that thief that stole my wallet, hanging out with the thugs.

Fight

There were four of them in total versus about fifteen of us.

While his three other thug friends did, he clearly didn't recognize me as I dropped my backpack and walked over to him in fight mode.

"Where's my wallet?" I abruptly asked.

"What? Who the hell are you, punk?" he asked as he spat and took a puff from his cigarette.

"You picked my pocket on the bus on Monday morning at the terminal!"

He seemed to be rewinding his memory.

"Oh, shoot. Yeah, yeah, that was you. Damn, you were pretty loaded for a schoolboy." He grinned with an uncaring stare, referring to the amount of cash I had in my wallet.

"I need my money back." I stared him down.

"What you say, fool?" he scoffed before he walked off and gave an order to his other thug friends. "Take this fool out!" Nobody budged. "I said take this punk-ass fool out!" he again ordered before I met him with a powerful sucker punch that sent him flying to the ground as his lit cigarette also flew from his mouth.

I jumped on top of him and started raining blows. His three thugs jumped me. My other classmates, except for the girl, jumped in, and yep, another street brawl was on. In no time, all four thugs, who were outnumbered, were on the ground, trying to fend off kicks and punches. They were finally rescued by a screeching car that pulled up next to us.

It was an unmarked civilian car; however, four uniformed soldiers exited. Three drew their service pistols and aimed it all of us, ordering us to stop. The fourth was unarmed. As I tried to quickly recompose myself out of fight mode, I realized that the fourth unarmed soldier was Assad.

The three armed soldiers held us at gunpoint and separated us. One was on his radio or phone or whatever, calling for backup.

"Yo, Street!" Assad gasped as he walked over. "What the heck is this?"

"You know him?" one of the soldiers asked.

"Yes! This is the Street I have been telling you guys about!" he replied as we greeted.

He again asked me what was going on, and I explained. Within minutes, two soldier jeeps and a cop car that we normally saw patrolling the area raced up to where we were located. At least eight heavily armed soldiers exited from their jump out jeep, and four heavily armed police officers exited from their vehicle.

It was routine for us in Jamaica to have both police and soldiers patrol jointly, especially in volatile communities, like where my school was located. Soldiers, however, didn't have the power to arrest anyone, so they just served as the "iron fist" to restore order or calm, and the cops in turn would then make the relevant arrests.

Within minutes, a crowd of onlookers had converged. Assad was told to step aside, and we were all separated and put in handcuffs while we were being thoroughly searched and interrogated.

"10/32! 10/32!" one of the officers, frisking the pickpocket's waistband, then shouted as he held his automatic weapon up to his face.

I later learned that was the police code for an illegal firearm being carried by someone. Yes, the pickpocket was armed and dangerous. My body jolted in shock that he could have shot and killed me during our earlier confrontation had I not left him semiconscious with that surprise sucker punch.

Other cop cars arrived, and by now all my classmates, even Willy, were clearly shaken and scared at how in one minute we were all just walking to school as we have done each morning but now were facing this!

Over an hour passed, and we were all now officially late for class, but nobody cared about class; we just didn't want to be arrested. Thankfully, even though I was the one who started the brawl by throwing the first punch, I clearly remembered the officer that interviewed me, explaining as he removed my handcuffs that the pickpocket actually started it not by picking my pocket but by issuing an order to take me out (give me a beat-down) and as such I just defended myself.

All four thugs were arrested for illegal possession of a firearm, and the rest of us were released with a warning.

Phew!

Assad and I talked some more as the rest of the combined patrol vehicles pulled off. Still shaken, everything we spoke about was going through one ear and coming through the other. But I did hear him say that, that was his new car he finally bought and it was having some issue with an upgraded engine. I just brushed him off nicely as I tried to recompose myself and told him to come see me on Friday at school for us to take a look at it, as that was the day we could bring in our personal vehicles to work on for free as part of our training.

He was ecstatic at the no labor cost and quickly agreed. And while it was great to see him after all these weeks, the mood was dampened by the earlier events.

Once we got to school, we were all summoned to the principal's office. Two police officers were also there.

Our first two classes were cancelled for the day, and we were all given a lecture on good behavior and integrity, plus a letter of warning leading to suspension and even expulsion should our alliance of "one for all, all for one" continue.

Yes, that damn snitch from our class who was bent on getting me kicked out also informed the principal of our so-called gang. I still couldn't explain her dislike for me, even though we never even spoke. And I didn't care, because I couldn't stand her guts either. She started it!

Most of my schoolmates on the spot then threw in the towel and said that it was over and they wouldn't be hanging out with our group anymore because of serious consequences from their strict parents or guardians. Also, I guessed that the earlier incident with the fight, cops, soldiers, and us all being held at gunpoint and put in handcuffs was the breaking point, although, sadly, that had become *a day in the life* for me. Ironically, only Willy and I, plus two or three others, gave each other a wink of alliance.

A Familiar Face with an Unfamiliar Story

We all went through the rest of the day with an uneasy calm, as we officially broke our alliance with some students, and secretly kept it with others.

I went home, showered, had some me time, and met up with Michelle at the bus stop later that night.

Her tooth was all fixed and fine again as she updated me, but I dared not update her on how my week thus far has been. She hated all this fighting, so I didn't want her to get mad at me…again.

We boarded the bus to church, which had half empty seats as usual for that time of night, but as she went to sit at the back, as she said she preferred, I stopped with my back turned to her to speak with a familiar face; the bus driver.

Us Street Boys used to wait on his particular bus all the time based on where we were headed, because he always had the music going for our listening pleasure, unlike other bus drivers that didn't even have the radio on. At times we would even dance in the bus isle, much to the amusement of most of the passengers. But then we just never saw him again for months.

He then explained that he was away overseas on military duty, but since he returned just over a week ago, the company assigned him to our "tricky" new route which they gave him two days to learn, and which was giving him hell. He didn't even hesitate to admit that on many occasions, he lost his way: much to the annoyance of some passengers.

We had a brief animated chat, as I also updated him on the break-up of the Street Boys before we were interrupted by a passenger that stormed up to him, cursing that she rang the bell twice yet he still passed her stop.

He apologized, pulled over, and let her off.

We laughed it off chatted a bit more, and then I went to meet up with Michelle, who was sitting in the back seat next to the window, and as much as there were empty seats everywhere, there was this guy in a hoodie sitting too close for comfort next to her. At first, I grinned, as I brushed it off as just another dude trying to hit on my girl, but then I noticed the way she was looking at me as I approached.

My smiling face quickly transformed into an alert stare as we made eye contact.

As I got closer to the back seat, I followed her eyes as she looked down to her waist, and to my shock, I realized that the guy with his head down had a knife pointed in her hip.

Yes, she was being robbed!

I carefully sat next to the dude.

"Yo, can we have some privacy? I'm trying to have a conversation with my girl here," he then said with his back turned to me, his face facing her.

"Oh, my bad!" I played along with my options running at a million miles an hour as I contemplated my next move. She tried to turn and look at me, but he nudged her, and she looked back down at her lap.

It seemed like an eternity, but he then slowly slid his right hand down to her knee with the blade pointing at her chest. Then he used his left hand to retrieve her handbag resting on the seat between her and the window, opened it, and slowly started searching for anything of value.

Most people would have maintained their gaze at what valuables he pulled from the handbag with his left hand, but instead, my eyes were locked on his right hand. And no, not because it held the knife but because of a familiar tattoo I saw before on the back of his wrist—it was a skull and crossbone symbol.

And then it hit me like a brick in the face that not only had I seen this tattoo before, but I had also encountered this thug before. Yes, it was the same thief on the bus that tried to rob me several weeks back.

I had to think fast as I had an adrenaline rush.

"I'm going to count to three," I then whispered to him.

His body jolted as if he heard a ghost whisper a familiar line. He slowly turned around and looked at me.

"What you say, fool?" he asked as he turned to me.

229

"Don't let me count to three." I sighed heavily, as this fight in front of Michelle could now go any way because her presence would not let me go all out in full force and that could mean big trouble for me.

"One…" I then started counting as I grabbed his right wrist and pulled it away from Michelle.

He put up a scared resistance but didn't try to flinch.

"Two…" I gazed him down out of frustration and now fully in fight mode, not caring what Michelle was about to witness again or not.

"Street…" was the last thing I heard a now scared Michelle gasp from the encounter.

He didn't see it coming, but I gave him a swift powerful elbow to the throat that left him dry coughing and gasping for air, which made it easy for me to pry the knife from his hand.

I then dragged him to the isle and started raining blows to his face. And would you believe it? Michelle was the one who actually jumped me and hauled me off him, crying and begging me to stop. Women!

"Hey, driver! Stop the bus and call the cops!" I then shouted.

'Hey, what's going on back there?" the driver, gazing through his rearview mirror, questioned as he pulled over, as other curious passengers turned around and held their inquiring stare on us.

"What's going on back there?" the driver again asked as he made his way to the back of the bus.

"Please, please!" the thief begged in between dry coughs as he slouched in the isle. "I can't go back to jail. You don't know what they do especially to homeless men in jail. Not again!" he pleaded.

"Street, what the hell is going on?" the driver asked out of confusion.

"He tried to rob her," I abruptly answered.

All this time, Michelle, now back in her seat, was still shaken and at a loss for words.

"You tried to rob me a few weeks ago, remember? Now you trying to rob my girl when you could have simply asked her for some money!" I snapped as I draped him by his collar up to a kneeling position.

There was brief silence as his coughing calmed.

"I'm sorry. I'm sorry, ma'am," he said with a petrified glance at her. "You don't know my story. I'm a broken man, so this is what I have to do to survive."

"By robbing passengers on a bus when you don't know their story either?" I barked as I was about to punch him, but the driver caught my hand and restrained it.

The thief started crying. "I never chose to rob anyone. I lost everything ever since my woman of fifteen years kicked me out of my own house for another man she was cheating on me with and lied to my boss at work to get me fired. I have no family. I have no friends. I have nothing. So I turned to drugs to take my life when I realized I was hopeless and homeless," he said with an empty, lost stare into nowhere as he wiped his tears and runny nose. "People looked down on you as they did with me when I rode the bus as my shelter. I was looked down with scorn as I would sit beside a passenger and beg a few dollars for food. Some would even get up with scorn and move to another seat. So out of desperation, I started robbing people on the bus at knife point and quickly realized how these same people now looked up to me with fear and gave me everything I demanded."

"We all have a story, and that tattoo on your hand tells yours. You're a thief, and you're going to jail," I scoffed.

He started sobbing again, as the siren and flickering lights of two cop cars approached and pulled up behind the bus. I glanced at Michelle, trying not to take my gaze off him, and I saw her reach in her pocketbook, counted out some cash, and to my shock, gave it to him along with a flyer.

What the what!

"What are you doing?" I obviously questioned.

"Let he who is without sin cast the first stone." She exhaled heavily as I knew the whole incident that was still unfolding left her a bit traumatic.

The driver heard the banging on the bus door from the officers.

"This right here is too much for me, man, because you don't know the half of what I've seen while I was deployed or the stories I've heard," he said, reflecting. "I gotta go let these officers in, so what do you wanna do—prison or prayers?" he asked with a look at Michelle, whom he also knew from back in the days, and her purpose.

I didn't give him an answer fast enough, as one officer now came to the window with gun drawn, so the driver left and let them in.

"The next time I see you, it will be *three!*" I warned the thief, sensing that Michelle was now in a different mindset from mine.

"What's going on here?" one of the officers asked with hand poised on his holster as he walked down the bus isle and approached us.

"Please!" The thief started crying again.

Michelle let out a heavy exhalation.

"This guy lost his way and was trying to—" I started, but she interrupted.

"Was trying to beg me some money, but my boyfriend here thought he was trying to rob me," she finished.

Okay, so I was not sure whether I was mad at her for not saying he was in fact trying to rob her or if I was now blown away by her officially labeling me as her boyfriend! So I just sat there and listened to her and the cops go back and forth for a moment until they left.

"Thank you," the thief said, looking at her, not me, as he stood up.

I took his knife and, as was the case in the first incident, broke it again. But this time, I then handed it to him.

"The next time I see your face will be *three!*" I again warned.

"Buy yourself a nice hot meal, and oh, read that flyer. It could change your life," Michelle said to him with a sad, disappointed smile.

He exited the bus still shaken and looking somewhat confused at what just unfolded. He didn't know we were watching him, but as the bus was about to drive off, we watched as he counted the cash she gave him and stuck it in his pocket, read the flyer, crumpled it, and tossed it away before walking off.

"What was that?" I asked. "One minute, this thief held you up at knife point, and the next minute, you're voluntarily handing him cash?"

"I know, and I don't know what I was thinking." She sighed as she hugged my arm and rested her head on my shoulder. "Sometimes it's okay to do a good deed for someone without thinking twice, even if that someone is a person you didn't want to be in the company with."

We rode in silence for a bit.

"I invited him to our Youth Fellowship Crusade at church this weekend."

"You saw what he did with the flyer," I scoffed as we continued our journey in more silence until she rang the bus bell.

"The Gospel of Matthew warned us not to, out of pity, throw our jewelry to pigs in the mud because they don't know its value so won't appreciate our sacrifice," I warned her as we said good night to the driver and exited.

"You know your Bible well. I am impressed," she said with a sad smile. "Just because someone is in the mud doesn't make them a pig. You are a backslidden, searching soul in the mud, too, Street, yet here I am, 'throwing' myself at you. Does this make you my pig?"

Silence.

"This is your church?" I asked as I nudged her for that corny remark.

"Yes, what's up with that look on your face?"

There was brief silence as we crossed the street and entered the parking lot.

"This can't be real." I chuckled to myself. "I've been here before. This is the church I was telling you I spontaneously stopped at after the incident with that same guy on the bus, remember?"

"Are you serious? Oh my god, what are the odds?" she said excitedly. "But yeah, this is the church my father pastors at, and I have been a member since childhood."

We both entered from the back, and as she chatted briefly with some people hanging out on the corridors, a guy called her over. He was one of four dressed in the same jersey top, and although this was church, he didn't seem pleased at seeing her with another man.

They had a brief poorly disguised animated conversation while glancing at me at intervals before she finally walked back over to me.

"What was that?" I asked, noticing that she was a bit upset as she led me into the church.

"That was him, my ex. He still won't accept the fact that it's over, but I don't want to talk about it, because I'm done." She sighed. "He's a sore cocky loser, so he won't take this lightly, especially with you now in the picture."

"Should I rally my boys?"

"No, Street." She nudged me. "This is church, where there is no fighting or bloodshed!"

She wanted to sit further up front, but I led her to the same back bench I sat on that night I visited. It didn't take her long as she settled for her to notice a graffiti engraved on the back rest of the bench in front of us which had the names Street and Michelle with a heart between them.

She stared at me with a smirk for the graffiti.

"Proof of my love for you, or maybe I was just bored," I whispered as she nudged me to shush as we stood to sing a hymn.

Her dad, the pastor, then gave a breakdown of the itinerary for the youth fellowship crusade starting on Friday, and he asked that committee members to meet with him to discuss further in an adjoining room while another presenter took the stage.

"I'll be back," she said. She was on the committee. Then she leaned over to give me a warm kiss and then stood and left.

My gaze followed her but was interrupted by those four guys sitting on the opposite side across from us, one of whom was the one she went to speak to earlier.

He stood and walked over to where she was sitting beside me. It was only then that I noticed that they all had on the same hoodie with the name "Sardonyx" printed big and bold on the back. I guessed that was the name of their group or crew or whatever. Just when I thought I had heard and seen it all, here was a church—yes, a church—with its own set of jocks and their fraternity.

Wow!

"Hey, man, bro," he scoffed. "I don't know what you and Michelle have going on, but I just saw that kiss." He exhaled. "Now I can't stop your sorry-ass rotten soul from coming here to church to try to get *saved*." He chuckled. "But that's my girl. I can save you a whole lot of trouble. Stay the hell away from her, or very, very, very bad things will happen to you. Oh, and she ain't no trophy girl. I hit it first!" He ended with an evil grin.

I kinda laughed to myself at his threat because here I was at church supposedly among saved and holy peacemakers, but I was being threatened? So I was like, really!

Sigh.

"Are you wearing women's perfume?" I finally asked without care for his threat, as I had been down this road a million times, but he was leaning over close to me and whispering and did reek of a girly perfume, and I also noticed he wore a dangling feather earring in his right ear.

Yes, past street brawls and retaliations made me a profiler from thugs we had fights with in the past to avoid being surprised and jumped (get a surprised attack) in the future. As Street Boys, we had another very simple rule—pay attention to detail to any person threatening you or fighting you: their tattoos, their walk, jewelry, hairstyle, even their scent.

So don't call me silly, but even though I was at church, this punk just threatened me, so I immediately started to profile him. He waved a warning finger at me, slowly got up with a hateful smirk, and left without saying another word.

I was beside myself.

What is it about life sometimes that you just can't seem to escape trouble? You can't just dance without trouble. You can't make a cordial visit to a girl's house without trouble. You can't be chilling at home without trouble. You can't just go to school without trouble. You can't just ride the bus without trouble. And damn. now you can't even just attend church without trouble?

I waited for her but didn't say anything about me and her ex's encounter or even questioned what he meant by saying, "I hit it first."

Scare tactics, maybe, as she did tell me she was a virgin. She was too innocent and excited about the crusade for me to ruin her mood, as she even said she signed me up for the mini soccer tournament the upcoming Saturday.

Memories

If only pictures, the fond ones, when you stare at them long enough, could then become a time warp machine, which takes you back to the moment that photo was taken and make you relive it all over again. Agree?

So the night ended quietly, and so went the next couple days also until Assad turned up at my school as expected that Friday evening for us to work on his new turbo-charged car.

After my teacher and another geek engineer looked at it, they determined that his car could not "fly" as he wanted the speed to get up to because he was missing integral components to complete the turbo charged mechanism. They made him a list of parts he needed to get, and he said based on his income and allowance, he would be back in a couple weeks with everything.

"So I guess we gonna make this turbocharged baby fly eventually," I said as we both hopped into his car. "Just don't push it to the limit and kill yourself or get anyone else killed," I warned with laughter as we dabbed and drove off.

He gave me a ride home after stopping at the deli for beers and smoke. After checking in on his house, he came over, and we had a few beers and caught up on happenings. He told me that, according to his cop friend, the punks that hung out at the open lot near to our school would all receive between five and seven years minimum for gun possession. I guessed I wouldn't ever have to worry about seeing their sorry asses again, as I would have long graduated from that college by then, making it one less future street fright to worry about.

We concurred that Stoke had not been in contact, and Bob hadn't returned any calls left on his school's messaging system.

To break the solemn vibe, I put some break dance music on, as we both listened and bobbed in the chair as we normally would to get charged up mentally before practice or a dance-off.

"Guess it's just me and you against the world now, Street." He rocked to the beat, as it got intense as he rapped along.

"I just exhaled with a smile," I said as I bobbed. "Remember that night? We killed it!" I pointed to the picture my eye caught, which was the night we won the golden break dance championship belt, one of many pictures of the Street Boys in action our promoter friend would give us from time to time.

Assad cracked up laughing and playfully shoved me aside as he remembered that night well because his pants crotch had ripped, which he did a great job disguising after trying this crazy new windmill move.

We looked around and pointed at some other pictures I had of us around the living room, all this time laughing and happy in loving recollection of the story each picture told. We pointed and laughed hysterically at times at some other pictures, each time narrating and reliving the moment, until the song ended.

Funny enough, that was the last song on my tape, so there was a brief silence as I lit a cigarette and chugged on my beer a bit, as I was in no hurry to get up, open the tape deck, flip the tape around, and hit Play.

I guessed it was because "play time," as those pictures reminded us, was over for us Street Boys.

Have there been circumstances in your life where you didn't or couldn't hit the Play button?

It's funny how, however long ago the photo was taken, one look at a picture of yourself or in the company of others, and you can recall the exact occasion and, at times, still get emotional in reminiscence.

Our laughter and hysteria soon quitened, as the mood changed to a bittersweet moment of recollection and hit us at how fast things, and life had changed, propelling us Street Boys to go our separate ways and grow up in the fast lane, to us now just becoming a distant memory.

There was a moment of somber silence.

I'd heard stories of the *"forever young"* wish from parents who didn't want their kids to grow up because they wanted to forever cherish those childhood moments or of best friends who hugged and bawled their eyes out at their school's graduation ceremony when they accepted the fact that they might never see each other again, as before they knew it, all those wonderful years spent, lived, and loved together would in time evaporate to just being a distant memory.

That moment made me realize that I was a loner. The Street Boys were no more, school friends never invited me over and were always too busy to accept my invitation, my brother and his girl came whenever, Michelle came over sometimes. Mom was in a foreign country. Dad was dead.

"Choose three!" I simply said to Assad.

"What?" he asked, confused.

As the leader of the Street Boys, I kept the championship belts and whatever other trophies, pictures, etc. there was of us. There were twelve pictures of us all over the living room.

"Choose your best three photos of us Street Boys," I pointed out, "except that one, the night we won the golden championship belt. It's my favorite!" I smiled. "Whichever other three you choose is yours. Just make sure you pin or hang them up—in memory of the good ole days."

"Really?" he asked surprisingly, as I was overly protective of those photos, which I always joked would one day be hung up in the Break Dance Hall of Fame! Well, that was if one was ever to be established.

He placed his beer down, rubbed his palms together, and excitedly stood to select.

"Okay, okay," he said to my amusement, as it was obvious it was hard for him to select. "Damn, this is great of you, Street. Now people on base don't just have to be convinced by my stories. I will have pictures to prove it!"

He looked at them all close up, and I could see his mood going on a rollercoaster ride, reliving the moments each picture told all over again.

"Okay, so you said not that one?" he questioned at the one that was off limits.

I gave him a "Don't even think about it" nod.

"Okay, okay. Damn, this is hard!" he screamed with a happy laugh before finally selecting three. He sat beside me and just gazed at them with the biggest grin I have ever seen on his face. "I love you, Street. You are the brother I never had."

"And I don't care if you are a soldier now. I'll still kick your ass in a minute," I said, and we both laughed. "You and I always had the most disagreements in the Street Boys, but your resilience made me stronger. I salute you, soldier!" I saluted him.

He looked away with a grin, had a chug from his beer, and spoke: "You're supposed to stand up to salute." He then laughed.

I gave him a shoulder-to-shoulder tackle as we both laughed. Then I put my beer down, stood, he stood, and then I spoke again.

"I salute you soldier, my friend, my brother!" I saluted.

There was brief silence, ruined only by a heavy sigh from us both as his eyes got glossy.

"I'll try to see if I can reach Bob or Stoke, but boy, are they gonna be mad when I tell them you gave me three of our best break dance moments pics from your archive." He laughed as he wiped his eyes.

I looked around the room and counted the remaining pictures of us.

"I still got nine left," I sighed with a smile. "If you make contact, tell them to holla at me so I can send them their best three also; just not that one," I laughed.

We bear hugged and he left, as he had combat training back on base in a couple hours.

I gazed at the pictures while finishing my beer, locked up and went to bed where I was greeted by yet another priceless picture by my bedside table ; this time, of Michelle.

I gazed long and hard at it, kissed it, turned the lights off and went to bed.

Youth Fellowship Crusade

It was opening night of the Youth Fellowship Retreat. Assad said he would give us a ride to church, so as I glanced up at the clock at the wall, I didn't want to be late so went to take a shower.

As usual, that moment was my time of reflection; as steam filled the bath, I just rested my arms up on the wall, rested my head between them, closed my eyes, and just let the shower rain down on me.

I wasn't happy with my life and recent events. So I was in contemplative mode. Was this night one of the Youth Fellowship Crusade my turning point to return to a life of living for Christ and being a church boy all over again? I was tired of fighting. I was tired of having an attitude with my God. I was just tired, and there and then decided that I was going to go to this crusade and have a blast, let go, let all, and just let God's will be done for my resurgence.

I whispered that prayer and then said, "Amen!"

To my shock, I heard another voice whisper, "Amen."

I popped my eyes open, turned around, and to my surprise, it was Michelle, who snuck into the bathroom, popped her head in the shower, and was watching me for who knew how long, as her hair and face were getting wet from the shower sprays.

"Didn't mean to sneak up on you, but Assad was outside, so I thought I'd be a bit mischievous," she said as she stroked my face and kissed me.

"How much did you see?" I asked, looking down at my naked body covered in a spray of steamy water.

"I didn't get a chance to look...down." She giggled. "Because the minute I pulled the shower curtains, I saw you praying and froze and prayed with you." Her mood suddenly changed. "I don't remember saying 'Thank you' for that night you prayed for me and my broken tooth." She sighed. "Yes, I heard you praying in tongues and everything. All this time, I was a missionary praying for you, yet that night when I was down and out, against all odds, I heard you praying for me. And then the pain was gone!" she ended as a tear rolled from her eye.

"It's gonna cost you a buck fifty as my prayers don't come cheap," I said, trying to make light of the matter, as I didn't want to be categorized as a church boy all over again. I was just trying to do what the Lord told me to do when caught up in bad situations: "Having done all, don't just stand—pray!"

I splashed some water on her, and she did the same at me. We had a mini make out and water fight, as she laughed and cried for a brief moment.

But after a final kiss, she dropped a bombshell question.

CHAPTER 13

BLOOD ON THE CHURCH GROUND

"What's going on with you and my ex?"

I turned the shower off with a now upset look on my face as I reached for the towel and started to dry myself.

"I heard you two had a bit of a run-in." She sighed as she leaned into my towel to dry her face. "Street! Street!" she snapped as she pulled my chin up so I could make eye contact. "Vick is the most popular guy at church. His father is in charge of our accounts department. Vick and his Sardonyx crew are the desire of every teen to be a part of. Everybody loves him and is either his friend or wants to be his friend. I broke up with him because he has gotten so cocky. He thinks he's a god that he wanted me to bow to. I said no and walked away. Don't get into any confrontations with him. You won't win, so just walk away because I know you have no intentions of being his friend."

Silence.

"I just wanted to come back to church." I sighed.

"I know. I sensed your heart," she said as she hugged me, a bit emotional.

I just stood there and honestly didn't even hug her back because of the insult for my "welcome back party."

"You told me you settle your scores by fighting. Promise me there will be no blood on the church ground," she whispered as she buried her face in my neck.

I stayed silent as I remembered his threat.

"Promise me!" she said as she hugged and jolted my body.

More silence.

Then I finally spoke. "I promise."

"Thank you." She hugged me.

"Not on the church ground," I then added.

"Street," she gasped as she hugged my face, kissed me, and started to sob, because she knew my history of violence.

"Hey, hey! Stop." I calmed her down as I brushed her hair from her face and kissed her. "I promise—no blood on the church ground." I gave her my word to not fight him at church.

We were interrupted by Assad.

"Yo, Street, I'll be back," he said with a knock on the door. "Running over to my crib to get some stuff." He left.

We went to my bedroom and made out a bit for a few minutes until once again, amidst her heavy erotic panting, which confirmed that she was ready to give me her all, she stopped me.

Really!

"Not now, not yet," she whispered as she kissed me and rolled me off her.

She left for the kitchen to get some juice, and I started getting ready. She reentered my bedroom and helped to get me dressed by suggesting I wear the T-shirt she got me and my golden break dance championship belt, as she claimed I had many fans at her church.

We met Assad at his car and left for church. She gave me a peck as we entered the church ground and then took off to meet up with her other committee members to start the night's proceedings. Assad decided to linger for a while, so we both sat at the back.

They made their formal announcements and introductions and then asked all the newcomers to stand. There were almost two hundred of us at church. Assad and I, along with about twenty others in the congregation, stood as Michelle took the podium and asked us all to tell our names and a fun fact about ourselves, starting with the front row.

We were seated at the back, so we were last.

Damn You, Drummer Boy

Assad was all decked out in his military gear, as he had to report back to base that night, so he introduced himself as a soldier serving our country and that his company (a group of soldiers) were about to travel to Africa soon for more training. He would have his first tour of duty in collaborating with the United Nations armed forces. He received a resounding ovation.

I looked around and realized that I was the last man standing.

All of a sudden, the buzz in the crowd turned to excitement as many in the congregation started talking aloud and inaudibly to the point where I could make out a few lines.

"Oh my god, it's Street!" one male voice said.

"Me and my girls came to all your break dance competitions," a female voice said.

"What the! You guys won the Golden Championship belt?" another male voice asked amidst numerous ongoing conversations about my presence.

"Really, dude, you didn't know that? Which rock did you just crawl from under?" another male voice joked. "Look, he's even wearing the belt!"

"I'm your biggest fan!" a female voice screamed to the applause from many in the congregation.

Michelle was not surprised by the welcoming reception and had a hard time telling most in the congregation to hush and settle down. It took about a minute for them to do so, but they finally did.

"Okay," Michelle said, grinning from ear to ear and trying to maintain her composure. "So I guess you don't need to introduce yourself, mister." She smiled. "But go ahead anyway."

I, too, had to take a moment to recompose myself as I was caught off guard and a bit flabbergasted by the surprise reception, but I also noticed that while most cheered, we also got a few looks of scorn, including from the Sardonyx crew, sitting in the isle across from us.

We have been booed off stage in many dance contests before when we just formed our group and started competing, so we were used to the scorn. I ignored them! Bite me!

"Hey," I said, much to the amusement of many in the congregation, "I'm Street."

There was a chorus of happy "Duh!" and laughter across the room.

"I am—was—leader of the Street Boys," I corrected myself as I nudged Assad to stand up.

"What! It's Assad!" a male voice shouted. "Damn, dude. You looked so different in army gear and without your crazy hairstyle," he continued, stirring up more euphoria, before Michelle once again had to settle them.

Assad returned a hand clap to them and sat back down.

"I said I *was* the leader of the Street Boys as…the Street Boys are no more."

"You guys broke up! Why?" a male voice shouted, stirring the buzz across the room even louder.

I slowly raised both my palms to calm them.

"No! Why?" another concerned female voice shouted.

"Would you like to come to the podium, Street?" Michelle suggested, sensing the sudden change in the atmosphere.

"No, I'm good," I declined.

"Well, can you speak a bit louder, Street?" a female voice three isles over requested.

I complied. "We…" I sighed. "The Street Boys didn't break up. We grew up and simply started pursuing our careers in different directions," I started. "Bob and I are in college on separate sides of the country, Stoke migrated to the United States, and as you just heard, Assad joined the army and will be on a tour of duty in Africa for only God knows how long. So I guess I am now the last man standing."

"So does that mean we will never see the Street Boys in action again?" a male voice across the aisle shouted. "I was hoping you guys would compete for the new Break Dance Platinum Belt they are launching next summer."

"I'll see if us Street Boys can have a reunion to compete for that," I said with a glance at Assad, which caused crazy cheers from most in the congregation.

There was more buzz in the room until Michelle hushed them, and then said the unthinkable. "Okay, so this wasn't part of our agenda for tonight, but based on what you just heard, since this is the last night you will all be seeing what is left of the Street boys together, how about you two come up here and give us a final farewell cameo performance? Whadda ya say, guys?" she shouted, spreading both arms wide to stir them up.

It worked. Michelle then beckoned for us to come to the podium. The congregation joined in with loud cheers. Assad nudged me. I followed his gaze at his attire, which would make it difficult for him to perform a routine break dance. I agreed but nudged him back to comply.

"I didn't come to church for this," he gasped as he reluctantly stood and slowly walked to the podium.

Michelle removed the microphone from the stand and was about to hand it to me, but Assad took it. He gestured for them to calm down.

"Okay, okay, hey, listen." He tried to hush them. "Sure, like yeah, sure we would love to do a li'l cameo for you guys, but…but we can't break dance to piano music," he said as an excuse with a glance at the piano to the left of the podium. "And plus, look at me. I'm not dressed to break dance."

There were murmurs and groans of disappointment until I saw a huddled conversation between three guys at the other side of the podium. Two held guitars and the other sat around the drum set. The drummer then stood and boldly walked over to us, took the mike from Assad, and spoke.

"I am one of your biggest fans!" He introduced himself. "And who said you had to break dance to piano music?" he continued with a smirk as he signaled to the audio controller, handed back the microphone, and walked back to the drum set, sat, took his drum sticks up, and eventually, started playing some popular break dance beats.

The congregation rose in excitement as the audio tech turned the volume up, and then turned on the synthesizer to collaborate with some cool break dance beats.

"Let's make this your last farewell," Michelle said as she walked back over and hugged me side to side after a glance from some of the elders in the church who were sitting in a corner of the podium for their approval of what she was about to do.

They concurred.

"Really, Michelle," I gasped, as we had been in impromptu break-dance performances before but never at a church.

She couldn't contain her laughter as she kept swinging her right hand from side to side to arouse the congregation even more while poking me in the side. The look of love and happiness she gave me during all that was priceless, as she kept nudging me to start dancing.

For a moment, I blocked out all the cheers because my world stood still; for the first time in my life, I was about to break dance with the Street, Boys maybe for the last time ever, in front of the woman I loved. And yes, I was in, and I believed in love all over again. But of all places, all this was going down in church?

Guess it's true what they say: "God does have a sense of humor!"

"One last time—for your fans, for the Street Boys, for me, for you," she said as her demeanor had a flash of emotion.

Assad interrupted our gaze with a nudge that meant no.

I looked at the cheering congregation, then back at Michelle as the drummer and music kept on playing.

"Okay, one last time," I said to her. Then I turned to Assad. "One last time," I echoed to him as I started to remove my championship belt and prepped my attire. "One last time—for the Street Boys." I stared him down.

He took a heavy sigh of compliance and then removed his army jacket, combat belt, and boots.

The crowd went wild as we moved some furniture from the stage to have a bigger room. And then we started to break-dance with exhaling energy of what was and what would never be again, nailing all our signature moves to the uproar of most in the congregation. I included some of Stoke's moves, and Assad included some of Bob's signature moves.

Everyone was on their feet, cheering! Even the drummer broke one of his drum sticks and had to quickly retrieve a replacement because he was playing the drums with such excitement.

"We danced like David danced" (2 Samuel) without a care of who was watching, unimpressed, or who was cheering on top of their lungs.

Minutes later, we ended our dance routine. We got a standing ovation. But instead of the usual hype at the end of our dance when we competed, Assad and I gave each other a solemn breathless look, knowing that this was finally the end of the Street Boys in performance…at least for now. Would there ever be a reunion to compete for the coveted Break Dance Platinum Championship Belt? The promoter, who was one of our biggest fans, would go all out on travel expenses to get us reunited to compete for that because there was big money involved. But although this was about his break dance competition and us Street Boys would be clear favorites, there were some things in life that only time and God could decide.

Assad and I went outside and chatted for a bit and gave each other a bear hug, and then he left for base.

The Staircase

I didn't reenter the church, but instead I just sat on a staircase at the back in a moment of reflection. I could still hear everything that was going on. I was at church but not in church, and it felt good. Baby steps, if you know what I mean.

I was at church again, feeling God again, feeling love again! I had a smile on my face as I gazed at my golden Break Dance Championship belt before slowly putting it back on.

So it was the official start of the crusade, and it was a happy moment. I guessed that they took a break, as a couple of the youths walked back and forth with a happy wave at me or a dab or a high five.

"There you are!" a female voice interrupted my greetings. It was Michelle. She took a quick look around to see if anyone could see us and then gave me a quick passionate kiss.

"Thank you for what you guys just pulled off. I didn't know you were so popular." She smiled as we both sat on the staircase.

"I didn't know church kids were into break dance, too, so I am equally surprised." I smiled.

We chatted for a bit.

"You have an influence on these kids' lives. Make it a positive one." She smiled as she stood. "I have to go. Wait for me here at the end." She gave me a peck and went back inside.

I remained on the staircase as I could hear all that was going on. They had some musical presentations, a mini sermon, and then a buffet at the end. Michelle was the presenter for that night and was excited that it went flawless. She thanked everyone, including us Street Boys for our cameo performance, which resonated in huge cheers.

She came back out and introduced me to a few of her friends; we took some finger food and went for a walk at the back of the church. We sat on a bench in this park area around the back, and as I listened to our conversation back and forth, I actually felt comfortable that this church vibe was not so bad after all.

It actually felt good being back.

Some time passed, and we eventually got ready to leave. I walked her to the ladies' room and waited by the entrance to the adjoining men's room. She came out sometime after, and we hugged playfully and then kissed, only to be interrupted by someone exiting the men's room. It was her ex, who saw the embrace and kiss.

If looks could kill, I'd be dead, judging by the way he stared at me.

He tried about two or three times to beckon her over so they could have a chat, but she refused. It was more fuel to his fire, as I could see his frustration as he finally stormed off. Trouble was coming! And yes, even while at church!

Sports Day

Okay, so I never signed up for this, but Saturday came, and it was a big fanfare as it was sports day! There were four teams—red, blue, green, and gold. I was on the red team.

There were numerous competitions, like egg and spoon race, potato sack race, toss the water balloon, track and field, volley ball, and stuff that made it a really fun day. I didn't compete in any much to the frustration of Michelle, but I was still enjoying the moment.

It was around four later that afternoon for the final competition of the evening—the six-a-side soccer final. All teams played earlier as we were split in two groups. The gold team won to reach the finals, and so did our red team, which I reluctantly geared up for as a substitute.

This soccer final drew a large buzzing crowd for whatever reason until I found out that Michelle's ex was the captain of the gold team, along with the rest of his Sardonyx crew. Everyone at church was their biggest fans as they attempted to win a fifth straight title.

Michelle and the drummer boy came over to me and begged me to play. I said no. By now I could tell she was disappointed at me. The game started. It was pretty exciting, but after twenty minutes, the first half ended 0-0.

Michelle came over again.

"Okay, so I know this is not break dancing, but you are embarrassing me, Street. Everyone here is expecting you to compete in at least one competition, and this is the last one for the day," she said as she gave me a vexed poke in my side. "It doesn't always have to be about you, Street. The gold team is going to win as always, so please, just go on as a substitute and play. Damn, even break dance with the ball if you have to." She laughed. "Do this for me."

And for the first time ever, she hugged me by the back of my head, pulled me in, and kissed me in front of the over a hundred spectators. I was not sure how many saw, but one person did, who just happened to be walking by to head back on the field—her ex.

We stared each other down, and at that point, my competitive spirit kicked in. I was not sure if I wanted to win the game or just wanted this self-righteous cocky bastard to lose, but I accepted her request.

"Okay, go tell our team captain I want to come on as a sub," I said as I stood and started to warm up on the spot.

She hugged me happily, put a number sticker on my back as show that I was now part of the soccer squad, and went to talk to the team captain, who immediately beckoned me over.

"You want to go on as a sub now?" he blatantly asked. "We win this, red team wins sports day. We gave nothing in the first half. We got twenty minutes to see what you got, and to beat these show-offs, or I will sub your ass too." He laughed.

Michelle gave me a playful nudge. I looked at her ex and his boys preparing for kickoff. "Yes."

I took to the field to loud cheers. The second half started, and within a minute, they hit our goalpost with a powerful shot from her ex.

It was game on.

Honestly, my team couldn't play soccer for shit. They were just playing for fun, and I get it! It was sports day at church, not an official competition. But I don't compete for fun—I compete to win!

I was the striker and gave a simple instruction for them to get me the ball. It was easier said than done, however, with time ticking and around five minutes remaining before a penalty shoot-out.

I was tackled even when I didn't have the ball.

What the what!

It then became obvious that I was being targeted and, as such, avoided rough tackles from the Sardonyx crew. They were bombarding our goal with shots that were either wide or blocked until I had a lucky break. The gold team had a throw-in, which one of my team members intercepted. Surprisingly, he made a superb pass to me at the halfway line. I started charging at the gold team's goalpost on the right wing, one-on-one with the keeper. I could hear the gold team players charging at me from behind like a hoard of wild horses, so in order to avoid a brutal tackle, I looked, aimed, and took a powerful shot at the goal.

The keeper fumbled, and I scored!

Goal!

There was shock and euphoria from the crowd, but without being able to explain why and as strange as it might sound, I didn't even celebrate. I just smiled when I saw Michelle and her girls on the sidelines, jumping and screaming, making it obvious which team they were cheering for.

The game resumed, and with three minutes to go, they were pressing for an equalizer. As luck would have it, a frantic wild clearance from our goalkeeper found me again. I charged at the gold team keeper—yep, one-on-one again—as they were pressing high. I slowed and sidestepped his wild lunge at me, as if he wanted to break my leg, and calmly slotted the ball into an empty net for a second goal.

Goal!

Pandemonium!

This time, I cheered as my teammates and I frantically embraced, and scores of our supporters stormed the pitch in jubilant celebration. I guessed it was a shocker that us underdogs were leading 2-0 in a final against the favorites, which would end their unbeaten run. Pride was at stake.

It took a couple of minutes for the referee to clear the field, and the game finally resumed in extra time.

Our keeper collected another shot blasted straight at him and cleared it to the half line. I saw Michelle's ex charging in but went up to compete for a header and was clobbered by his deliberate elbow with a blow to my left cheek.

I crashed to the ground, and for a moment, everything went silent and blurred. I revived to a medical staff around me, dressing the wound as my face had a gash and was bleeding. I could hear frantic arguing among opposing spectators as to whether it was accidental or intentional. I was eventually helped back to my feet.

Her ex was given a red card. Out of frustration, the minute the game resumed and the ball was passed, the referee blew the whistle to end it.

It was a bittersweet moment as, not sure if I won, but the red team did.

Michelle rushed over, we hugged, and I was taken to a room and given further treatment.

It Was an Accident

Back home later that evening, I had a big ole bandage covering half my face. My brother was furious, but he counted to ten—or maybe like a thousand—to calm his retaliatory temper. Michelle and even my brother's girlfriend kind of sided with the thought that it was a rough tackle, yes, that it was not deliberate, that it was an accident! My brother and I couldn't decide for sure. We debated on the subject for a while in the living room over dinner until my brother gave his ruling.

"Anybody else and I would agree that this was an accident, if it was with some random guy. But this was your ex, who is obviously mad that you two are now dating. So what are the odds that this was really an accident?" He finished the last of his plate and popped a beer open. "Time will tell if it was, bro," he continued. "I can't believe I'm gonna say this, because we are talking about church here, but if there is another *accident* between you and this dude, what me and my boys are gonna do to him will be no accident."

Michelle got scared. "Please, G, don't fuel Street's rage. I have seen what he and you guys can do, and I don't want any bloodshed at church. We are talking about *church* here. Please," she pleaded. "He should know better than to mess with you, Street, because they all have heard and know about your and the Street Boys' reputation not just as break dancers but as street brawlers too. It was an accident!"

"Time will tell if it was, Michelle," my brother again said as he lit a cigarette and passed it to me. Then he lit one for himself.

I thought he was upset and felt bad for me that I was trying to do right by going to church yet trouble still found me, even at church!

"And if it wasn't an accident and shit goes down at church, just look the other way, girl," his girlfriend then said as she patted her on her lap. "They say, 'Choose your battles.' But sometimes, that choice is not left up to you, because there may come a time when you have to defend yourself against the enemy, even if you are in the house of God."

There was an uneasy silence.

She looked at the clock on the wall. "You two ready to go?" she then asked with an unhappy smile. She offered us a ride back to church for the sports day's awards ceremony, which was going to be held later that night.

We cleaned up and left. She and my brother stayed at church as I discreetly pointed out to them who the Sardonyx bastards were and, more importantly, who Michelle's ex was.

I went up to receive my award for Man of the Match for the soccer game. There were cheers. I smiled and thanked them and forced myself to believe that maybe it really was just an accident—or not!

G and his girlfriend eventually left as they had to meet up with their respective study group back on campus. I mixed and mingled with the youths for a while and then just went outside to sit on the staircase for some fresh air after lingering and realizing Michelle was busy.

I went to the restroom and, on my way out, ran into the Sardonyx. They all cracked up laughing when they saw the bandage on my cheek.

"Oh, poor baby. Street got a boo-boo," Michelle's ex teased, laughing.

I just stared him down as he got up in my face.

"Stay away from her, or there will be more 'accidents,'" he threatened before they all walked off laughing at me.

I counted to ten, as I wanted to attack him. Well, more like I counted to a hundred to calm my rage.

Sigh.

Crystal

I lit a cigarette and decided to take a stroll in the parking lot to wait for the next bus so I could head home. Then a female voice shout my name.

"Hey, Street!"

It was Crystal. Yes, she did catch my eye during the soccer match earlier. She was one of our cheerleaders and also a cheerleader at her university, where she was an exchange student from Sweden.

If Michelle was a 10, she was a 10 too. She was gorgeous for a white girl. But she and Michelle never got along.

"How you feeling?" she asked as she closed her car door and walked over to me, staring at my bandage.

"I've had worst days." I smiled.

She decided to take a stroll with me, and we had a casual conversation. She said she admired me from that night she and a few of her friends came to watch us win the Break Dance Championship's golden belt.

I didn't even know she was there.

"So what's up with you and Michelle?" she then abruptly asked. "Are you two officially dating? Because if so, you just walked into the lion's den. I hope you know that what happened earlier with that busted face of yours was no accident."

I just listened as she went on to tell me what she heard about the many times Michelle and her ex had broken up and that when other guys tried to date her, there would be an *accident* until she was forced to get back together with him.

Doubt

And then she dropped a bombshell. "I heard they broke up again for the umpteenth time while on their mission in England, but the biggest gossip is, I heard they also had sex!"

The cigarette fell from my hand out of shock at what I just heard.

"So the Virgin Mary—I mean the virgin Michelle—may no longer be a virgin after all, and for all I care is just playing the both of you."

"They had sex?" I gasped.

"That's the rumor." She dryly smiled. "And strangely, the details of their night of drunken love, as told by her boyfriend, make that rumor sound true."

What the what!

We were interrupted by another voice. "Street, Street! I've been looking all over for you!"

It was Michelle walking toward us.

"Oh, ooh, here comes your damsel! This is the part where I say good night," Crystal said as she discreetly took out a pen and wrote her telephone number in my palm.

"Call me if you want to be with a real woman instead of her—a female player," she whispered as she walked away, deliberately bumping into Michelle, who finally approached us.

They exchanged a few angry words. There was definitely bad blood between them both, but I didn't care about that, as I was numb at the so-called rumor that she had sex with her ex.

"What was that about? Street! Street!" Michelle said as she shoved me in a temper.

I didn't answer.

"I told you she and I don't speak, so why are you out here, up close and personal, talking with her?"

I still didn't answer.

She thumped me in the chest. We stared each other down for a moment. I could tell she was jealous or more like just mad at me.

"Did you sleep with him?" I then abruptly asked.

"What?" she replied, confused.

"Your so-called ex. Did you sleep with him in England?"

Her body jolted for a moment without a reply until she turned the tables on me as I used my hand to pat the bandage on my cheek and she saw the telephone number in my palm.

"What is that? What is this?" she screamed at me. "Did you sleep with her? Are you sleeping with that bitch Crystal?" she screamed, thumping me in the chest even harder again before she started to sob quietly.

There was uneasy silence filled only with the sounds of her sobbing as it started to drizzle.

"No, I'm not. No, I didn't," I said as I looked at the number, spat in my palm, and rubbed it on my thigh until the number was erased.

She noticed and held my palm with a gaze to ensure that it was completely erased.

"Your turn. Did you make love to him?"

Her body jolted even more as she wiped tears from her eyes.

"Michelle! Michelle! There you are," one of her girlfriends shouted. "We've been looking for you. Come say closing prayer so we can get out of here before this rain."

"Give me a second!" Michelle replied with a gaze in my eyes. "No, I did not make love to him! Stay away from Crystal, or I will stay away from you." Then she recomposed herself._"Are you coming?" She started heading back inside.

"I'll be right there," I said.

Talk about being in limbo. I thought about lighting a cigarette, but it started raining. I didn't go back inside. I didn't want to hear her pray because I still had doubts and was just beside myself.

Don't Let Me Count to Three…Again

The rest of the week went by fast. I tried to put the whole thing behind me and gave her the benefit of the doubt after I heard her deliver a sermon—or more like a motivational speech—one night. I had no more run-ins with the Sardonyx. I did a couple more solo break dance performances. I tried out with the youth choir as a tenor. Epic fail. I had everyone cracking up at how terrible a singer I was.

But Michelle was a great spiritual dancer and received resounding applause for the nights she performed. She and I even performed a skit together. I had put the rumors behind me and was happy to be, not just at church, but actively in church again.

Isn't it funny how, sometimes in life, when you find yourself in a certain tumultuous situation with a loved one that gives you doubt, there comes a point where after the back-and-forth arguing, you don't even want to know the truth anymore? You instead just choose to believe your own scenario so as to give yourself peace of mind.

The final night came for the youth fellowship crusade, and I surprised myself by going up for altar call. As much as I was labeled as a bad boy, I wanted to get back on the right track with God. I had made my peace with Him.

As others and I stood at the altar, we were asked to hold hands so they could pray for us. As I reached across to hold the hand of a guy standing on my right, I looked down and realized a familiar tattoo. It was the wrist with the crossbones and skeleton face. Yep, it was the thief from the bus encounters with Michelle and me.

We just stared at each other in surprise for a bit.

"So does this count as three?" he asked nervously, remembering my threat, as he held me with trembling hands.

"No. We're cool." I smiled, holding back my own tears as I saw tears streaming from his face.

We were both two lost souls at the altar, on a mission to make things right.

I remembered the scripture in the book of Romans 7:24–25: "O wretched man that I am! Who will deliver me from this body of death? I thank God through Jesus Christ our Lord. So then, with the mind I myself serve the law of God, but with the flesh the law of sin."

Sigh.

It was a somber moment as the pastor prayed and some deacons in the group of about twenty of us standing at the altar walked around, rested their palm on our forehead, and also prayed for us.

Amen.

The pastor, Michelle's dad, welcomed us as new family members to his church and told us that we were in safe and good hands and that becoming members would let us experience the best years of our lives.

I was happy! We clapped in hope of a better future henceforth. At the end, as we went back to our seats and as the choir sang, the thief and I chatted a bit. And yes, I never even asked his name or told him mine. But he told me that he had turned his life around, got a job on a construction site, was working things out with his girlfriend (who moved him back in), and that, for his first paycheck, he had bought himself a brand-new bicycle to commute so he no longer took the bus.

It all sounded so simple and routine, but in his eyes, it seemed as if he had won the lottery. That moment humbled me into thinking that we should never look down on anyone's progress or success in life—however mediocre—just because ours are levels higher than theirs.

I was proud of him! I made up my mind to become a believer again and enroll as a member of their church. But not so fast, as I was about to have my intention thrown right back in my face.

Michelle Caught in the Act

Church was in full swing with a musical concert when I snuck out to use the restroom. To my shock, I saw Michelle pinned against the wall with her ex groping her. He forcefully kissed her for a bit until she started to fight him off.

What the what!

She was visibly upset and trying to fight him off, but she was no match, as he was huge and was easily overpowering her.

"Hey! Hey!" I shouted as he pinned both her hands against the wall, pressed his body against hers, and tried to kiss her again. She frantically avoided his attempts by swaying her head from side to side.

I stormed over as he finally landed a kiss on her lips. But she bit him. He got mad and thrust her against the wall even more and was about to slap her. But I screamed at him again.

"Hey! Let her go! I said let her go!" I screamed.

"Mind your business, asshole," he said as he wiped blood from his lips caused by her bite and groped her some more.

Wow. With that entire beautiful vibes I got from the altar just now, I went into shutdown mode and came to my old self—fight mode!

It is incomprehensible how, one moment in life, you are happy and at peace with yourself, feeling like Mr. Goody Two Shoes, and then the next moment, in the blink of an eye, some jerk ticks you off and makes you mad to the point where you wanna shove one of those Goody Two Shoes down their throat.

"Don't let me count to three!" I barked in a rage with clenched fists, as I was ready to beat the crap out of this guy.

"What you say, fool!" He laughed, finally giving me attention.

"One!" I started as I removed my hoodie. "Two!" I walked up to him.

"Street, please," Michelle sobbed, knowing what was about to go down.

He started to release her to confront me, and she kneed him in the crotch and shoved him off her.

"Really, bitch! To be continued." He pointed at her, groaning as he limped off, clutching his groin. "You're a dead man!" he then threatened me as he left.

I paused for a moment as she covered her face and sobbed. I eventually walked over to her after retrieving my hoodie.

"What was that about?" I asked.

No reply. Instead, silence, filled only by her sobbing.

"Are you okay?"

"No!" she cried as she hugged me, buried her face in my chest, and sobbed even harder.

My doubt had escalated into what I just saw and what Crystal told me. Call it what you might, but as I consoled her, my mind was not on her; it was on her ex and finally having to do what I do best to put an end to what has now been escalated to his sexual assault on her.

She eventually calmed and went inside to report the incident to her father and church security. I was beside myself, so I sat on the staircase and lit a cigarette. Crystal was passing by, headed to the ladies' room, and she stopped to say hi. We chatted for a bit as she took a few puffs from my cigarette.

"That girl is trouble, and you are going to be in big trouble if you don't walk away from her." She sighed, unaware of what just went down but still in feud mode with Michelle.

I didn't reply, as I knew the rivalry between them both and didn't even care to ask what triggered it.

"Sometimes by the actions of these church members, I have had to ask myself if this place is a church or a cult group," she continued. "There are some very righteous folks here that make you feel blessed and welcomed, but evil lurks here as well. My major is in law, as a prosecutor. I've seen things that should not be happening, especially at church." She puffed on the cigarette.

Her girlfriend walked over and interrupted us. "Hey, girl," she greeted.

"Remember to call me if you need me," Crystal finally said as she stroked my cheek and surprisingly kissed the much tinier Band-Aid I was still wearing. With a stare and a smile, she handed the cigarette back to me and walked off to the ladies' room.

Moments later, they passed by again. This time, she didn't say a word but instead just gave me a soft smile, a wink, and a "Call me" gesture by holding her hand to her ear.

She looked amazing in her skinny jeans, heels, and T-shirt, yet still I returned an empty smile. The cigarette had burned out in my hand without me even realizing, as I had been in deep thought. I only noticed because I looked at my palm, where she wrote her number, before I erased it to avoid a confrontation with Michelle.

Have you ever tried your best to diffuse a confrontation, yet it still happened? That night taught me a valuable lesson, that when you find yourself in that situation where you know it is looming, having done all, stand, brace yourself, be on guard, and wait for it so you won't be caught off guard.

Love let me drop my guard, though. As I rose to use the restroom, I was in a contemplative mode by being lovestruck with Michelle and trying to get to the bottom of what was going on with her and her ex. Plus now I was distracted by Crystal, who was easily a tie with Michelle for the hottest girl at church. Plus, I just went to altar call and decided to turn my life around once again and live for Christ.

Sigh.

The Restroom

I didn't see it coming when I entered the restroom.

As I washed my hands, the lights suddenly turned off, turning everything pitch-black, and all I could hear were footsteps charging at me. I was tackled to the ground, and as much as I fought back, I admit that I got a good beat-down from multiple people. I couldn't see who they were as they had flashlights shining at me as they punched, kicked, and stomped me for a good minute or so before finally running off and exiting the restroom.

Wow!

I lay there in the darkness and in a daze for a bit, trying not to lose consciousness as I spat blood and wiped more from my face. I could smell my blood. I could taste my blood as it streamed from my nose. My mouth was also busted up. It seemed like an eternity, but I eventually managed to drag myself to my feet and wobbled over to turn the lights back on.

I stood there for a while to regain my strength and trying to make sense of what just happened, especially at the safest place you could ever be—in church.

Yes, I was just jumped and got a beat-down at church!

I stumbled over to the mirror and gave it an empty gaze as I looked at my bloodied face and busted head with blood still streaming down my face. I stood there for another minute or so to regain my strength. I checked myself and realized that I still had my wallet and my jewelry, so this was no robbery. I looked around on the floor for any evidence that would make sense of what just happened, and in a splatter of blood, I saw a familiar earring. It was the one I saw Michelle's ex wearing that night he first threatened me.

I must have yanked it from his ear as I fought to defend myself. I slowly picked it up and then, without washing up, I did the inconceivable—I staggered off into the church.

Michelle's father was in the middle of his sermon as I entered from the back and slowly staggered down the aisle, all battered, bloodied and bruised, which slowly grew the attention of everyone.

Some came to my rescue, but I shoved them aside.

"Is this how you welcome newcomers to this church, to this damn cult?" I asked as I spat blood. "Is this your idea of telling us we are safe here as you did earlier at altar call?" I shouted as I spat more blood and stumbled again.

More people from the congregation came to my aid again, but I shoved them away, as by now the whole congregation was standing and trying to get a glimpse of me, talking among themselves as to what happened.

The pastor rushed down and met me. He caught me as I was about to fall again. "Oh my god! Street, what happened? Who did this to you?" he questioned in shock.

I spat more blood as I gave him Michelle ex's earring. His eyes grew wide as he recognized it too.

"Come. Let our medical team take a look at you," he said as he tried to help me back to my feet. "I'm calling the police because this nonsense has gone too far!"

"No. No police. I got this!" I vowed in street-justice mode. "I just want to go home." I stood.

"She told me what he did to her earlier. He will pay *dearly* for all of this," he whispered as he helped me up.

"I just wanna go home. Can someone please call my brother to come get me?"

"I'll take you home," a voice from behind said. It was Crystal. She had an angry look on her face as a tear streamed from her eye when she saw my bloodied state.

"Where are the Sardonyx?" I questioned the pastor.

"Sardonyx! Sardonyx! Get your asses over here!" he ordered without compliance.

"This is their usual spot to sit, but they are not here," an old lady uttered, gesturing at the half-empty bench beside her. "They all left a while ago and haven't come back since."

"Where's Michelle?" I asked the pastor.

"She was so shaken up about the assault with him earlier that I sent her home," he said with an angry gasp.

"Come, let me take you home," Crystal again offered.

I got help to a back room, where they cleaned and patched me up a bit, and then I hopped in her car and directed her for the ride home. It was a clear, starry night as I rested my head against the front passenger window and gazed at the stars.

"What have I done to deserve this welcome back, Jesus?" I whispered to myself as a tear rolled from my eye. There was no answer. Guess He abandoned me again. I sobbed discreetly as Crystal spoke, but I didn't hear a word she was saying.

We arrived home. Crystal helped me to the door. I knocked, and my brother opened the door. He was shocked at my appearance.

"What happened? Bro, what the... What happened?" he asked as he helped me inside.

His girlfriend ran from the kitchen when she heard the commotion.

"They jumped me," I said as he helped me to the couch to sit.

"Who? Willy and his boys?" he asked as he angrily started to get dressed to go to Willy's house and, yes, to fight!

"No. The Sardonyx." I sighed.

There was tense silence until he started punching the wall. His girlfriend tried to restrain him, but he shoved her away.

"I told you! I told you that was no accident during the soccer match!" he screamed at her.

She looked frightened; she had probably never seen him so angry. He thumped the wall some more until she cautiously hugged him from behind to calm him down.

"Where is she?" he questioned about Michelle's whereabouts, assuming she was behind it. "And who are you?" he angrily questioned Crystal.

"This is Crystal," I introduced.

"Hi," she said nervously, still standing by the doorway. "So I think I should go. I'll see you at church, Street," she said, rubbing her hands together, sensing the tension.

"No, no," I said as I sat up, "No. You will never see me at church again." I tried to hold back the tears.

There was empty silence as she, too, wiped a tear from her eyes.

"Will I... Can I see you again?" she choked.

More silence.

"What's today?" I tried to remember. "Friday. Yeah, you wanna come crash with me tomorrow?"

"I'll be out of town until late tomorrow, but I can come over Sunday around noon." She smiled.

"Okay."

"Okay." She smiled back as she said good night and nervously left.

"What happened?" my brother returned to anger mode and asked.

I told them everything. His girlfriend got her first-aid kit, removed my bloodied T-shirt, sat in the sofa as I sat on the floor between her legs, leaned my head back, and had her remove the bandages and administer her own treatment.

"So what happens now?" she asked as she replaced a bandage and glanced at my brother.

He didn't reply. He just went to the kitchen, returned with two beers, and handed me one. Then he sat, sipped on his, and gazed into space. There was an uneasy silence as she finished patching me up, hugged me around the neck, and kissed me on the top of my head.

"I don't care if this is church. You didn't start this, so go do what you do best. Nail it!" she whispered in a vengeful tone.

My brother gave me a gaze of consent. We eventually retired to bed. Saturday morning came and, with it, something that not even a gambler could predict.

I Don't Remember

Your life is not determined by what other people label or profile you as; it is instead determined by what you see yourself as each time you look in the mirror. Always remember that!

Willy was having a cookout that started at noon. My brother, his girlfriend, and I, plus a few of his friends as "security," just in case anything flared up with Willy's brother, all got there around three.

I told Willy what happened at church after he noticed the bandages. He vowed to join me in revenge. My mind was in fight mode, plotting my revenge while taking shots with Willy. He eventually went off to talk with other people, which gave his baby mother, "the devil in the red dress," the opportunity to walk over.

"What happened?' she asked, rubbing her pregnant belly.

"I let my guard down," I replied as I took a sip from my beer.

"What happened, Street?" she again asked out of concern, staring at my bruised face.

We gazed at each other for a bit, and I could tell that she really had strong feelings for me.

"Soccer match incident at church. Don't wanna talk about it," I finally said.

We chatted for a bit. She then made a shocking confession that even after all these months, whenever she and Willy made love, she had to keep her eyes open, as each time she closed them, all she saw was my face as I had made love to her that night. She again reminded me that the baby could be mine and again begged me to keep it our secret. I gave her my word, as in those days no one even thought or cared about having a paternity test; you just wanted to know that you were going to be a mommy or daddy, whether you planned to step up to the role or not.

Willy's mom called her over to help out with something, so she left. But there I stood, thinking that with all that was going on in my life, I could also be a father, and the worst part was, I would never know.

I Remember…Well, Maybe Not

My mind was all over the place, so I did the unusual and just started having more shots with my beer. Mixing drinks was asking for trouble, as I started getting very tipsy.

I noticed my brother and his girlfriend walking over from Michelle's house with her. Yep, they went to get her to cheer up my mood. We talked about the incident at church. She hugged and kissed me in front of everyone, which attracted a few stares. We slow-danced as I continued to take shots and have a smoke.

I was just enjoying myself to clear my head.

Sigh.

So?

I eventually got wasted. I remember Michelle and G helping me as I wobbled up our driveway. I remember both of them were laughing as they helped me to my room, and then I crashed onto my bed. I remember my brother closing the door as he exited. I remember the worst feeling you could ever get from being drunk; lying on my back and watching the ceiling wobble and spin in slow motion as Michelle fought to remove my boots and jeans and then my T-shirt. I remember her getting undressed to just her panties and bra and then putting on one of my T-shirts before snuggling beside me. I remember us kissing, and I once again tried to make my move.

I couldn't remember anything after that.

That night taught me a very valuable lesson. No, it was not just to never mix alcohol when you were out drinking, as it makes you drunk faster, but the lesson was that drinking in excess and passing out made you a vulnerable prey to predators if you were in the wrong company. G's girlfriend told me many stories about girls on campus that did just that at parties. They passed out after a while, and multiple guys took advantage of them sexually. The next morning, they knew they were gang-raped but was too embarrassed to report it, because it would be very difficult to prove their case that it was not consensual.

Wow!

Luckily for me, I was home in bed with Michelle.

The next morning, I awoke and felt for her, but she was gone. I lifted the sheet to check how last night went down, and I still had my underwear on. I have had sex before while still clothed, but I just couldn't remember anything about whether we did it or not. It was a dreaded consequence of consuming too much alcohol.

My moment of recollection soon turned into a moment of meditation.

Interestingly, priests from the Roman Catholic Church freely smoked cigarettes simply because the Bible was *silent* about smoking. So that habit became a matter of conscience. The Bible was, however, very vocal on drinking, with numerous chapters commenting on it. In fact, according to John 2, the very first miracle Jesus performed was to turn water into wine at a wedding. First Timothy 5 took it even further and instructed us to not just drink water but have a little wine for our stomach's sake.

So it was official that even as Christians, it would be okay for us to consume alcohol, but the key word in the latter verse was *little*. Ephesians 5:18 urged us not to be drunk with wine, and 1 Peter 5:8 warned us to be *sober* and vigilant because our adversary, the devil, as a roaring lion, walked about, seeking whom he might devour.

How? Countless women would get raped while drunk and would be too ashamed to report it the next morning when they sobered up. Most men would do stupid-dare devil stunts and get robbed or hurt, or have stupid fist fights and wake up in a hospital bed or in jail the next morning. Not to mention the consequences of drunk driving...

So to put it simply, we should do all things in moderation.

But last night, I hadn't. I liked beer; I only drank beer. But I tried to keep up with Willy plus my brother and his crew by doing shots, and this was the end result. It could have, however, been worse, but at least I woke up in my bed with no strangers around.

My room door opened, and it was my brother, He had a big grin on his face as he quietly shut it and sat on my bed next to me.

"Finally?" he questioned with a big grin on his face as he thumped me with a pillow.

I knew exactly what he was asking—about what happened with Michelle and I last night. I just let out a heavy exhalation as I grabbed the pillow from him and covered my face in disappointment. He gasped, got up, opened my dresser drawer, and searched the area he knew I kept the blue pills he gave me. He popped the bottle open, threw the pills in his palm, and counted them with his eyes.

"Bro, like, really!" he gasped, realizing that I haven't used one since.

"Babe," his girlfriend called, "breakfast is ready!"

"Okay, I'm coming," he replied with a disappointed stare at me. He walked over to my bed and sat down. "You wanna talk about it?"

"Talk about what?" I questioned.

"Down there," he said, using his eyes to point at my groin. "You told me you couldn't get it up for Clair, and with all due respect, thank God for that. But look at Michelle, man. What's wrong with you?"

"I was drunk, bro. Plus, she keeps begging me to respect her and her virginity. You know how these virgins are, man. Even if they're with the right guy, they still wanna wait for that right moment. Add to that the fact that she is also a devoted Christian."

"True. But just look at her, bro. You might be playing Mr. Nice Guy, but not all guys play like that, especially when it comes to a body like that," he said. "Plus, it's Christmas, so you will have many more parties to attend. But unlike last night, why don't you get her drunk the next time? Just like on campus, she will wake up the next morning and won't even remember what happened. I have even had girls do that to me as a freshman. I remember this one time after a frat party, I woke up the next morning naked in the female dorm with two naked chicks next to me in bed sleeping, and I still can't remember what happened." He grinned.

"You know I'm not that guy," I said as I slapped him with my pillow, which started a playful pillow fight, only to be interrupted by his girlfriend standing at the door with folded arms.

"Hey, Street," she greeted. "So are you two gonna join us for breakfast or should I join in?"

Us?

My brother didn't give me a chance to make sense of that as he threw a pillow at her. I followed up by sailing one that smacked her right in the face.

"Really!" She laughed as she picked up both pillows and charged at us.

Our laughter filled the room, as it was two against one until she screamed for back-up.

"Mich, I need your help. Come!" she screamed as we playfully clobbered her with pillows.

I was surprisingly hit from behind with a pillow, and when I turned around, it was Michelle. She apparently didn't leave for home yet but was in the kitchen, helping with breakfast. I rolled her over onto the bed, and the pillow fight went on for a while until my brother and I, realizing that it was going to end in a draw, turned the tables on them by tossing our pillows and started tickling them.

It was hilarious. I had never laughed so hard.

I was happy.

We eventually got exhausted and were breathing heavily, just sprawled out while still laughing.

"I need to pee," G's girlfriend said with gasps of laughter as she dragged herself up from the bed and wobbled to the bathroom.

"Let me leave you two love birds alone," my brother said as he also exited after a parting pillow blow at Michelle and me, which she returned.

Michelle, who was now dressed in one of my pajama pants, was lying across my belly, stroking my chest.

"You guys are fun," she said as she crawled up to my face, stroked it, and kissed me. Then she buried her face in my neck.

We had a moment of happy silence.

"I thought you had left."

"It's Sunday. No morning service at church today, so I just thought I'd hang with you guys a bit before I head home, because dad won't be back home until afternoon."

More silence.

"So did we?" I started, trying to confirm.

"Did we what?"

"You know what I'm talking about," I said as I started tickling her again.

Then she pinned me to the bed. She looked so beautiful as she knelt on top of me and then used one hand to brush her hair from her face. She took a heavy exhalation and then spoke.

"The very first time I tried drinking, I guess I had one glass too many and..." she paused, burying her chin in her chest.

"And what?" I asked to break the uneasy silence.

She looked back up at me with a long gaze.

"And and let's just say it didn't end well." She sighed. "But last night you had one drink too many, and let's just say, it ended well." She sighed.

Unsure silence. I was now more curious about her episode, not mine.

"When was this that you had one drink too many? I didn't even know you drink," I queried.

Sad silence.

"Talk to me!" I snapped her back into reality, as I knew her mind had drifted.

"England," she finally spoke. "A few days before I returned from our crusade."

"Was this with your ex?" I questioned as I eased her off me and sat up out of curiosity and a brewing anger.

Silence.

"Just tell me what happened," I said, remembering the incident with her and Willy, and Assad.

With a long sigh and glossy eyes, she looked like she was trying to hold back the tears.

"Hey, are you guys coming to eat or what?" my brother's girl-friend said as she entered my room.

She saw the look on my face and Michelle wiping a tear from her eye, gave an apologetic and confused look, exited, and softly closed the door.

"I'm listening," I then said, trying to drop the mush.

She took a few deep breaths and sat up in the bed. "It was his birthday the night before you called and I told you I broke up with him," she started. "We normally went as a group to eat, but on this occasion, he begged me and the others to just let it be us two at a separate diner to celebrate his occasion. We agreed. Dinner went well. He ordered a bottle of wine to toast his birthday. I reluctantly accepted a glass, and we toasted. He urged me to have a few sips as we conversed. I complied, thinking I was in good hands. One sip led to another, and then one glass led to another." She sighed. "By halfway the third glass, my head was in a spin, and I was ready to leave. He complied, realizing that I was half drunk and just wanted my bed."

"Instead, the next morning, I woke up in his, which is a few doors down the hallway from my room," she continued as she gazed at my stone face for a comment.

"I'm listening," I exhaled.

Silence.

"I remember getting back to the hotel lobby. I remember him trying to kiss me in the elevator, but I stopped him. I remember his getting me into what I thought was my room because all these hotel rooms are decorated the same. But the next thing I knew, I woke up with him snoring beside me," she continued with an angry look on her face.

"Go on," I pressed.

"I lifted the sheets and realized we were both naked. My body shook in shock when I rose and saw a small pool of blood in the center of the bed that was poorly cleaned up. I started fighting him, screaming, 'What did you do to me!' He woke up in a daze, fending me off, and to this day, he has not admitted to anything. And I don't remember anything, but I know he took advantage of me while I was passed out," she softly sobbed.

Long silence.

"I'm sorry," she said as she rose and started getting dressed. "I didn't tell you before because I didn't know what to tell you, and I don't want to lose you. I have since learned that, in certain situations, I should never let my guard down, even when I am around people I think I can trust."

She finished getting dressed, came over to kiss me goodbye, but I fended her off. She backed off and stood by my bedside for what seemed like an eternity.

"Say something. Street! Please say something," she pleaded.

"You slept with him?"

"No. He raped me while I was passed out."

Long silence.

"Say something."

"Get out!" I finally said as I turned my back to her and covered my face with a pillow.

"Street, please…" I heard her starting to sob again. Then she walked off, and I heard my door closed.

I wasn't crying, but my pillow was slowly getting saturated by tears rolling from my eyes.

A few minutes later, my brother and his girlfriend came and sat by my bed to enquire what just went down as they said they saw her leave while crying.

I told them.

"Bitch!" my brother grunted, only to be nudge by his girlfriend to shut up.

He liked Michelle but, at the same time, never liked her because he thought she was just a "Miss Goody Two Shoes," which was just too good to be true.

His girlfriend made a long sigh before she spoke. "So one minute I laughed so hard I was crying because I was having the best pillow fight ever, and not even ten minutes later, this—tears for a totally different reason."

My brother consoled her, as he knew Michelle and her were forming a bond.

"So what now?" he asked.

Contemplative silence.

"Technically, he was her boyfriend. That's his alibi." She sighed.

I caressed the bandage on my head. "Now I need a beer, a smoke, and some fresh air. Let the chips fall where they may!" I said as I rose, dressed, got a beer and my cigarettes, and went to the front porch.

They gave me my space as I sat there for a few minutes, wondering if I should blame her or go beat the crap out of her boyfriend. I noticed our neighbor doing his gardening and cussing as he ripped thick batches of love bush from his side of the hedge and threw them into a trash heap.

Strangely, I halted my thoughts, walked over to his house with a greeting, and started helping him to remove the love bush, as I felt it was love lost.

CHAPTER 15

SEDUCTION

I had breakfast after and went back to bed. It was around noon when my brother was sitting by my bedside, shaking me to wake me up.

"What, yo!" I yawned as I finally awoke, shrugging him off.

"You got company, tiger. Get your ass up," he simply said as he rose and left the room.

I figured it was Michelle coming back to apologize again. I slowly became fully awake and remembered what happened the night before. I was semi-dressed when I went out to see Michelle—or so I thought it was her.

But it was Crystal.

What the what!

I could tell she was drinking, and then I did remember her saying she was going to come by on Sunday, so ignore that last "What the what!"

We chatted for a bit, and I told her what went down with Michelle and me and that we were officially over. Surprisingly, she scoffed and leaned over to kiss me. I didn't stop her. It was the very first time I was kissing a white girl. It felt different; I had my eyes opened, staring at her beautiful face. But then once I closed my eyes, she just became another pretty face I was kissing.

It's funny how color or race don't matter when you close your eyes while standing in front of the couple. But there are some racists out there that criticize these interracial relationships with their eyes wide shut, meaning they only see what they want to see from their own pathetic perspective.

The Unexpected

"Her loss, my gain," she said. Then she shocked me as she suddenly undressed herself, and then me.

Long story short, we made love. Yep, just like that, out of the blue. She literally jumped me! It was passionate. It was awkward because she was the last person I expected to be in bed with like this, so it was intense and awesome, like another trophy that my body won but my mind wasn't even competing for.

Have you ever kissed someone you never imagined you would in a million years? Worse still, you took that kiss even further and all you can whisper to your naked self while you're getting dressed all over again after that moment of passion is "What the what! I can't believe that just happened?" And then that "moment" that just "happened," although it shouldn't have in a million years, becomes your best-kept dirty little secret, which you try your best not even to remind yourself of.

Sigh.

I couldn't close my eyes as she took me, as each time I would see Michelle's face. It became rough and loud, as I guessed I just wanted to vent. She was also having her own moment. It went on for quite a while until she and I both hit the ultimate moment of lovemaking.

We lay in bed, breathless, for a while. We both took a shower afterward. As I stood in the shower with the water spraying me, I asked myself if this was going to be my new love, but my heart was still on Michelle. Crystal confessed that I was her first black guy, so her curiosity about being with a black man fuelled the secret crush she had on me. I was maybe just a fantasy of hers—nothing more.

Sigh.

We went out back to sit on the swings, and Crystal had a look of regret on her face, too, about what just happened.

"You okay?" I asked.

"No." She sighed.

There was an uneasy silence as she slowly swung.

"I'm listening," I said as we both lit cigarettes and had a beer.

I knew there was something she wanted to tell me or, as we say, "get off her chest," so I zipped my mouth closed and just listened. I learned at a very young age that sometimes it was okay to just shut up and listen!

"I have been in this country for a year and three months as an exchange student," she started. "Guys have hit on me every single day since maybe because I'm a white girl and their fantasy or because everyone wants to date a cheerleader. But since I have been here, in over a year, I never once even kissed another guy because I promised my boyfriend back home, the love of my life, whom I hope to marry one day and start a family with, that I would never cheat on him. That's why I started going to church instead of the nightclubs and bars to keep myself safe and to honor my promise. But he has gotten distant of late for whatever reason he's not telling me. I became a confused soul. And then came you, and then you made me break my promise just now, willingly. And now I'm just confused whether to blush at the fact that I slept with you, Street, my break dance idol, whom every girl wants to be with, or whether to regret it because I cheated on my boyfriend." She exhaled heavily.

There was an uneasy silence between us, as I had no plausible response.

"I have to go in a minute, as I have to call him," she said as she rose and went to her car. She came back a couple of minutes later, cursing at herself.

"What?" I queried.

"I was all about coming to see you, so I left my damn phone at my girlfriend's house," she explained, in deep thought. "They were having a brunch party. Not even sure where I left it. Shit!"

"I have to go. She's an hour away, and I have to call him. I call him every Sunday, so he's expecting my call as we speak. Shit!" she screamed.

"There's a phone booth a couple minutes from here that you could use," I suggested. "Just tell him you left your phone at your girlfriend's house."

She thought for a moment and then agreed. She drove us to the deli to get quarters, and then I directed her to the phone booth. A familiar face, the old lady, just finished her call, and we greeted and wished each other happy holidays.

Crystal went into the phone booth and closed the door and made her call.

To Each His Own

I lit a cigarette and paced the lot, momentarily glancing at her. She was conversing with her man with a smile as she caressed the phone booth. It went on for a few minutes until her demeanor changed, and to my shock, she started crying. I was tempted to go check on her, but I gave her space, as I could hear her screaming and cussing at him.

The conversation finally ended when she slammed the receiver down several times before finally hanging up on him and storming out.

She walked right past me without saying a word and went to her car and sobbed. I slowly got in as she sobbed and kept punching the steering wheel.

"Hey, hey! What's going on?" I asked out of obvious concern as I tried to restrain her.

No response. There was only silence, interrupted by more intermediate sobbing.

"Talk to me," I pleaded.

More silence.

"He...he...he told me that... He told me that he...that he met someone," she finally cried. "He just broke up with me," she cried.

What the what! I was at a loss for words.

"What the heck was his reason? And not making any excuses for him, but it's been a year since you two have seen each other. A whole lot of stuff can happen when couples spend a year apart from each other."

Silence.

"So what happens now? Kiss and make up when you go back, or is this the chapter in your life when you just walk away?" I asked.

After a short pause, she said, "I'm gonna finish my semester, go back home, and my brothers and I are gonna kick him and this guy's ass." Then she started the car and drove off.

"Guy?" I asked.

"Yes!" she said as she braked, pulled over, and resumed thumping the steering wheel. "Can you believe he dumped me for another *man!*" she sobbed. "It's bad enough if it was for another woman, but what's a girl to do when your man dumps you for another man?"

What the what!

I was in shock and at a loss for words as I gave her a moment to cry it out.

Wow.

"I always suspected he was gay or at least bisexual because he and this one friend in particular were too close for comfort every time I saw them together. He would even cancel dates with me to go hang out with him," she sobbed. "I'm gonna kick both their asses. Just watch."

"Hey, let it be. Us Jamaicans are very homophobic, so much so that, here, you get thrown in jail if you are openly gay. But I mind my business. Whomever or whatever you choose to have as your sexual partner behind closed doors is your business, just like how you made me swear after sex this morning behind my closed doors not to tell anyone. At least he came out and told you." I tried to calm her down. "Just look at you. You can get any man you want. They do a poor job of disguising it, but I see how the guys drool at you at church, so I can just imagine your fan club at school. You'll be all right."

There was a long moment of silence as she recomposed herself. She said, venting, "I'm no angel, Street. I have been beaten up for sleeping with this chick's boyfriend in high school. And me and my girls have beat the crap out of at least two or three girls in college for sleeping with my man. But what do you do as a woman when you find out that your man is…is cheating…is…is cheating on you with…with another man!" She sobbed uncontrollably.

I was stumped by that question. I had no answer, as I was just a teenager that didn't want to pretend that I had an answer for everything.

But then I remembered a chapter in the Bible.

"Just walk away and don't look back." I sighed, rubbing her hand. "Wish him, them, nothing but the best in life and let them work out their own salvation with fear and trembling. That will give you closure and peace of mind."

She stroked my face while still sobbing.

"Read Romans chapter 1, verse 27." I sighed. "Just walk away, and don't you ever look back, lest you turn into a pillar of salt. Against all odds, I went to church to find Christ all over again but got beaten the hell out of church and instead found you." I sighed again. "Just walk away."

"I'll try, but it's going to be hard! I've been with this guy from when I was thirteen. The only guy I ever knew, the only guy I ever loved…" She started crying again. "He took my virginity and claimed he couldn't wait for us to have our first child and a family. And now he's dumping me for another man."

"Hey, hey," I said as I searched her glove compartment, took out a couple napkins, and gave them to her so she could wipe her eyes and blow her nose. "So what about us?" I asked, thinking that a new relationship was in the making.

"There's no *us*, Street. You can have Michelle," she said as she wiped her nose, sniffling.

It was not the answer I wanted, but knowing her turmoil, I decided to give her space and some time to have this conversation again in the near future. There was silence for the rest of the ride as she took me home.

"You not coming in?" I asked as she pulled up to my house.

"No. I need some space. I'll probably go sit by the river and just breathe a bit and absorb all that I just heard from that bastard," she said as she patted my leg and wiped her eyes.

"When can I see you again?" I asked.

She shook her head with an "I don't know" gesture. "I dunno. You were fantasy—the first black guy I have ever been with. I slept with Street! Wow!" She laughed and cried at the same time. "But there is more to love and life than fulfilling a fantasy!" she replied. "Don't feel bad, but while making love to you this morning, he was on my mind the whole time. I gave my body to you, but my mind knows I was cheating on him. I was experiencing physical pleasure in the midst of mental turmoil." She sobbed. "But for what it's worth, you're an awesome guy, and I'll never forget you."

"So are you saying this is it?" I asked.

"Street, please! This is too much too soon for me," she said with a heavy exhalation. "Plus…"

Silence.

"Plus what?" I asked.

"Plus…plus my parents would never accept the fact that I was dating," she explained with a heavy sigh, "that I was dating a…that I was dating a…a black guy. I'm sorry, but this will never work between us." Tears were streaming from her eyes.

There was embarrassed silence from my end, while she sobbed.

"I have to go," she said, as she started the car again, and started sobbing again, leaned over, kissed me and just held my face against hers for a moment. I got out of the car and she drove off.

As I stood there watching her drive off and wiping her tears from my cheek, I was beside myself all over again.

Wow! So first her boyfriend cheated on her with another, not woman, but man. Her family would not accept me because of the color of my skin. And Michelle slept with her so-called ex; yes, my beloved Michelle.

I looked at Assad's house, and down the street to Stoke, and Bob's house, and asked myself, where did my once happy, simple life go? And then I noticed that the love bush started growing on my side of the hedge.

Take Me

Hours later, I was home alone, in the living room watching TV and having a beer and smoke when I heard a knock at my door.

I thought Crystal had changed her mind and come back to spend some more time with me. But it was Michelle.

With all that just happened with Crystal, my mind was just in a swirl, so I let her in. We talked for a bit, or it was more like she talked for a bit, being very apologetic.

"Just shut up and kiss me!" I said to shut her up.

She complied.

I rested the cigarette in the ash stray and put my beer down, and we started making out passionately. To my surprise, she started to remove her clothes and then mine. Eventually, she was down to only her panties, and I was down to only my boxers when she finally gasped the magic words.

"Take me!" she said as she held my hand to her naked breasts. Tears streamed down her face. "I have failed God. I have failed you. I have failed myself by him having sex with me. I am a sinner. I am nothing. And I give up," she cried.

I hugged her as she wept.

"Why did God allow this to happen to me, especially on a mission doing His work?" she sobbed. "All I wanted to do was make Him proud of me and do His will for my life, which is why I became a missionary—to save and win souls for Him instead of becoming a cheerleader on the side, like some people I know."

I stayed silent.

"And why did God allow this to happen to you, Street? I saw your heart, and all you wanted to do was come back to church," she continued, looking at my bruised face. She sobbed uncontrollably for a moment. It was clear that she doubted her faith.

"All I ever wanted to do was be in break dance champions, make my mom and brother proud, go back to church, and last but not least, find and settle with the love of my life." I sighed.

We were silent as she cuddled me.

"The first ambition, us Street Boys have achieved," I continued. "The second is so far, so good. The third…" I paused. "The third I attempted but may not happen again anytime soon. And as for the fourth…then came you."

Silence. Then she cuddled me even tighter.

"Take me!" she again ordered as we kissed passionately. "I have failed! But I don't want to fail you."

"No! God is still and will always be with you. Always! Even when at times you can't make sense of the bad stuff that's happening to you," I said as she sat in my lap, and I gave her a bear hug and had her bawl it out. "You might have stumbled in a situation that you had no intentions of being in, but you didn't fall from grace."

What the what! Was I preaching here when the love of my life was almost naked and just asked me to take her? Yet I resisted?

Have you ever had a moment when you just wanted to bitch-slap yourself because you couldn't make sense of your actions?

Sigh.

She eventually calmed down and recomposed herself. "So do you want to? I've always hoped that you would be the first," she asked with a trembling voice as she hugged herself. "You will still be my first—that I remember."

"Yes. But not like this. Don't make love to me out of duress," I replied.

"Just make love to me." She sighed as she stood, took my hand, and led me to the bedroom. We made out some more on the bed until things finally started getting heated. But then she stopped me with one word.

"Condom," she simply said as a tear rolled from her eye.

I paused. "Are you sure you wanna do this?" I asked as I wiped a tear from her cheek.

"Just take me," she said, giving me a gentle shove to go get it, and then she closed her eyes.

I got up reluctantly to go get a condom as I knew her mind wasn't in the right place. But hey, this was the moment I had been dreaming of. I checked my drawer. I was out. I went to my broth-er's room and checked where he usually kept his. He was out too. I checked the living room drawers, where we would keep some for girls that wouldn't even make it to the bedroom before things got hot and steamy. But there was none also.

This went on for a few minutes until I just paused and won-dered, *What are the odds?*

I decided to go get a pack at the deli and went into my room to tell her, but she was falling asleep. I just gazed at her beautiful body for a while.

Okay, correction: Michelle was a 10, but Crystal was a 9, and I felt like I won the lottery because here I was, about to make love to the both of them in the same day.

Wow!

She was lying on her side, so I lay down and hugged her from behind. She pulled my arm over so I could hug her closer. We just lay there for a bit.

"I didn't find any," I finally whispered as I kissed the back of her neck.

"They are in my bag on the sofa. I picked up a pack on the way over." She sighed, falling deeper into sleep.

"You wanna go get it?" she whispered.

I took an eternity to answer before I finally did.

"No. Not yet. Not like this," I said as I hugged her tighter.

There was a moment of silence until she burst out crying again.

"Thank you," she sobbed. "You're a good man, Street. I feel safe with you," she continued as she squeezed my hand.

Long silence.

Isn't it funny how you can be wishing for something for the longest while and yet when the opportunity comes, for whatever reason, you decline?

Hmmm.

"They have football practice every Wednesday evening at five, on the school soccer field next to our church. This is not the church ground, so do whatever you have to do to get justice for yourself and for what that bastard did to me," she said and then dozed off.

She finally fell asleep, and I must have dosed off with her because nothing happened. Yes, nothing happened.

Rainy Day Brawl...Postponed

A few days passed. I told my brother and Willy about my plan of revenge. We were on Christmas break from school. Wednesday evening finally came. It was raining like crazy, but true to Michelle's words, there were the Sardonyx and some other guys playing six-a-side soccer in the downpour.

I rode with my brother and his girlfriend. He had another car with five of his bicycle crew following behind us. The plan was simple, but it didn't go down as planned.

We parked. I got out, pulled my hoodie over my head, walked over, and sat on a bench in the mini stand on the sideline of the field. They didn't recognize me as I watched them play, waiting for my moment. A thunderstorm was looming closer and closer, and they would cheer each time a thunder clapped.

I was alone, but across from me by the other mini stand were a group of girls laughing and chatting and cheering the Sardonyx on. To my surprise, one of the girls, also wearing a raincoat hoodie, jogged over to me.

"Hey," she said as she sat and lifted the hoodie off her head.

It was Crystal.

"What are you doing here?" she asked.

I was caught off guard, so I had to think fast, as I was surprised to see her.

"How did you know it was me?" I asked.

"Who else wears gold sneakers?" She laughed as she used her shoulder to playfully shove me.

"Umm, I...I came to... I came to watch practice," I lied.

"To watch who practice—me or them?" she asked, unaware of my true intent.

"You. Just wanted to see you in action as a cheerleader."

"Well, definitely not today with this thunderstorm." She laughed before letting out a scream as another thunder clapped.

"I think they gonna call the match in a bit, and we all come back tomorrow, same time," she said.

I exhaled heavily, as I figured my next move. She screamed again and hugged me as thunder rang out, and she pointed at the lightning bolt in the distance.

The Sardonyx and the rest of the soccer team called the match off, chatted a bit, and then all ran to their respective cars. And yes, these buggers all drove cars, owned by their parents or whoever, yet I rode the bus.

Jealousy? No. Envy? No. So what is it then, Street? I questioned myself. These spoilt rich kids thought they owned the world and that they owned church and could do what they wanted with whomever they wanted. And I was gonna prove them wrong; I was going to crumble their Sardonyx empire.

Yes. I was talking to myself.

Haven't you ever done that, like you were two persons in one, arguing or reasoning back and forth?

To be continued, I guess. I exhaled.

It's funny how these guys were there laughing, playing, and enjoying a soccer match, not even aware that my boys and I were present, waiting for the right moment to give them the beat-down of their lives. We had all been there—just going about our daily routine, doing our thing, and then out of nowhere, boom!

"Are you even listening to me?" Crystal asked with a chuckle, as she realized my mind had drifted.

"I have to go. And you should go too," she said as she started to get up. "I know you guys have your hurricane season every year, so you're probably used to this. Rain, I can handle. Thunderstorms, I don't think so." She laughed as she put the hoodie back over her head.

Her wet hair was all over her face. Damn, she was beautiful, even with smudged make-up caused by the rain.

Okay, fine. If Michelle was a 10, Crystal was a 10 too. I couldn't decide!

"Come home with me," I abruptly said as I took her hand.

"Wait, what?" She giggled, as I had caught her off guard.

"Let's grab some beer and go chill at my crib," I said as I gently squeezed her hand, "one last time."

"Street," she begged as she squeezed my hand back. "Please."

"One last time," I begged, gazing into her beautiful blue eyes as my mind switched off from fight mode.

"Stop. We talked about this," she said as she released my grip. "You're killing me." She then laughed. "Go home, get drunk, and don't get struck by—" Another scream as thunder clapped and interrupted her sentence. "And don't get struck by lightning," she said as she laughed and ran off to her friends, who were beckoning to her.

"One last time!" I shouted.

She stopped, turned, and stared at me for a second, shook her head with a smile, and then went to speak with her girlfriends. I stood there for a moment, watching her chatting with them as the rain beat down on me. They all eventually went to their respective vehicles.

Nobody had driven off yet.

I slowly walked over to where my brother and his girl were parked. He got out of the car. His friends from the other car got out, too, and took the "attack stance" as we had a chat in the pouring rain, as they figured it was show time.

"What's going on? You still wanna do this?" G asked.

I thought for a moment.

"They will be back tomorrow. Let's save it for tomorrow." I sighed.

"You sure you just don't want to get this over with?" he asked as he handed me his cigarette and huddled his baseball bat under his arm. "Look at those punks. We can take those fools out in less than a minute," he growled with a deadly gaze at them as the Sardonyx, and a couple other guys were all goofing around in the rain.

"Tomorrow. I asked Crystal to come over," I said as I took a couple of puffs from his rain-speckled cigarette and then tossed it aside. "My fight mode is shutdown."

My brother cracked up.

"So one minute you came to fight, and the next minute you wanna...?" he started asking as a car pulled up behind me.

It was Crystal.

"Okay." She simply smiled in a sad way as she rolled the window halfway down, "One last time."

My brother caught on and went over and talked briefly with his boys. They all hopped in and left.

"We'll be right behind you," I said as we dabbed, and he hopped into his girl's car.

I rode with Crystal.

He arrived home first. We checked the mailbox, and we all went in and got dried up. My brother's girlfriend and Crystal chatted for a bit in the kitchen while he and I stayed out on the front porch.

It was still pouring rain.

The Breakup

"It's a note from Michelle," he said to me as he handed it and sifted through the other mail. "Mom's allowance, and bills…"

I opened and read.

To my surprise, she said she couldn't see me anymore for a while. What the what!

She confessed to her dad about what happened with her ex in England, plus the fact that she and I were dating. He got mad and even slapped her across the face for disgracing him, if word was to ever get out. So now she was grounded indefinitely, and her dad planned to have the cops press charges against her ex for sexual assault.

Wow.

She ended by saying she would do her best to see me again as soon as possible, but if her dad had his way, it was going to be over between us.

Double wow.

My brother saw my demeanor as his girlfriend walked out and brought us two beers.

She also noticed. "What's going on?" she asked as she handed us our drinks.

We didn't answer.

"Is she breaking up with you again?" G asked.

I didn't answer also but instead just took a gulp from my beer and handed him her note. He read it and then crushed it and handed it back to me.

"Bitch!" my brother then barked before being nudged by his girlfriend to shut up.

"What's going on?" she again asked.

Silence.

"Michelle. Again!" my brother replied. "But for what it's worth, Crystal looks fine for a fallback girl," he continued, gesturing slightly to my bedroom, where Crystal was.

"Wow. I don't know what to say, Street," his girlfriend said as she gave me a slight cheer-up hug and took a sip from my beer. "You succeed at break dancing. You kick ass in street brawls. You are excelling in college. But when it comes to love and church, you suck!" She laughed to herself.

This time, my brother was the one who nudged her to shut up.

"We staying the night. So let's just get into chill mode," G said. "Go start dinner, babe. I'll be right there to help." He nudged her.

They smooched, and she went back inside.

Silence. He and I just stood there gazing at nothing, just watching the pouring rain as we had a drink and smoke.

"Okay, so tomorrow, same time, same place to take down those fools?" he asked in revenge mode.

"Yes," I nodded.

As much as he knew, I was a badass who could defend myself. I was still his little brother, which, thanks to Mom, made him overly protective. He would charge to my rescue and fight you in a heartbeat if you messed with me.

"She staying the night?" He finally asked about Crystal.

"I dunno," I said with thoughts of Michelle still on my mind.

He left for a minute. I went to check in on Crystal. She was sitting up in bed, just in her undies and one of my T-shirts; she had hung her wet clothes on my clothes rack to dry. She was having a heated conversation on her phone. She gave me a look and gesture to give her some privacy to complete the call. I complied and went back out on the front porch.

"I think she is," I said, and G went to his room for a moment and then came back out to the front porch.

He jokingly squeezed my cheeks to open my mouth and then popped one of his blue pills in my mouth and then held my beer to my lips.

I took a gulp and swallowed it. He then handed me a pack of condoms.

"Forget Michelle, bro." He sighed as we sat. "I was right. Guess she was too good to be true, after all. You got more important things in life to focus on than church boy love."

Silence.

Isn't it funny how, in some cases, when you decide to just date random people with no strings attached, you are happy and calling all the shots, but the minute you decide to fall in love and settle with this one person, your "rewards" are doubt, drama, and regret.

Sigh.

Most of us have all lived or know of someone who had lived that regret. Yes, I said regret—when you find yourself at a stage in your life where you have *lived, loved,* and *lost!*

So that being said, it's not rocket science that not all marriages, love, and relationships will have a happy ending. And all of you can confess or relate to that statement! Correct?

I just stared at the rainfall. G handed me a $20 bill.

"I'll cash mom's money order tomorrow and give you your allowance, but this should keep you for now in case you two wanna go grab some drinks and such later."

"She's a high-end girl. She only drinks shots, fine wine, and champagne."

He reached for his pocket and handed me another $20 bill.

"Well, go get that fine lady whatever she wants. But that's a loan." He smiled with a nudge, trying to bring a smile to my face.

"What's up with that chunk of love bush on our side of the hedge now, bro?" he asked as we smoked and drank. "Mom is coming in a few weeks. Take care of it, because like you, I don't want to get a cuss out from her either."

I just gazed at the love bush, thinking that it was just a plant, another form of life that we choose to kill as humans either because they are a pest, a nuisance, a hunting game or because they put food on our plate. Sorry, I was always told that I was deep and had a bad habit of always overthinking simple stuff, especially in my current mood.

"Let's just get this over with tomorrow. I have a project I have to turn in, first week in January. Nine days. I need some time to stop skipping out on my study group and focus on that," G said as he gazed into the rain and puffed on his cigarette.

Sometimes I felt like a burden to him because he would at times drop everything and focus on my situation.

"I love you, you piece a shit," I said after a gulp and a nudge with my shoulder.

Silence.

"I can't stand your guts either, but I love you, too, you annoying li'l bro." He laughed as we nudged shoulders and toasted each other.

We were interrupted by Crystal, now donned in my pajamas.

My brother noticed her look.

"Hey, you doing okay?" he asked.

Silence.

"I need a drink. Do you have wine?" she then asked as she took my beer and gulped until it was finished.

"You know what. I do have a bottle of champagne that I was saving for Christmas dinner, bro. No need to head back out in this weather. You guys can have it but make sure you replace it before Christmas," he said as he rose and toasted me again.

"Let me leave you two alone," G then said as he stood and left, only to briefly return a couple of minutes later with a beer for me and a glass of champagne for her. "The rest of the bottle is in your room. You're staying for dinner. That's an order!" he joked, which drew a sad smile from her.

"Okay." She smiled sadly.

Silence. I knew she had a lot of processing to do in her head after that phone call.

"You wanna talk about it?" I abruptly asked, sensing her demeanor, as G left us.

There was only silence as she gulped her champagne. I knew she didn't smoke, but she still took my cigarette, took a puff, choked and coughed, and then handed it back to me.

More silence. Then I noticed a tear roll from her eye.

One Last Time

"I couldn't wait until next Sunday, so I called him." She sighed, referring to her boyfriend. "And that piece of shit had the nerve to again confirm that he and Trey were dating, as he just wanted to *explore* his sexuality." She broke down crying. "I cussed his ass out, hung up, blocked his number, and then erased it. I guess that is the last time I will ever hear his voice."

I said nothing.

"Can we go inside? I need a refill." she asked. "I could use a few shots, too, if you have any vodka."

She went to my room. I went to the kitchen and returned with a shot glass and a half bottle of Jamaican rum. She took two shots back to back.

I said nothing, as I empathized with her. She said nothing either as she refilled her glass from the champagne on my bedside table. There was a framed picture of Michelle next to it.

"What are you smiling at, bitch?" She burped, talking to the photo, and then she used her finger to tip it over so it could rest face down.

After the fourth or fifth, I took the bottle away, as I noticed she just wanted to drown her sorrow in alcohol.

We sat there for a while, just staring into the rainfall through my bedroom window, not saying a word, until she spoke.

"Take me," she simply said as she stood up with a bit of a wobble and started to undress. You could tell she was beside herself and very tipsy. She undressed.

Then she undressed me sensually and made her move, and unlike Michelle, I took her! Yes! I took her. We made passionate love together.

It was long and loud, so much so that when we finally ended and I exited my room to go shower, I saw G and his girlfriend in the living room, watching a movie. He threw a cushion at me with muffled laughter and gave me a thumbs up in approval to what they were overhearing coming from my bedroom. I showered and exited the bathroom. Then he called me over and handed me a letter he had opened.

It was from my college—our quarterly semester report. I held my breath. I had gotten straight As. My arms trembled a bit as I read it with joy.

"Straight As. Mom's gonna be so proud of me," I gasped.

"No, I'm so proud of you because…of what we heard coming from your room for the past hour was a straight A!" he joked.

His girlfriend nudged him with a smirk to shut up, and then she gave me a wink.

"Hey, Street, is it okay if I take a shower?" a drained Crystal asked as she slowly exited my room, dressed in my pajamas again.

She did, and then we all had dinner, chatted in the living room for a bit, and then went to our separate rooms. We had a few drinks, but as I lit a cigarette, she requested that we go sit out on the front porch for more ventilation, as she didn't want her asthma to start acting up. We did. She had a couple more shots and then a beer as we just casually chatted and gazed into the sporadic downpour. I was amazed at how much she could hold her liquor, as I would have been passed out by now.

"So what's your story, now that you know mine?" I asked her.

She gazed into nowhere for a bit, and after another shot, she finally spoke. "I got a scholarship for winning a cheerleading competition," she joked before turning stone-faced again. "My boyfriend was a gofer in a street gang. One night after a party, they jumped this rival gang, beat them up really bad," she started. "One evening, as I was walking home, members of the rival gang jumped me, tried to drag me off to this abandoned building, and—who knows?—gang-

293

rape me, I guess. That's what they do. They go after your family and loved ones first to make you suffer mentally and emotionally, and then they go after you."

Silence.

"Luckily, some coworkers from my father's construction site were passing by and chased them off. I told my father. He and some of them went for revenge. We gave them a good-ass whooping, but then came the death threats," she continued. "My boyfriend got beaten up really bad. He ended up in the hospital, where his now lover, Trey, was there every day by his side. The lame-ass cops' only advice for us was to leave town, as my father would be gone for weeks at a time, travelling all over the country to work at various construction sites, leaving me home alone, which the cops warned wasn't safe anymore. Dad agreed. We feared for our lives, so we did. I got this student exchange opportunity, and my dad, who knew that I was still a target for these gangsters, helped me to pack. And here I am. Three more years to go, and he said, by the time I get back, they would have found another town to settle on the other side of the country, where my mom lives. I think they're getting back together."

More silence.

"And that's why I am majoring in law—to become a prosecutor to rid our streets back home of these thugs when I return and to bring down the bad cops they have an alliance with. Because there are some fights you can never win with your fists, especially as a woman, but you can in a court of law. It's never just good enough to be a self-righteous missionary and try to be the blah, blah, blah savoir of all. Sometimes you have to fight!"

I thought she took a jab at Michelle, but I didn't dare say a word.

Silence.

She was right. But as the Bible said, "Having done *all*, stand." Well, "all" for me was to fight with my fists first in conflicts as a last resort, and then I would "stand," if things still weren't settled.

She stayed the night. We made drunken love all night. And yes, again she made me promise not to say a word to anyone, because there were people at church that were close associates with her parents and they would talk on a regular basis.

I made her promise me that she wouldn't show up for practice the next day. She suspected that I was up to something, as she claimed she didn't like Michelle's ex guts either so wouldn't.

The next day, we woke up around noon and made love once again—this time, without a condom. She was curled up in my arms after as she dozed off afterward. I brushed her hair from her face and softly kissed her. She stirred, kissed me back, and smiled, saying her parents would kill her but that she hoped I was ready to be a father if she got pregnant because we didn't use any protection.

Our eyes spoke to each other's between kisses, as there were no other words exchanged for a while until, with a yawn, she asked what time it was.

"Almost lunch." I smiled.

"What?" she said as she stretched and looked at the clock on the wall. "Shit! Shit!" she fumed as she staggered up and hurriedly started to get dressed.

"What is it?" I asked.

"I am late for my study group *again*. They're gonna kill me!" she said as she fought to put on her booths. Then she leaned over to kiss me, grabbed her bag, and ran out.

I wasn't sure if I would ever see her again, but I knew I had to, even if I was to return to church.

I must have just rolled over and gone back to sleep from my hangover because I was awakened by someone who playfully hit me with a pillow.

"Your young men will see visions, your old men will dream dreams" (Acts 2:17).

"Wake up, sleepy head," the familiar voice said.

To my surprise, as I turned around, I saw that it was Michelle. What the what!

I was still half asleep and at a loss for words as she playfully jumped on the bed and cuddled me.

"I thought you said I would never see you again." I sighed.

"I know, but dad said he would be gone all day, so I just thought I would sneak out and come see you for a bit."

I hugged her.

"Come, we don't have much time," she said as she sprung off the bed and quickly started to undress.

"What are you doing?" I asked.

"Why is my picture face down?" she asked, ignoring my question as she stood it up.

Think fast!

"Oh, aah, I must have knocked it over in my sleep."

She bought it, got fully undressed, and then removed my boxers. She climbed on top, and we kissed.

"How did you get in?"

"Duh! Didn't you show me where you hid your spare key under that brick by our lucky tree?" She kissed me.

"Wait, wait, Michelle, are you sure you want to do this?"

Too late, she took me!

"Hush. And let me take you," she said between moans. "We don't have much time, because my dad would kill me and then you if he found out I was here and we were doing this."

For a moment, I just gazed at the ceiling as she kissed my neck and caressed me. Why? Because I was about to break one of my golden rules by fornicating with a church girl. As I feared, God would give me an ass whooping for doing that, considering the millions of other women out there to choose from who were not interested in living a righteous life for Him.

I didn't know what I was thinking as Michelle, in between passionate kisses, gave me her all, so I in turn gave her my all after she reminded me that this might be my last chance ever.

I closed my eyes from my gaze, rolled her over, and gave her an even-deeper love. It was painful for her; she was loud and erotic as her screams filled the room. I was sure my neighbor from next door could hear her, as just a short waist-high hedge fence separated where my room was from where his backyard gazebo, where he always hung out, was located.

Our lovemaking was interrupted by a sound on the outside of my room window that alerted me. I glanced up for a second to see if it was my nosy neighbor being a peeping tom again by watching me in the act. Yep, I had caught him doing so before.

But to my surprise, it was Crystal.

What the what!

Before I could say anything, she spoke as a tear rolled down her cheek. "I left my phone," she simply said with a tearful voice as she pointed to the dresser with her eyes.

I looked, and it was there.

Everything was happening so fast, because by the time I could even roll off Michelle, my bedroom door violently swung open.

"Dad!" was all I heard Michelle scream as she sat up and grabbed the sheet to cover her nakedness.

"Get off my daughter! What are you doing to my daughter?" he barked as he pulled his firearm and aimed it at me.

What!

"I warned you!" was all he said with an angry gaze, as her screams not to do it fell on deaf ears.

I raised my hand and begged him also, but he fired a shot that hit me in the chest! I immediately jumped up, screaming and breathing heavily, clutching my chest as I felt it for the gunshot wound. Michelle was fast, as she was nowhere to be seen. Her dad was gone too. And how the hell did Crystal move so fast? I looked at the dresser, and both she and her phone were gone.

I was trembling, still checking myself for an entry wound and blood, but there was nothing. It then finally hit me that it was just a crazy dream I had when I fell back asleep after Crystal left.

Sweet sigh of relief.

"You okay over there, Street?" my nosy neighbor came to the fence and asked. "Sounds like you met your match this time and someone has *you* finally screaming and tapping out for a change." He chuckled as he pruned the hedge in his backyard.

"I'm fine," I said, trying to recompose myself.

I sat up in bed for what seemed like an eternity, still trying to recompose myself and wondering if I did get shot for real and had died and if this was my "purgatory white light" experience as punishment from God.

I awkwardly tried to get up using my bedside table as support, but my hand slipped, and I knocked the champagne bottle and glass over, which in turn knocked Michelle's photo over, breaking the frame and the champagne glass, which all fell to the ground.

"Really!" I sighed as I stood and accidentally stepped on a broken piece of the champagne glass.

"Ouch! Ouch! Ouch!" I griped. I leaned against the wall to remove the bit of broken glass that was lodged in my heel.

I saw and felt blood, I thought to myself, *so this must be reality, not a dream.* I sighed.

As crazy as it sounded, I had never been so happy to see myself bleeding, because I would have taken that because of stepping on a piece of broken glass any day versus being shot in the chest, as I was in that dream.

I dressed my wound and cleaned the mess up and realized I needed to get a replacement picture frame—or maybe not if I was never going to see Michelle again. I had a bad habit of using my lighter to simply burn pictures of exes I had broken up with. I simply didn't need the visual memories.

I checked both front and back doors. They were locked. I grabbed a beer and a smoke and went to the backyard, stopped at our lucky tree, and saw that the key was still there.

What a crazy dream!

I went for a slow swing. I just gazed into nowhere as I took a sip from my beer and smoked. I reflected on my situation. How could I have had sexual encounters with three women in a matter of months, yet here I was alone, swinging by myself and daring not to harbor a feeling of loneliness. I just started meditating.

And what was that sexual encounter with Michelle about in my dream? Was that me having a lustful dream, or was this God's way of saying that this was the only way I was gonna get some or "I am gonna get you!" But if that was the case, half his church members would be in trouble like me, because it was an open secret that even today millions of churchgoers fornicated or committed adultery with an outsider or, worse, a fellow church member. And yes, this included church elders and leaders.

Sorry. I didn't mean to ruffle any feathers. I just didn't want you to be so quick to paint me *only* as the bad guy.

Sigh.

Then I thought, Just because everyone else is committing a sin doesn't give you a pass or a right to join in, because that will be no excuse on the day of judgment when we are instructed to "work out our *own* salvation with fear and trembling" (Philippians 2:12).

Maybe I should just leave all church girls alone—well, except for Crystal, who never was really into church and all and didn't even wanted to be converted. Church was just her sanctuary so as not to be lured into other places to hang out at. That was still good for her, though, right?

And what was the meaning in my dream of Michelle's father shooting me? Was that or will that be a form of God's wrath for people who mess with his followers?

"But because of your hard and impenitent heart, you are storing up wrath for yourself on the day of wrath, when God's righteous judgment will be revealed" (Romans 2:5).

My thoughts were broken by a clap of lightning in the distance, as it started to drizzle. Rain was coming.

And why did her father, a preacher man, carry a pistol when countless scriptures talk about God being our protector and guide? So why would we have to protect ourselves then when God would be here for us?

And then I remembered the story about the time when the Roman soldiers came to arrest Jesus (John 18:1–11). Verse 10 speaks of how Simon Peter, who was easily Jesus's favorite disciple, drew his sword in protest, swung it, and cut off the right ear of Malchus, the high priest's slave.

Hmmm.

So for all of you who thought Peter was that skilled and precise, like a samurai swordsman, to just cut off his ear as a warning, you are wrong. Peter was devastated by the arrest and wanted to protect and defend Jesus at all cost, so he swung for the bastard's neck to chop his head off! But just like in these action movies, Malchus probably ducked sideways for his life, and the sword just skimmed his head, catching only his ear.

Simon Peter was a badass, but Jesus never judged him for his actions, which was why he healed Malchus; he judged his heart and admired him so much that, in Matthew 16:18, he said to him, "Now I say to you that you are Peter (which means 'rock'), and upon this rock I will build my church, and all the powers of hell will not conquer it."

Wow.

Maybe that's why I am still here, I thought to myself. I raised my cigarette to take a puff, but it had all burned out, leaving only a long trail of ash. I had been so deep in thought. Is there a long trail of ash in your life, based on your past, but for whatever reason, you are still here because Jesus sees your heart also instead of the long journey you took to get this far?

There was thunder and a sudden downpour. I ran in and got prepped for my brawl with the Sardonyx the next day. I prayed that God would see my heart, too, and not judge me for my actions tomorrow.

CHAPTER 16

RAINY DAY BRAWL

There was a heavy downpour again when I arrived at the playfield the next day, but this time, it was not a thunderstorm, just torrential rainfall. And yes, in Jamaica, on those days during hurricane season, as they called it, we would get heavy rainfall for several days at a time. No one complained about it, simply because the rain was as a result of the outer bands of a hurricane way out at sea that missed our island.

G and I had our game plan. It was just two car loads of us—my brother, his girl, and five of his thug friends. We pulled up on the opposite side of the field in a grassy area where the parking lot was. I noticed an unusually large amount of vehicles, considering the downpour, but I shrugged it off and watched as the Sardonyx had soccer practice against another team.

I flipped my hoodie raincoat over my head and slowly walked to a bench close to the sidelines and sat. Rain dripped heavily off the hoodie, covering my head, and fell onto my clasped arms and legs as I contemplated when to make my move. I gazed at the raindrops beating down on the mud puddles.

You don't have to do this, Street. You can get back in that car, lick your wounds, and walk away, a voice said in my head.

What would Jesus do? another voice asked.

Have you ever been in a situation where you literally have an argument with yourself over a decision, a life-changing decision, that your mind and heart are split over?

I remembered those cartoons where a tiny devil whispered in one ear about what you should do, while in the other ear, an angel from Heaven whispered the opposite.

Sigh.

Maybe that was more than just a cartoon.

Do unto others as they did unto you, I mocked the voice in my head, which was a powerful phrase us Street Boys used to get our adrenaline pumping just before a revenge street brawl. *So what would you have me do?* I mocked.

No response. I buried my chin in my chest and cracked my knuckles.

"Hey! Hey, Street!" I heard a female voice shout.

I looked up and saw a female trotting over to me. She was holding a hoodie over her head, so I didn't recognize her until I saw her ring. It was Crystal!

What the what!

"Hey!" She gasped as she stood before me, still holding the hoodie over her head.

"What are you doing here?" I started. "I told you not to—"

"Yes, I know, but we had cheerleading practice today. I couldn't reach most of the girls, so I just came to tell whoever turned up that it was cancelled," she explained.

I bought it.

"So now you can go," I urged.

"I will because this rain is crazy," she said. "But we don't start until three, so I'm gonna wait until then and I'm outa here."

"Just go now," I again urged.

She looked at her watch. "Why don't you want me here? I can sit with you and watch practice."

I gave her a look.

"Okay, okay. Eleven more minutes, and I will go." She sighed. "Can I sit with you until?" she asked.

I said no, but she still sat next to me.

"I said no!"

"Okay, okay! What's wrong with you?"

"I just came to watch them practice. Might join the team if I like what I see," I replied. "Go wait in your car. I'll be playing in these conditions if I join, so I'm good right here."

"Okay, guess I'll be seeing you around then," she said, obviously suspicious, as her demeanor suddenly changed because of my resentment. Then she slowly trotted off.

I didn't know whether it was coincidence or what, but as soon as she got near her car, the ball went out of play and slowly hit her car. I couldn't make out who it was, but a guy went to retrieve it and spoke to her briefly. She hopped in, and the game resumed.

The soccer game went on for another minute or so. I could hear them playing but didn't really watch them. My chin was again buried in my chest as I watched raindrops fill a mud puddle. And no, I wasn't enjoying the rainfall, but just like a predator in the wild on a hunt, I was just waiting instinctively for that right moment to pounce.

My thoughts were interrupted suddenly when the ball went out of play and came to a stop close to my feet. I reached over and picked it up.

"Hey!" a voice barked.

I didn't reply.

"I said, 'Hey, fool!' Can we get our ball back!"

Without looking up or replying, I let it roll from my palms into a mud puddle at my feet.

"You know what!" the person then angrily said, stormed over, grabbed the ball, and shoved me.

There was no backrest, so I fell off the bench backward into another puddle. He kicked the ball in for them to resume the game.

"Hey! Hey!" I shouted as he walked toward them. "You forgot to say thank you." I sighed as I took my hoodie off and stood.

Yep, that was the signal to my crew.

Fight

"You!" he said as he also took his hoodie off.

To my surprise, it was Michelle's ex. What were the odds? There were twelve guys playing six-a-side soccer, yet he was the one to come and retrieve the ball.

"What you doing here, punk?" he said as he spat. "Came for yet another beat-down?" He let out an evil chuckle.

"No. Just came to watch you sissies play with the hope of joining the team," I spat. "But you should let the cheerleaders play, and you li'l punks put your miniskirts on and go cheerlead."

He got mad and swung a punch, which caught me across the chin. I didn't see it coming.

"Is that all you got 'cuz your crew isn't here with you?" I asked as I spat blood.

"Oh, they're here. They're all here!" he shouted as he punched me again.

This time, I deliberately braced for it. Yes. I deliberately made him hit me twice *first*, because I could then simply claim self-defense, if the cops were to get involved, for the beat-down he was about to get. I spat more blood. But just when he was about to punch me across the face a third time, I saw it coming and went in for the kill.

I ducked his swing, stepped back, and gave him a powerful judo kick in the chest, which sent him flying back, crashing onto his back. His knees were up in the air, and before he could catch his breath, I rushed over and gave him an equally powerful stomp in his crotch. He screamed like a girl as he held his crotch and rolled from side to side, screaming for help.

"That was for Michelle!" I said as I steadied him and knelt over his chest.

I glanced to my right and could see all his buddies, twenty or more, charging to his rescue. I glanced to my right, and I saw G and his boys charging to my rescue. We were outnumbered three to one, but I didn't care. I didn't back down, because it wasn't the first time. I had about ten seconds or so to finish this church boy rapist off before an all-out brawl would ensue.

"Now say hello to my two best friends!" I grunted as I clenched both fists and pummeled his face with punches—right, left, right, left, right left, right left, right—until I was football-tackled off him by one of the Sardonyx.

Michelle's ex's was coughing out blood, and it gushed from his mouth and nose and splashed in my face. Good thing he wasn't a zombie, or I would have turned. And when I was tackled by his friend, I crashed face down in a mud puddle, so I was temporarily blinded.

Kicks, stomps, and punches rained down on me as I got into the protective beat-down curl. But a powerful kick to the back of my head left me semiconscious. With all the sound of the heavy rainfall and the sounds of intense fighting happening all around me, every-thing suddenly became peacefully quiet. I was not sure how long I was out for, but I started to drift. I could literally feel my spirit leav-ing my body until I heard someone screaming my name.

It was faint, but the scream gradually got louder and louder as I slowly regained consciousness.

I still couldn't open my eyes to see with the pool of blood and mud covering them, so I weakly rolled over onto my back, positioned my head to the heavens, and let the heavy downpour slowly wash my face. I opened my palms to get them washed also.

I was dazed, but it was working. It worked! After frantically wiping the dirt from my eyes, I could see again. I looked to my right and saw the fighting continuing around me, and surprisingly, the first blurred person I saw in the distance, who was on her phone, crying in a frantic conversation, was Crystal. She hurriedly got in her car and sped off.

I turned my head to the right and saw that my brother was down, so I knew I had to get back up!

Have you ever been in that situation where you were down and out for the count but then you realize there's someone down and out also, in a worse condition than you, so just when you think it's over, you have to muster up all the energy and courage to get up and con-tinue the fight all over again?

There were bodies sprawled out in the muddy playfield every-where, groaning and writhing in pain. G was fending off two of the Sardonyx. We never thought about bringing in all his seventy-plus vicious bicycle crew members because we underestimated the fact that these church boys could fight!

Don't ever underestimate your enemy, especially when you have no background check on them!

One of the Sardonyx members noticed me and, with an evil grin, spat blood from his mouth and staggered over to me. I tried to get up but had not fully regained my strength yet.

For someone who was so devoted to the church, the look on his face I saw as he stood next to my chest was a look of pure evil. He spat at my face. He gave me a devilish chuckle, mustered up all his strength, and then tried to stomp on my chest with his right foot, but with all my energy, I lifted my shoulder ninety degrees, which caused his foot to just graze me and hit the mud puddle instead. He was overweight and clumsy during soccer practice, so I used his own weight against him. I used both hands to grab and forcefully hold that foot in place, and then mustering up even more strength, I let out a mighty roar, positioned my right insole against his left ankle, and violently shoved it all the way back. He let out a thunderous fart and did a perfect split as he fell and crashed to the ground. He then screamed in pain like a girl's choir.

Remembering what he just tried to do to me and knowing that he had now been rendered incapacitated with strained or torn groin injuries in both legs from that perfect split, I scooped up two handfuls of mud, wobbled to my feet, spat at his face, and trotted over to where G, who had clearly lost his wind, was still fending off another Sardonyx.

The brawl started out as a three against one, but once they took out one of us, the ratio went in their favor, so we had to take them out faster in order to minimize how many of them we each had to take on at once. It was like a pack of wolves attacking seven hikers; if six successfully escaped, the entire pack turned on and attacked the last hiker. Luckily, we took out most of the pack before they could launch one final attack.

G was desperately fending off a Sardonyx member, trying to regain his strength, but his attacker saw me coming, so he charged at me and took a swing. Yeah! Good for G. I was a diversion, but I was still bleeding badly from my head wound, dazed, and a bit wobbly. I swayed back to miss his punch, but still not at full strength, I slipped and fell onto my back.

He quickly tried to take advantage and pounced on top of me, kneeling over my torso.

Big mistake!

Just because your enemy is down doesn't mean you've won. The fight's never over until not *you* but your enemy is down and out!

He growled and raised his arm to punch me. I didn't scream like a girl; I fought like a girl. How? In a split-second life-or-death situation, I gouged both his eyes with the handful of mud I had scooped up earlier and used my thumbs to violently rub the mud into his eyes. Then I shoved him off me. I got so mad I in turn mustered up some strength, knelt on top of him, and started scooping more and more mud onto his face. Then I started punching him, over and over and over again, with my elbows.

He started coughing up mud and blood at the same time and then passed out. I knew he had no fight left in him. I went to G's rescue as another church boy was attacking him.

These dudes were just defending their friend and themselves, church boy or not, and I could totally respect that. Just like in a boxing match, where both opponents hug and complement each other at the end of the fight, we were just trying to win too. Only this time, there would be no hugs and handshakes at the end.

He was the last of the Sardonyx crew standing. The downpour didn't allow him to hear me coming toward him from behind, but G glanced at me, which made him turn around. In a flash, I swung a life-or-death powerful elbow at him, which caught him on his chin, causing his head to swing violently to the right. I saw a tooth fly from his mouth as he rocked back like he was doing a salsa dance, and then he crashed backward into a mud puddle.

We beat the crap out of all of them. Even my brother's girlfriend was in on the action, beating and fending off one of the punks with her umbrella. He took off running when I screamed at him and he made eye contact with me. Strangely, others from the Sardonyx crew wobbled to their feet and took off running, too, after helping others to their feet. And yes, they didn't even run to their respective vehicles; they just scattered and took off running. To this day, I still wonder where they were running to. They just scattered everywhere. I guess in a flight-or-fight situation, if you choose to flee, you just run! Others were too injured to even stand up, let alone run off.

I looked around and saw that some of G's friends were tending to the two of ours that were still down. The fight was officially over.

I crashed beside G as the downpour became heavier. He just lay there as the rain beat on his face.

"Is there any more?" he asked as he turned his face sideways to spit blood.

Silence.

Have you ever been in a situation where, after being in a fight, whatever your situation or interpretation of that fight is, you still asked if there are any more enemies because you simply want that fight to be over with once and for all?

Sigh.

"No." I sighed in sweet relief. "Whoever's not licking their wounds took off running."

"For reinforcement?" He exhaled, mustering up his energy for retaliation.

"Nah. I've seen it all, bro. I can tell when during a fight, someone runs away for backup or to save their life. It's over!" I calmed him and then crazily lay beside him in the mud and just let the downpour massage our bloodied and bruised bodies.

There was a brief moment of silence as we recomposed ourselves. His girlfriend soon ran over, swearing, and she kicked another Sardonyx member who was still lying in the mud and writhing in pain.

"You guys okay? Josh is busted up really bad." She was gasping as she knelt beside us.

"Shit. I told him he shouldn't eat a whole large pizza and drink that many beers before a fight." G grunted and laughed as he spat blood again. "He was probably out after the first punch, but he can take a punch. He should have listened. He'll be all right," G said as he spat more blood.

There will be consequences in life if you don't listen to sound advice and take heed, even if it's comical advice, like not eating a large pizza and having beers before a fight.

She tended to him. He was in pain but eventually sat up. She then had me remove my hoodie, remove my T-shirt, and use it as a bandage to tie around my head to stop the bleeding. She opened her umbrella as a shelter and didn't care to be cute and just sat there in the muddy playfield with us as we scanned the battle scene. There was no more talking as I could tell we were all in our own contemplative mode. I was in mine as usual, as I sometimes was in the shower, but strangely, I didn't want to make sense of what just happened because it shouldn't have. After all, this was supposed to be a *playfield*!

But sometimes you just had to fight back to not be bullied, and if you couldn't win on your own, then you should get reinforcements and support so as to stop being bullied by any means necessary.

Have you sometimes been in certain situations where you just didn't even want to think or make sense of it, where you instead just wanted closure?

A minute or two passed before we were alerted to quickly stand to our feet by a car that sped and stopped nearby.

Oh, boy, reinforcements? I thought. But thankfully, no, it was the pastor along with a couple of deacons. And yes, Crystal was the driver.

The pastor was mad and brushed a deacon's umbrella away as he reprimanded us all on top of his voice and scolded us to leave and that there would be consequences for our shameful behavior. I was not sure who called them, but the cops arrived shortly after.

To my surprise, Crystal never once came over to check up on me, but instead she spent the whole time checking up on Michelle's ex.

What the what!

The pastor and two cops spoke to the Sardonyx boys first. The cops took notes, and then they came over to us for our version. By the look on their faces, our story seemed more believable to the point where one of the cops asked if we wanted to press charges.

I took a glance at G and then said, "Yes!"

Let them shit their pants for a bit and humble themselves, and then I will drop all charges, I thought to myself.

The ploy worked, as the pastor took the lead to ensure that there was never going to be another confrontation between us and the Sardonyx after that, with the threat of expulsion from church. The church was their hangout spot; it was their life, I was told, although they didn't quite live up to the expected lifestyle of being church boys.

We made eye contact with them as they were rounded up. We were instructed to leave first so there would be no road rage. They had a look of defeat and embarrassment. We had a look of "Bring it whenever you're ready for a rematch." We then left and eventually arrived home.

The Agony of Victory

Have you ever been successful in accomplishing something you set out to do but there was no celebration because your triumph came at a price, which gives you no reason to celebrate?

G was sitting on the floor between his girl's legs, having a beer as she dressed his wounds. I was in the other sofa, having a beer and smoke. We were all showered and were now being patched up.

There was only silence, and we were in a contemplative mood until G spoke.

"So, bro, I've seen you Street Boys fight before. Violent. Vicious. Bloody!" he said and then took a sip from his beer. "You guys are like me and my crew. Nobody would want to mess with us, or there will be blood—their blood!" He sipped his beer again. "You dance to win. You fight to win. But today I saw one of your new recruits, a Street Girl, showing how much of a badass she is, too, winning by beating a guy with, of all things, her flimsy umbrella! I thought only old ladies did that."

There was a brief silence, and then we all burst out laughing.

"Really, G." His girl laughed uncontrollably, slapping him, knowing that he was referring to her taking on one of the guys earlier.

"Look," she said as she showed him a broken bandaged fingernail, "I took out one of them by clawing the skin from his face. But after I broke this nail in the process, I just went for my umbrella and started swinging."

We all laughed some more, remembering the frantic crazy brawl, and gave her a high five because we all now knew what the saying "A sinking man will clutch at straws" meant. Anyone would clutch onto anything in a fight for survival.

She slapped him in the back of the neck after treatment, took his beer, and finished it. Then it was my turn.

"So what happens now, Street?" she asked as she dressed me and wrapped a bandage around my head.

Silence. We all returned to contemplative mode.

"No more church," I finally spoke after a meditative sip from my beer. "I will find other ways to make my peace with my Creator. Television evangelism maybe—I don't know. There is this constant 'calling' in my head that I am tormented by to make my life right with Christ, so I just want to make it right so that I can be at peace with myself and with my God. We fought and got our revenge for Bob. We fought and got our revenge for me today. But I am getting weary of fighting. I missed the days when all I looked forward to was to prepare for a break dance competition instead of now, where I prepare myself for yet another fight."

Even if it was for a just and reasonable cause, be it emotionally, mentally, or physically, have you ever just grown weary of fighting?

There was a long solemn silence to the point where G got up and returned with two beers for us.

Then I laughed. "I'm gonna go to school, keep on getting those straight As, make you guys proud of me—besides us Street Boys winning break dance competitions. Oh, and buy you a new umbrella for Christmas." I laughed.

Silence. Then we all burst out laughing again as his girlfriend started a playful pillow fight with us.

"Next time, pop the trunk, and get the crow bar or a lug tool. Anything, babe, except an umbrella," G teased as we laughed and horse-played some more.

"Follow your heart, Street. I love you like the little brother I never had to the point where I will fight for you and I will fight *with* you," his girlfriend said surprisingly, almost emotionally. "I know you. I see your heart. I wish I had this *calling* from Jesus that you are talking about, but I don't. Maybe it's not my turn yet. I'll wait. But until then, you keep on following in His footsteps, and I will follow in yours," she said as she broke down crying.

"Babe," G said out of surprise, and he dropped everything and went over to console her.

I didn't see that coming either. I reached over, took her hand, and gently squeezed it. She returned the squeeze as she sobbed in my brother's chest.

You would be surprised how many people, though they would never admit it, saw you as a mentor and their inspiration based on your, though not perfect, but positive lifestyle. I was surprised that she saw me as hers.

"You better keep your word about getting me a new umbrella because that one shattered with that last blow over that punk's head." She sniffled, laughing and crying at the same time.

Silence. Then we all burst out laughing again. It lasted for a moment, and then there was silence again, only interrupted by her sniffles.

Then she finally spoke. "No love lost, G. You are the love of my life, and I will ride or die with you too. But, Street, you are my inspiration! The passion and perseverance and will I saw you put into some of those break dance competitions gave me goose bumps out of admiration." She playfully thumped my shoulder. "Most people say, 'Que sera sera,' but I saw how badly you took defeat. I saw how jubilant you were in victory. And now all these fights. Yes, you lost some, but you always win the main events. It's like David taking on Goliath, but even outnumbered, you never once backed down. I can't tell you how many times I would tremble and cry all night until G got back on campus safely when I knew he and his boys were going to meet up to join you Street Boys for a brawl with some other gang."

G hugged her closer.

"I prayed for the day when he would never have to do that again—not to abandon you, but I, too, have gotten weary of all this fighting. I just want to graduate, get a kickass career, make my family proud, and have G walk me down the aisle. And someday make you an uncle and just live happily ever after." She sobbed.

The silence was filled only by her sniffles.

G kissed her and gently wiped tears from her cheeks. A tear rolled from my eye. I never saw G cry before, but he did a sloppy job of trying to discreetly wipe a tear from his eye too. Minutes went by as we just sat there in a moment of assessing and auditing ourselves and our lifestyle.

"I lost my faith after I lost my friend back then in church and after constantly playing my stupid game of proof test, where I prayed but God never answered." I chuckled sadly. "But you have always had an answer to my problems. And it was always the right answer. You and G have been my rock because of your inspirational words to me, especially each time you were dressing my wounds. And, G, with all due respect to you, knowing that I am a badass, I or us the Street Boys wouldn't have won half of our fights and street brawls if we did not have back-up from you and your crew. You have been my knight in rusty armor." I chuckled as a tear rolled from my eye.

They both chuckled as he hit me with a cushion.

"I love you, guys," I finally said as we huddled.

"I love you, too, my annoying, always-getting-into-trouble brother. And I love you, too, my princess," G said as he kissed her.

Heavy contemplative exhalations filled the room. There was only small instead of deep talk after that as we shook off the somber mood to get more drinks. G and I had a deep brother-to-brother conversation as his girl made us dinner. Interestingly, during the conversation, he told me that *love* had made me weak; *love* had made me lose my will to fight.

It finally hit me what it meant to be blinded by love.

Traitor

There was a knock on the door. I opened and saw that it was Crystal. She looked visibly upset but said hello to everyone, and then she and I sat on the front porch.

"You okay?" she asked, almost spaced out, as we watched the rain and listened to thunder in the distance.

"Now you decide to ask?" I replied as I tossed my old cigarette and lit a new one.

She didn't reply as she took it and had a puff. She then led me to the kitchen while giving G and his girl, who were watching TV, an empty smile. She instructed me to get her a drink and had a couple shots.

"It's my dad," she said after a third shot.

"Why did you stop to check on him first?" I asked, ignoring her comment.

"What?" she asked, confused.

"After the fight earlier, why did you stop to check on that punk first instead of me?" I vented.

"Really, Street!" she snapped. "Because he was right there. And by the time I was about to come check up on you, the pastor told you all to leave. Jesus, are you for real right now?" she cussed. After a pause, she said, "I'm going back home to Sweden tomorrow. Not sure for how long. It's my dad."

"What's going on?" I asked in an almost distant tone.

"He fell," she said heavily, "from a two-story on a construction site. Nobody wants to tell me the true nature of his injuries. All they said was that he keeps asking for me so I should go home immediately. Mom sent me a ticket for tomorrow night."

I remained silent.

"In this country, we ask on the phone if you're sitting down before we break bad news. In my culture, we meet up with you in person, so I fear the worst," she said as she started crying before taking another shot.

I just hugged her as I was at a loss for words.

"I'm sorry," I said with an even tighter hug of faith.

"I should go. I'll be on a plane heading back home in twenty-four hours, so I need to call my school plus so many other places and people, because only God knows how long I'll be gone for. Plus, I need to pack. I have so much to do. I am so distraught right now, Street," she sobbed.

I hugged her tighter, and then we exchanged a parting kiss.

"I have to confess. I betrayed you today," she cried.

I looked at her with curious eyes.

"Rumor had it that you were planning revenge with the Sardonyx. You confirmed the day when you told me not to show up for practice. These guys are my friends, so...so I gave them a heads-up."

"You're kidding me, right?" I asked out of surprise.

"Nothing that started from me coming over and even sitting down next to you to confirm your identity earlier was a coincidence," she said as a trail of tears streamed from her face. "I'm not a good girl! But I was hoping and praying that you guys would have just talked things over and finally make your peace with each other. But instead I will never forget that brawl I saw earlier."

I just stared at her in disbelief that she snitched. She tried to kiss me. I kissed her back.

"The kiss of Judas," I said as I pulled away.

She slapped me across the face.

"I'm not the perfect girl you thought I was. I am a hot mess, but I am no Judas!" she screamed. "You were more than a fantasy to me, unlike half these girls even here at church that wanted to be with you! I can tell the world that I have been with you many times, not for bragging rights. I did fall for you, Street, although dating you, a black man, is taboo in my culture! And for all I care, I could now be pregnant with your child!"

So just a quick "food for thought" question, before I get back to my story, what's your view on interracial relationships?

Silence.

"You guys okay?" G interrupted as he walked into the kitchen after hearing the commotion.

"Okay, I don't know what's going on with you two, but I thought we left the fight at the playground earlier," his girlfriend said, following behind him.

"We're fine. I should go," Crystal said, wiping her eyes. "The youth fellowship is keeping a prayer service at church for me tomorrow night before I head to the airport. Yes, news travels fast. It would be nice to see you there for—who knows—maybe one last time," she said as she rubbed my shoulder.

I didn't reply. She did a lousy job holding back more tears.

"I pray I will see you again and even be with you again. But it may never happen, because my prayers have, let's just say, never been answered." She sadly laughed and cried at the same time. "But if you make me a mom, I'll write to you and let you know, and we'll take it from there."

She kissed my cheek, broke down crying even harder as she exited after one final long hug, and then left.

Wow.

"What was that about?" my brother's girlfriend asked out of concern.

Silence.

"Bro!" my brother urged me to speak up.

I never mentioned the possibility of her being pregnant.

"Her dad is sick. She's flying back home tomorrow," I started. "She set us up today. The Sardonyx were expecting us, which is why they almost won. She snitched!"

Have you ever expected something to happen and even braced for it but when it did, you still flopped because you weren't fully prepared?

"Bitch!" my brother barked.

"Bitch!" his girlfriend, for the first time, surprisingly echoed at the fact that she betrayed us.

We both looked at her funny, as she was always telling G never to use the *B* word.

"We won the fight earlier, and based on what the pastor said, it's over." She exhaled heavily. "Let's just hope and pray that her father is okay. And let's just resume normal programming with our lives."

Silence.

We all made our plates for dinner. The rest of the night ended quietly, and the next night, I did attend church but purposely only did so at the end of the prayer service for Crystal's father. I had picked up a bottle of Jamaican rum for her as a soother and just had a smoke on the staircase until the service ended.

In my book, it was okay to forgive someone even after they betrayed or failed you based on the circumstances, especially when you knew you might never see them again. I had heard of many stories of people who had lost loved ones and grieved bitterly because they never had a chance to say "I love you" or "I forgive you" or even just to have a memorable conversation that was "happy" for a change.

I was at the back of the church, looking out for her, but had no luck until the church was empty. I knew she must have been somewhere, hanging out with the girls, so I just lingered patiently on the church steps. I soon got restless and decided to go to the back of the church to have another smoke. But then I noticed a couple passionately kissing.

At first, it was no big deal, but then my heart skipped a beat as it crossed my mind that it could have been Michelle, who had dumped me. And now Crystal was leaving for her home half a world away. Only God knows when, or if, I would ever see any of them again.

My thoughts were interrupted when the guy said something funny and then looked away from her and made eye contact with me. He held my gaze. To my surprise, it was Michelle's ex.

Okay, so my heart raced—until the girl with her strong Swedish accent said something and turned around to follow his stare. To my shock, it was Crystal.

What the what!

The bottle of Jamaican rum I had in a bag fell from my hand and shattered. She, too, eventually realized it was me. He tried to restrain her, but either in shock or shame, she shoved him off and ran to her car. He and I held an angry gaze at each other until he eventually walked off in the opposite direction so he wouldn't have to walk past me.

Crystal not only betrayed me but was intimate with this punk too?

Wow. My world was shattered.

I stooped to clean up the broken bottle, with my mind still trying to process what I just saw, when a car pulled up. It was Crystal, in tears.

"What was that?" I asked angrily. "Are you sleeping with that punk too?"

She didn't reply but just banged her head at the steering wheel in distress as she sobbed uncontrollably, used her cell phone to thump the dashboard, raised her head, brushed her hair from her face, looked at me in shame, and simply said, "I'm sorry. I lied. I was a gang member also with my boyfriend. I'm a very bad girl, Street. You don't want to know my true story, my child's father-to-be, if God's will be done. Just trying to do right, but it's hard, boo. I think I have lost my way," she cried.

"Did you sleep with him?" I dryly asked.

Silence.

"Answer me!"

"No. I just made out with him a few times to get back at that bitch Michelle to make her jealous. You got all of me countless times, but he just got a few kisses. He knows I am headed to the airport, so that was a goodbye kiss, which I now regret because you caught us," she said emotionally.

Wow!

So you felt guilty, only because you got caught?

"You are the only man I have ever slept with besides my boyfriend back home. Forgive me for what you just saw."

Strangely, I could be wrong, but I believed her based on her demeanor.

She removed her lucky charm hanging from her rearview mirror and handed it to me. "All of this is too much too soon. I will never forget you, Street. And I hope you will forgive and never forget me," she sobbed as she sped off.

"Crystal!" I said as she kept driving and burnt tires as she hit the road and sped off.

I just stood there, shaking out of shock that I caught her making out with the one guy I hated more than Willy's brother. I looked at my palm, at her lucky charm; it was a holy rosary. I threw it in the nearby garbage bin with the rest of the broken bottle and walked off.

I stopped halfway, looked to the heavens, and just exhaled heavily. I returned to the trash bin, retrieved the holy rosary, tucked it in my pocket, and left.

That was the last time I ever heard from her or saw Crystal again.

Wow!

Merry Christmas...or Not

My head was in a spin. In less than six months, I had four girls in my bed. I was in love with one and slept with two, yet there I was, on the eve of Christmas Day, alone and single.

Sigh.

I eventually got home to the house in darkness and a note from my brother on the fridge door. He reminded me that he was going to be away until New Year's Eve, as usual, as he and his girlfriend were going to be vacationing at their usual Christmas getaway hotel resort on the north end of the island.

I never had a problem being alone, but this time, I grew lonely. Have you ever been there?

I made a toast to Clair and Willy's girl. I was missing Michelle and had no comment about Crystal.

Christmas came and went. No one knocked on my door. I did not receive a single "Merry Christmas!" from anyone, not even my nosy neighbor.

The Proof Test All Over Again

"Jesus, full of the Holy Spirit, left Jordan and was led by the Spirit into the wilderness, where for forty days he was tempted by the devil. He ate nothing during those days, and at the end of them he was hungry" (Luke 4:1–2).

Have you ever been going through some situations where the only company you want to be around with is "me, myself, and I"—in short, just wanting some alone time?

I was sad, and for days, I just locked myself in and drowned my sorrow in beer. I just lay in bed. The TV was on, but I never watched or cared to watch it; it was just on to add life to the house and drown out the deafening silence. I didn't even shower or groom myself for a couple of days, as I had no one to look clean or handsome for. Everyone handles depression differently based on their own unique situation. That was the first time I knew what it felt like to be depressed, based on what I was going through.

I slept it off.

It was on New Year's Eve, around 7:30 p.m., when I heard an annoying constant bang on my room window.

"Yo, Street! Open up, yo! I know you're in there! I can smell cigarette smoke in there," the voice persistently shouted.

I ignored, lit a cigarette, and took a sip from my half-finished beer. More banging. Then I finally answered out of frustration, because it was a familiar voice; it was Assad. I barely opened the windowpane, and he spoke.

"I see you had an early start to ring in the new year!" He laughed with a grin, thinking that I had some girl over and was why I took so long to answer. My room light was off, so he couldn't confirm.

"I'm home alone. So much for a happy new year," I scoffed as I chugged and coughed on my beer and smoke.

"You're alone?" he asked, surprised. "On New Year's Eve?" Then he chuckled. "That's a first! Okay, okay, I will share. Damn!"

"What?"

"I will share! Now just shut that hole up above your chin and come to the front door," he urged.

"What?" I again asked, trying to wake myself from my depressing slumber and make sense of his request.

He let out a frustrating exhalation. "You said we are brothers, right? So I will share one with you to ensure that you ring in the new year on a happy note." He softly barked. "Now get your ass to the front door before I go around and kick it in." He then marched off.

I wasn't sure what was going on, but I complied.

As I neared the front door to open it, I heard two half-drunk female voices questioning him about where he went and what took him so long, only for them both to be smothered by his kisses.

I snapped back to reality. Now I knew what he meant; there were two girls on my front porch with him, and he was willing to give one to me for the night. But instead of being excited, I freaked out. I looked a hot mess. I had not shaved or showered for days; plus, there were empty beer cans and delivered food containers everywhere. There was no way I was going to let them in.

Have you ever felt ugly? The devil is a liar! You're not! It takes a lot of self-motivation to convince yourself when you look in the mirror that you are one of God's most beautiful creations. All you have to do is believe!

The lights were off, so in order for them not to see me in my sorry state, I made sure to quietly put the security door latch on and then crack the door open.

"There he is!" Assad finally said as both girls groped him and kissed him all over. "Ladies, this is my 'brother,' Street, official leader of the Street Boys—from those stories and pictures I showed you." He gently shoved one of them forward. I guessed that was the one he was going to share me with me for the night.

"Oh my gosh, it's you! I've heard so much about you, Street." She giggled as she beckoned me closer and stroked my unshaved cheek.

"Open the door, yo!" Assad laughed and wondered why I wasn't letting them in.

I smiled and bowed my head in embarrassment at the opportunity that was standing right before me and then raised it with an ever bigger empty fake smile.

Have you ever done that when an unexpected chance caught you off guard? Have you ever spoken to someone by choice through a closed door?

Sigh.

"NCD, bro, HM," I said to him in code, meaning "No can do," as in I couldn't because of HM, which meant that my place and, worse, myself were a hot mess. "Your place. Give me an hour!"

He gazed at me with a shock, blank stare, hoping that the girls wouldn't pick up on our coded conversation.

"NCD. HM for me too, bro," he grunted, saying his place was a hot mess too.

Okay, so let's be honest here. Have you in the past refused to have an uninvited guest enter your dwelling because you were unprepared and because, in your view, the place was messy?

In the past, us Street Boys took that chance with girls, and some saw the mess, were turned off, and abruptly left. Lesson learned!

"What's up with all these army terms, guys? I need a drink," one of the girls said.

"And I am so disappointed," the one closest to Assad said with a devilish glance at me at her being uninvited in. She wobbled off down my driveway.

He beckoned to her, but she ignored him. The other girl, who was her friend, went after her.

"Damn. You're a hot mess," he said, noticing me through the darkened silhouette. "I'll buy you some time and go get some more drinks. One hour and I'll be back! Get your shit in order until, Street!" he ordered before he went to meet up with them, and they all left.

I had never cleaned up so fast. I even found time to dust and wipe up beer splatter. I showered, groomed, and put some music on. I even snuck into my brother's room, took out and lit one of his "groovy" candles, popped a beer (but didn't light a smoke to kill the aroma), and waited.

But an hour passed, and they never came back. I waited another forty-five minutes or so, but nothing.

I finally went by his house, which was in total darkness. I called out for him in our special call code beckon, but there was no answer. I was sad as I guessed that they were having so much fun that they forgot about me after. So I left.

Assad later confirmed some days after that he hadn't taken them back over to his messy place but instead stopped by the corner deli, grabbed some drinks, and then went by the open lot by the now-infamous phone booth, which was quiet with just a few people waiting to make calls. He had no way of reaching me, so they pulled up in a poorly lit corner near the phone booth. The three of them had some beers, and then one of the girls surprised him by lighting and passing around in circles her marijuana. Afterward, all three of them just got down and dirty until his car windows all became hot and steamy.

I went back home and had a few beers, and it was around 10:50 p.m. in the night when I finally decided to drag my butt off the sofa and then headed out to a club to ring in the new year.

By around 11:25 p.m., I was at my usual club, where I had met the devil in the red dress. Remember her? Willy's girl?

It was packed as expected. I was a familiar face there with VIP access and all as the manager frequently used us Street Boys to get sold-out nights by having us on the roster to perform. But tonight there were no Street Boys, just me, and I didn't even have a date. A lot of our fans came over, and we exchanged well-wishes and cheers. But it all felt so empty, as I soon got weary of greeting them with a "plastic" smile.

A few girls, one after another, came over and wanted to hang out with me, but I politely turned down their advances. Both Crystal and Michelle had hurt me. I wasn't looking for sex or a date that night. In fact, during those hours, I wasn't even sure what I was looking for.

Have you ever been there, where you had so much on your mind that, to appease yourself, you dress and leave the house to take a drive or walk to nowhere?

Sigh.

After a few beers, I went outside, lit a cigarette, and stared at the night sky. It could have been tipsy from having one beer too many, but I saw a shooting star and made a wish. And then I played my stupid game again.

"God, if you can hear me, save me! And send me a beautiful woman that I can take home tonight, because your own Word in the Bible says, 'It's not good for man to be alone,'" I whispered.

There was nothing in response for what seemed like an eternity.

But God was not to be mocked! At least eleven girls hit on me earlier that night who would have been more than willing to come and spend the night with me, yet I turned down their advances, and there I was, toying with God again with this stupid proof test!

I waited, and nothing happened.

"Fine. Forget you then," I finally said to God because I was tipsy and not thinking right as I drank and smoked. "Devil, if you can hear me, send me a—" I then started a few minutes later, but I was interrupted by a young lady.

"Please tell me you don't have a date tonight, because I could use you as mine," she said as she walked up.

She was my type—body, pretty face, and all. But something was off, although she did look sexy in her glittering mini dress.

"I don't!" I smiled.

"Well, now you do." She smiled as she took my cigarette and smoked.

"What's your name?" I asked, trying to start a conversation.

"Everyone calls me One Hundred Dollars because with that, you can have whatever you like." She puffed as she groped and tried to kiss me.

Our lips met, but then I backed off.

"I'm sorry, I'm not that guy." I chuckled. "I don't pay to play."

"Really! You college kids pay my bills because every night you wait in line to take me, one after another. So what's *your* problem?" she scoffed.

"Why don't you pay me to take you?" I bragged in an uncaring manner as I took out another cigarette.

"Probably can't afford me anyway," she scoffed as she got mad and walked off to two other guys several meters away that were smoking and checking her out.

I smoked and sipped on my beer. For whatever reason, I watched her as she took the cigarette from one of them, puffed on it, and then kissed the other, who reached for his wallet, counted out some cash, and gave it to her. They both hugged her while laughing and chatting, and all three of them walked off and disappeared into a dark back alley.

I soon got disgusted at the loud moans and groans from what they were doing back there that followed after. I had seen and had enough for the night, so I walked to the bus stop and waited, as buses ran all night because of the occasion.

It was close to midnight, so based on my mom's old tradition, I did the inconceivable and decided to ring in the new year by stopping by at church.

Really, dude!

The bus arrived. I paid and entered, looking for a cozy seat, as half of them were empty. A familiar face, sitting two rows from the back caught my attention. He did promise me he would never take the bus again, so I tried to muster up fight mode. He didn't notice me, and he looked bruised like he was in a fight. But I learned a long time ago to look the other way at times so as not to draw attention to yourself from someone who was battered and bruised because they might just snap and take out their vengeance and revenge on you.

I looked the other way and made my way to the back seat. He noticed me and, with an awkward smile, patted the empty seat beside him as a gesture for me to sit.

It was the bus thief.

I thought that time at church at the altar was the last time I would ever see him, but here he was again. I figured he had ditched his bicycle and was back to his old ways of robbing unsuspecting passengers on a bus and got beaten up by one of them.

Sigh.

Still, I sat beside him. "I thought you said no more busses because you bought a brand-new bicycle?"

"I did. But it broke." He laughed as I glanced through the corner of my eyes at his bruises.

Silence.

"So what happened?" I finally asked as curiosity got the better of me.

Silence.

"Where you headed?" He finally smiled, ignoring the question.

"Church. You?" I replied.

"Church! Wow, that's cool. I want to ring in the new year with God on my side." He smiled even brighter.

Thoughts ran through my head. Every time I saw him on the bus, it was to rob someone, so I was quick to judge his intent. But then a voice calmed me.

Everybody has a past or a rap sheet, I thought to myself, *but sometimes, instead of being quick to judge, for our conscience and peace of mind, it is better to ask than assume, especially when the person is right there next to you.*

Silence.

"So what happened?" I again asked, glancing at his bruises.

He chuckled but didn't reply.

The bus's bell rang. An old lady across from us struggled to get up to exit. I saw him glance at her purse.

"One…" I started to count.

"Wait, what?" He coughed out of confusion.

"Should I count to three again?" I exhaled out of weariness.

"Three! Four! Five! Six! Seven! Heaven!" he snapped as he looked me dead in the eyes.

His eyes weren't sad and empty anymore. I saw faith and belief in them. I was about to say something, but he interrupted me.

"The Lord is the light of my salvation, so whom shall I fear? The Lord is the strength of my life, so of whom shall I be afraid?" he quoted from the scriptures. "Three. Three!" He taunted me to attack him.

There was silence followed by an almost simultaneous heavy exhalation from us both.

"What's going on? Look at those bruises on you? What happened?" I asked in tense anxiety at his response.

He spoke after a brief pause. "I was downtown two days ago, trying to pop a wheelie to impress some friends, and I lost control of my bicycle. I almost got ran over by an oncoming bus, so I jumped off, landed awkwardly, and crashed face down. I'm lucky to be alive, but my bicycle wasn't so lucky."

Silence.

"A wheelie dude?" I started laughing.

We both laughed some more as the atmosphere calmed, and he went on to tell me about his lifelong passion to enter the local annual bicycle Tricks and Wow Competition, which was coming up at spring break in a couple months, so he was just getting some practice in public. He said his girlfriend, whom he had finally gotten back together with, promised to get him a new bicycle for the tournament once she got her delayed Christmas bonus.

He was bruised but happy.

Have you ever been bruised but happy after losing that one last fight but finally winning the battle?

Ecclesiastes 9:11 states, "The race of life is not based on the swift; but who can endure."

Don't ever compare yourselves with others in the journey of life. Why? They might be running a hundred-meter sprint and might speed past you, making you feel bad, until you feel better knowing that you are in a different race of life, a marathon, and a few miles later down the road, you slowly jog past them to your destiny.

I believed him and told him my brother did attend that tournament but that I never did.

We burst out laughing some more as he explained how he flew off the bicycle like a superman to avoid being hit by the bus. He asked me to come as a supporter for the competition. It would be strange, as I was always the one on stage performing and being cheered on by supporters, but this time, it would be the opposite. I agreed with a smile.

We chatted some more on the ride to church, talking about stuff in general, until he brought up his girlfriend again.

"She's pregnant! One month."

"Damn. Good for you, man. Good for you!" I happily nudged him on the shoulder.

Strangely, he didn't seem happy. There was only silence from him until he again spoke. "She said after we broke up that she started seeing this other guy she met at a house party in your neighborhood," he continued with a heavy exhalation. "Says he had just gotten out of jail, so I knew it wasn't you. They had a one-night stand at the party, which turned into an affair. She was sleeping with both of us at the same time, trying to decide whom to settle with, because she had doubts about my sincerity that I had turned my life around."

I silently listened. "One night, he told her that he had another girl that was pregnant. She cussed him out, he hit her, she called the cops and had him kicked out. Haven't seen him since." He sighed. "So now she doesn't know who the father of her baby is."

"I told her I was the father no matter what, as long as she promised me never to be in contact with this guy again," he continued. "She promised."

I stayed silent as it crossed my mind that this other guy fit the profile perfectly of someone I knew—Willy! But I dared not say a word to connect any dots.

We arrived at church and candidly chatted as we walked in from the back as usual.

It was a few minutes to midnight, and as is customary, they announced altar call to ring in the new year. I sat at the back bench as usual, but he never sat.

"Wish me well! Today marks the first day of the rest of my life." He smiled.

"You going?" I asked.

"Yeah. To pray that this baby is mine and that I will live a happy, healthy, prosperous life ever after." He smiled. "Just trying to save myself. Just trying to be saved." He exhaled as his eyes got glossy. "Wish me well, my friend." He choked up.

My body shook at the fact that he was now calling or wishing for me to be his friend.

"I wish you well…my friend," I replied.

The choir was singing "Amazing Grace," which got me teary-eyed as he slowly made his way to the altar. I should have been making my way to the altar too. But unlike some people, I couldn't go to church for show or do things in church for show.

Strangely, that was the last time I ever saw him.

I sat in the back bench as usual and, for whatever reason, started praying a simple prayer—that the last time I wanted to see or visualize family, friends, and loved ones was by watching them walking to the altar, to God, to heaven. I prayed likewise for myself.

My meditation was interrupted by an old lady who asked if she could sit next to me. I complied.

Then she spoke. "Hello, young man. You probably don't remember me, but I am an usher here." She smiled almost nervously. "For the longest while, I have been haunted by that night when we were taking up collections and instead of putting cash in my basket, you offered up a broken knife."

It clicked, and I remembered her. I was at church after my first encounter with my now friend on the bus, who was now being a converted man at the altar.

"I kept picking my brain, wondering, 'What evil did you commit? Why have you come to church for forgiveness and offered up that blood-stained knife?" she asked worriedly.

After a short silence, I finally spoke. "I committed no evil. But I may have caused more evil from being committed because that knife was not mine."

She let out a gasp and a confused look.

There was silence between us until the prayers from those that went up for altar call filled the room as the organist played.

"Is it okay if I pray for you?" she politely asked.

I finally looked up with empty eyes and looked at her nervous smiling face. "Yes," I simply said.

She held my hand and prayed for me and asked me to repeat after her. I complied. I had made my peace with God.

The next thing I knew was that there were jubilant greetings of "Happy New Year!" ringing out in the church.

NEED FOR SPEED

Back to school!

School had resumed. Willy was out all week with the flu.

That Friday evening, Assad showed up with the rest of the turbo parts for his car. A couple of us, including our instructor, worked after school hours to install everything. And at the end, he started it up, revved it a few times, and took it for a test drive around the block. It was a monster car!

Assad was ecstatic and acted as if he had won the lottery. He gave me a ride home, but obviously, we didn't go straight home, as he wanted to take it on the highway and all to give it a good test run. I had never seen him so happy, as he was always the serious one in the Street Boys.

I laughed at his silly excitement, and we both had a beer from his cooler in the back seat and drove back home.

He checked on his home and then came over for another drink. We sat on the front porch and had a few beers and smoked as he told me about this private soldier at the base that he was dating. He showed me her picture. She was pretty.

He was happy, not just for his turbo car finally being completed, but also that he had a full-time girlfriend, as he was the type that just never wanted to settle. Plus, his parents were very proud of him.

I told him about the revenge brawl at church. He got mad at me for not "inviting" him…again. He saw my bruises, but I told him we beat the crap out of them and that it was okay to watch the news.

And then he asked about Michelle. I told him everything. He was sad for me. I told him about Crystal, and he was happy for me. But then I told him how it ended, and he was sad for me again. But he encouraged me that I had a waiting list of women.

True. But have you ever been in a situation where so many people are interested in you but that one special person that you are interested in shows no interest or has lost interest?

Sigh.

He had to go back to the base, so we had a parting toast. I shouted his name for him to stop as he hopped in his car. Then I went to my room retrieved the holy rosary that I got from Crystal from off my dresser, squeezed it in assurance, and then walked out to his car.

He rolled the window down as he started it and revved the engine a few times with glee. I leaned in and simply hung it over his rearview mirror.

"Really, Street!" He laughed as he played with it for a bit. "What is this?" he asked as he toyed with it. "Who drives a muscle car with a holy rosary on their rearview mirror? Get me a naked bunny or a scull and cross bone!"

We both laughed.

"You tried to enroll in the army. I tried to enroll in church. You were successful. I was not." I sighed. "Keep this in memory of my attempt. Let's just call it…your lucky charm. Drive with it always."

"Okay, bro. I got you. You know I'm not big on these Jesus pieces and stuff, but cool. You keep on doing what you do best, and *win*!" he assured.

We dabbed, and he drove off.

"Hey! I saw that," I screamed. Yep, he was attempting to take the holy rosary down from his rearview mirror while driving off. "You keep that up there, soldier!" I ordered, laughing.

"Okay, okay!" He laughed back as he honked his horn, gave me a peace sign, and sped off.

I just stood there and smiled as I watched him burn some tires as he sped off, took a swerve on a corner, and was out of sight.

My life was at a standstill. It was funny how you could watch some people getting by life in the fast lane yet you had so much going on that you were pulled over on the soft shoulder.

I checked the mailbox. There was a letter from mom, this time, it was surprisingly telling us that she was coming home for her usual break next week and was asking us to pick her up at the airport. I figured she and her cop boyfriend had a fight, as he always got her. I guessed G and his girlfriend would get her this time. Or maybe I could impress her and give her the ride of her life by having Assad pick her up in his muscle car.

Broken

It was Friday night. I was home alone, so I went to the corner deli to grab some beers and chips. To my surprise, I saw Michelle and her dad in there as well. She just said hello, and her dad and I spoke for a bit. He gave me an update about the Sardonyx and asked if I wanted to drop the charges against them.

What did I hear? It came to me as a shocker, but Michelle's ex was expelled from the church.

What the what!

Why? Of all the reasons he gave, I thought it was over the fights, but the pastor dropped a bombshell by telling me that her ex's father, who was the accountant at the church, was expelled after numerous audits confirmed that he was stealing from the church fund.

Wow!

They didn't get the cops involved. They just expelled the entire family as a mute agreement. The rest of the Sardonyx, maybe out of patriotism, also left.

Wow!

I was beside myself at the news, but I had known from day one that there were many wolves in sheep's clothing among us, even in the church! But who am I to criticize? Jesus, when pressured to persecute the woman by allowing the mob to stone her to death, simply said, "Let who is without sin cast the first stone" (John 8:7). Not a single stone was thrown!

Wow!

But the bigger "wow factor" for me was the fact that this woman, a sinner, was ready to be stoned to death, which was a form of the death penalty back in those days. But Jesus spared her life! Yet Steven—a holy, righteous man of God—was stoned to death simply for preaching the gospel's truth.

Why did God pardon a sinner and spare her life yet had a holy man that lived and served Him fervently die in the same manner, stoned?

> When the council members heard Stephen's speech, they were angry and furious. But Stephen was filled with the Holy Spirit. He looked toward heaven, where he saw our glorious God and Jesus standing at his right side. Then Stephen said, "I see heaven open and the Son of Man standing at the right side of God!" The council members shouted and covered their ears. At once they all attacked Stephen and dragged him out of the city. Then they started throwing stones at him. The men who had brought charges against him put their coats at the feet of a young man named Saul. As Stephen was being stoned to death, he called out, "Lord Jesus, please welcome me!" He knelt down and shouted, "Lord, don't blame them for what they have done." Then he died. (Acts 7:54–60)

Wow!

So does it really pay to live a righteous life only to be "stoned to death" in the end? Or should we just live a sinful life and be pardoned by God in the end?

Answer:

> He has brought back their wickedness upon them
> And will destroy them in their evil; The LORD
> our God will destroy them. (Psalm 94:23)

> Blessed are those who are persecuted for righ-
> teousness' sake, for theirs is the kingdom of
> Heaven! (Matthew 5:10)

I had always told fellow believers that when I got to heaven, it would be okay for them to run off and live happily ever after for eternity. But on day one, I would first request a one-on-one meeting with my Creator to make sense of this chaotic world and head-scratching consequences we endured in our journey through life.

Sorry, Lord, you did say, "My ways are not your ways," so you are going to have some explaining to do.

I could be judged for fighting and having all these street brawls and for badly injuring multiple thugs over the years (some even had to be hospitalized). I could be judged for fornicating with multiple women, even in the church. I could go on and on, but as Matthew 7:1 said, "Judge not, lest ye be judged." I was not a thief stealing from the church fund, but I was guilty of other sins.

The pastor asked me again if I wanted to drop the charges.

I simply said, "Yes."

He let out a heavy exhalation. "She hasn't stopped whining about not being able to see you," he said, glancing at Michelle. "We lost her mother three years ago to cancer. I haven't tasted another woman's lips against mine since then, because I chose to be celibate in her honor. I was stupidly hoping she would follow suit. I am alone but not lonely, as my li'l girl here has become my rock and I feel her mom's presence around me every single day."

I stayed silent, reflecting over his words.

"I have given up on hearing her soft sobbing at nights over you. She has told me—well, more like confessed—to stories about you two. If this is not love, then maybe I have forgotten what love is.

With that, I give you my consent to date my daughter, but with strict conditions until I walk her down the aisle, if you guys last that long. Conditions I don't need to explain—you already know," he said as he stared me down.

I stayed silent. Wow, I was jubilant!

"Understood," I simply said, exhaling.

They hugged, and he kissed her on the forehead.

"You two go spend some time together. Let me go start dinner," he then said as he slowly walked off. "Don't break your curfew, or the deal is off." He smiled.

There was silence between us as Michelle and I just stood there for a moment, at a loss for words. We just stared at each other, as if our eyes had deeply missed whom we were both finally staring at all over again.

"Hey," I finally said with a bit of emotion.

"Hey." She chuckled as a sad tear rolled from her eye. She twiddled her thumbs.

"God, I've missed you." I was shaken.

Silence.

"Did you miss me?" I teared up.

She burst out crying. "You have no idea!" she sobbed as she ran to my arms.

We embraced and smothered each other with kisses and bear hugs.

Several minutes later, we were back at my crib, in my bed, exchanging passionate kisses as we rolled over each other in bed. I attempted to remove her clothing, but she stopped me.

"Street! Boo, stop, please," she said, panting heavily. She was clearly aroused, yet still she restrained me. "Remember our promise to Dad. Until we graduate, start a whole new chapter of our lives, and he walks me down the aisle to meet you. Remember my vow to God when I became a Christian."

I rolled my eyes. She playfully slapped me.

"Then all this will be mine?" I asked, glancing up and down her gorgeous body.

She kissed me then simply replied, "Every inch of me."

We passionately kissed some more before I reached over to my bedside table and chugged on my whole bottle of beer to calm down.

"Nice new frame." She smiled as I rested the bottle down next to her picture. She wiped a smear from it. "You should get me one of yourself so I can keep it by my bedside, too, to kiss every morning when I wake up and at night before I go to sleep. Where are the condoms?" she then asked, noticing that the condoms she had brought for me to take her that evening were no longer on the bedside table.

I froze and had to think fast, as I knew I had used them all on Crystal. "G took them," I lied with a heavy heart.

"Have you been a good boy, Street?" she asked as she cuddled in my arms.

I drained my beer. "No!" I finally exhaled, with the intent to confess. But the strangest thing happened that changed the whole subject of me confessing to cheating on her.

"My dad did press charges about what he did to me in England. The cops cut him a deal not to be extradited back there for an even longer prison term. So he confessed. He's going to court for the judge to decide his fate." She trembled as she played with the chain around my neck, speaking about her ex. "And I know you haven't been a good boy. I heard about that fight with you and them assholes by the soccer field."

She eased up and checked my face, neck, and chest for bruises. "I heard you kicked their asses good. Really good!" She then chuckled. "I listened to the news—church news gossip! Everybody is talking about it, even though they are all now gone. You are now even a bigger hero at church!"

We kissed.

Then she continued, "I heard about Crystal too. I couldn't stand her guts, but she's in my prayers over her father's death."

What the what!

"Word at church is that her mom and family are so devastated by his loss that they want her to be with them and plan to file a petition to end her studies here and continue in Sweden. So the last time we ever saw her may very well be the last time we ever see her again," she continued.

I stayed silent.

"First white girl I ever met and got to know. Didn't go down well, as different cultures play by different rules. But I pray that for her sake that all will be well." She sighed.

Although I was lying in bed, my body shook and slumped as I hugged her closer on hearing the news and updates. We just lay there for a long while, cuddling and staring into nowhere, until it was time for her to go. I decided to walk her home, and as we headed down my driveway, she walked over and picked a handful of love bush that was again in full bloom on our side of the hedge.

"Hmm. So now you know how I feel about you. Let's go find out how you feel about me." She smiled as we kissed and left.

We smiled and hugged side to side as I walked her home in silence. Just a few flirty words were exchanged. I was in her company but could not speak a word because my mind was elsewhere, still trying to process all that was said earlier.

Sigh.

We got to her house. She did the silly ritual with the love bush and tucked it into a section of her hedge. We made out a bit on her front porch before she said she was going to go help her dad with dinner.

"Them boys bothering you?" I asked as her eyes followed my stare at Willy's house.

"No," she replied after a long silence. "Willy has been keeping to himself. No more thugs hanging out over there. I can hear from here the daily cussing and screaming from his girl about this other girl he might have gotten pregnant. Too much drama for me. I hear his little brother is in jail and facing a lengthy prison sentence. Nobody is saying what he did. I don't care. At least that's one less thug I have to worry about running into when I am walking home alone."

Wow. So it could have very well been Willy, I thought, remembering that conversation with my now friend on the bus. Who knew? I had a bit of shock at what I just heard about his brother but was not surprised. Why? Some bad people chose their own destiny to the point where, when you heard of their fate, it would come as no surprise.

Sadly, I had lost many friends over the years, but because of their lifestyle, the eventual news of their foreseeable death didn't come as a shock to anyone.

We kissed, and then I left.

I surprisingly went the other long way to home to walk past Willy's house. I was hoping to see him to say hi and was wishing that he was over the flu. But there was no sign of anyone.

I never did see Willy again after that. I was told that he did return to school, but before we even got to lunch for us to meet up, I got word that he was busted selling drugs to another student in the welding room. It was a sting operation. Someone had set him up.

Wow.

Assad came by the next day to fine-tune a glitch with his exhaust system. We fixed it and told him to simply up the octane level for the gas he was buying and get another part to end the issue. I fulfilled his request to give him more speed.

As payment, he agreed to pick up my mom at the airport two nights later. G okayed it, and Michelle, who was surprisingly into muscle cars, wanted to come along for the thrill. My brother and his girl all exchanged hugs with us. It was a beautiful moment in the kitchen. They told me how proud they were of me, and just when I thought it was because of winning all three Break Dance Championship belts or finally having the winning outcome of all those street fights or returning to church or believing in love and relationship again thanks to Michelle, they finally flopped my mush by saying that they were all so proud of me for doing so well in school.

Really!

But that was all mom asked for—for me to stay out of trouble and do well in school. She was going to be so proud with the updates.

G then told me that he and his girlfriend were top of their respective classes also, and showed us certificates they received to prove it in some blah, blah, blah commemoration service they had at school recently.

Michelle told us that she was now officially ordained as a minister in the church by the executive board and, as such, would become the first ever female preacher at her church. That was her dream, her goal, her mission. We all hugged her in love.

And then came Assad's time to speak. He simply said he was doing so well as a new recruit in the army that they were considering promoting him to being a drill sergeant. He was ecstatic, but I guessed the army adored his tenacity. We all did.

All he ever wanted to do was make his father proud. He then said that when he told his father, who was back home for a few weeks from overseas duty, his dad was so proud of him that he hugged him and they had a happy cry together. Assad then recalled that it was the first time he could ever remember being hugged by his father. He did a poor job of holding back the tears.

We all hugged again, and Michelle said a subtle prayer.

When was the last time you were hugged by your father?

Sigh.

We all huddled and jumped, singing a silly chant praise after Michelle prayed. We gave God thanks and celebrated life and our respective accomplishments throughout our journey so far.

THE LAST THING I REMEMBERED

Around 8:20 p.m. that night, Assad picked up Michelle and me at home. We left after having a drink with G and his girlfriend, who were preparing dinner for mom.

Michelle and I were in the back seat; we left the front passenger seat for mom.

"Where is your lucky charm?" I questioned with a friendly jab at him as I noticed that the Holy Rosary "lucky charm" had been replaced by some other ornament.

"At the base, in my locker." He simply smiled. "If I don't pass this training coming up next week, a few of us, including myself, might not make drill sergeant! I keep it on the base so I can see it every time I go to my locker, which is a lot during our breaks, because I'm gonna need all the luck I can get with this upcoming underwater training."

I accepted his reasoning because I knew he couldn't swim.

The car lived up to its test and was flying past every other vehicle on the highway at over 100 miles an hour. In fact, I once clocked it going at 164 miles per hour!

Wow!

Michelle and I were thrilled, but Assad pushed it even further when we got to a railroad crossing.

In those days, there were no rails that came down to stop traffic; there was just a regular stop light telling drivers to stop when a train was coming.

Michelle was cuddled in my arms in the back seat. We all saw the train coming from a distance from our left. Ten out of ten times, every motorist simply stopped and waited for the train to pass and the green light, but tonight was different. Assad was drinking; plus, with a muscle car, he screamed the dreaded words.

"I'm going for it!" he screamed, meaning he was going to race the train and cross the railroad crossing before the train crossed our path.

Michelle hugged me tightly in nervous anticipation, as Assad let out a challenging adrenaline-rush scream and floored it. I glanced at his speedometer as it clocked at 187 miles per hour and counting.

"You not gonna make it, bro!" I shouted nervously as Michelle hugged me tighter. "Brake!" I shouted, sizing up the situation and using the laws of physics, not faith, to tell him we wouldn't make it across the track in time. "I said *brake*!"

"No, I got this, Street!" he screamed as he gunned it even more. "I got this!"

"No! Brake! *Brake*!" I screamed.

"Noooo! I got this!" he shouted, letting out a mighty scream as the train blasted its horn and screeched.

The big bright light of the train lit up our car amidst Michelle's deafening scream.

He did cross the railroad, but the hump from the railway tipped his car, and in that split second, the left side of the bumper got clipped by the train, which sent the car into a violent spin because of the speed we were going.

The car spun out violently for hundreds of meters as our screams drowned out the air. Then it slammed sideways into a light pole, sending Michelle flying from my arms. The impact was so great that she flew head first. She slammed into the door, which ripped it from its hinges, sending her flying from the car and crashing into a huge tree.

That was the last thing I saw amidst all the screeching and screaming. Everything went dark after that, followed by dead silence.

The Divine Encounter (Based on Actual Events)

It seemed like I was unconscious for an eternity. Everything was black until I saw a tiny white light above me. Confused, I started floating toward it as it got bigger and bigger, brighter and brighter. The next thing I knew was, instead of being in total darkness, I was blinded by this bright white light as I got even closer.

I was in confused silence until a voice finally spoke.

"Behold! You are here!"

I was panting heavily as I tried to regain full consciousness.

"Where am I?" I gasped.

"Where you earned yourself to belong," the voice answered.

"Am I dead?"

"No. You will be alive eternally."

"Am I in Heaven?"

"Not yet. You are on the pathway. Come! Let me take you there."

Silence. I was still trying to recompose myself.

"Come!" the sweet, gentle voice instructed again.

Silence. Then I broke down crying.

"Come!" the voice again beckoned.

More crying from me.

There was only silence from the voice.

"I can't." I finally sighed.

Silence. Then the voice urged, "Why not? Come! Come, Street. Come, Adrian!"

"I can't. I can't," I sobbed. "I remember now. There was an accident. Please, please let me go back to help them. I'm not ready."

"Street," the voice urged. "Adrian…"

The silence was only interrupted by my soft sobs.

"I can't. Please. *Please!*" I begged. "I need to go back and help my friends. Please. *Please!*"

"You are here." The voice assured me.

"Yes. Yes. Yes, but please! Please, I need to go back to help them." I was sobbing uncontrollably.

Silence. Then the voice urged again, "Come! Their faith will take care of them."

I would never forget those words.

"No! Please. I need to go back to help them," I replied to the blinding light. "I want to go back!"

"Are you sure?"

Silence. Then I continued to beg, "Yes. I want to go back."

"Are you sure, Street? Adrian, are you sure?"

"I don't know. I'm tired. I'm so tired, Lord. But...but, yes!" I cried. "I...I...I have...I have not done anything to earn this." I sobbed. "I have been through hell. I cursed God and wanted to die, yet He kept me alive. For what? Let me earn this. Please...let me earn this."

"I have been with you all the way throughout your journey as you call us your *guardian angels*. You did well, Street. But now it's over. I was instructed to come and take you. Just come. He's waiting," the voice again beckoned.

I was crying uncontrollably.

"I can't," I sobbed. "Exodus 23:15 says, 'No one is to appear before me empty-handed.' Don't let me appear before Him empty-handed. Let me do one last effort for Him to favor me as His son, to make Him proud of this wretched man that I am. Let me go back."

"Are you sure?"

Silence.

"Are you sure?" the voice asked again.

Silence.

"Yes," I said, breathing heavily, then repeated, "Yes." I recomposed myself. "Yes, Lord!"

Everything went silent. Then I felt myself descending as the blinding white light slowly turned into pitch-black surroundings.

There was a priceless, peaceful silence until I heard noises that gradually got louder and louder. The next thing I knew, I snapped back to consciousness.

I was confused and in shock. The horn from Assad's car was blaring. I gradually recouped myself and realized where I was and what was going on.

Assad was slouched over his steering wheel, all busted up, blood gushing from everywhere. His position was why the horn was blaring. I dragged myself up and struggled to gently lift him backward into a sitting position. He was unconscious, so I couldn't tell his status.

The horn stopped. There was silence. People from the train, which had stopped some distance away, were running to our aid.

I was banged up really bad, too, as there was blood streaming from my forehead, and I also coughed up blood a couple of times. It hurt. I again tried to recompose myself by taking a few deep breaths and then noticed the busted-out car door.

Where was Michelle?

I saw her leaning against the tree. She was about fifty feet away, so I dragged myself from the car and tried to stand, but collapsed. So I crawled on my belly to her rescue, using my knees and elbows to move.

When I got to her, I realized that she was in really bad shape and was semiconscious; blood was streaming from the back of her head and from her nose. Her eyes were closed, and her body violently shivered in sporadic shocks. I tried to talk to her, but she was unresponsive. Then suddenly and strangely enough, I heard her whispering. So I dragged myself up and rested my head closer to her bosom and listened, only to realize that she was softly praying in tongues.

I broke down crying again as I tried to assist her to get back on her feet, but she stopped me, as she wracked with pain at my efforts.

"I never knew my life would be cut this short." She exhaled with a heavy sigh as blood drained from her nose and head. "But God's will be done! They are waiting for me. I will never forget you, Street. I will never forget our journey—our *crazy* journey." She laughed and cried at the same time as she mustered up all her strength to use her hand to gently wipe the tears from my cheeks. "I love you!" she said as tears streamed from her eyes. She tried to lean forward to kiss me but couldn't because of the pain.

Then she took her last breath and stopped breathing.

I dragged myself upward even more and kissed her softly. "I love you too, boo. Michelle! Wake up! You hear the sirens? Help is coming. Michelle. Michelle! Wake up! Please wake up!" I cried and screamed even as I choked on my blood. I prodded and pleaded, nudging at her over and over again.

But there was no response from her.

I cried as I slumped back into her now lifeless bosom. I closed my eyes as I struggled to breathe but finally managed to hug her. I used her limp arm to hug me in return as I stared at the beautiful night sky. I did my best to stay conscious as I sobbed from the excruciating pain all over my body.

I remember trying to take slow deep breaths so as not to pass out—or die—as I listened to the sounds of sirens in the distance that was now getting closer and closer. I remember looking one last time back at Assad, who was motionless. Back then, his car wasn't outfitted with airbags, and he never wore a seatbelt, so his face had slammed into that steering wheel at almost a hundred and fifty miles an hour on impact. He was busted up really bad, and strangely, I sobbed as I blamed myself for his demise.

If I hadn't led the efforts to grant him his wish to supercharging his car to make it turbo fast, there was no way he would have dared to race that train across the tracks. There was no way tonight would have had happened! I wept out of regret at granting a friend his wish. It was still okay to say no sometimes when someone asked you to grant them their dream/wish.

I remember looking at some people from the train getting closer as they ran toward us to provide assistance. I was in and out of consciousness.

I remember thinking that, *Mom's gonna kill me for being late to pick her up. She must now be at a phone booth at the airport, talking with my brother's girl on her cell and asking where the hell we are.* And then I thought about how she would handle the news.

I thought of my brother, who would surely think of killing me, too, for being late to pick up mom. But then he would switch off and go into panic mode and freak out, thinking that we should be way early to do so because of Assad's fast car.

Mom would never forgive him if anything bad was to ever happen to me. He would live with regret and torment for the rest of his life because she would constantly remind him that this was all his fault and would never have happened if he and his girl had instead insisted on picking her up.

I remember envisioning G and his girl driving around en route to the airport, looking for us, freaking out and fearing the worst.

I remember looking at Michelle's face, her lifeless face, as tears streamed from my eyes. I remembered the day she was out back in the swing, powering away as far as she could go while fighting to keep her beautiful flowing hair from her face as she laughed out loud like a child at play. I remembered smiling at our lucky tree, which was in full bloom.

I remember looking at the heavens and the stars in the sky and wanted to play my "test game" all over again. But I didn't. I instead I just lay there, looking at the heavens, crying and begging and asking God, *Why? Why now? Why this way? Please...save us.*

But there was no answer—until I started whispering a prayer in tongues.

I remember praying, "Your will be done, Lord." And then I drifted in and out of consciousness. I briefly regained consciousness and painfully whispered, "It hurts!" I wept.

There was a long peaceful silence. Then people arrived and tried to revive us.

I was in serious pain, but strangely, I just stared at the beautiful starry skies, I exhaled heavily as I slowly drifted back into a state of unconsciousness, and simply whispered, "It hurts. It hurts no more."

That was the last thing I remembered.

The End

Adrian Nelson is a fifty-one-year old Jamaican male who started from humble beginnings and finally moved to the United States nine years ago. He is currently a contented single dad, a resident of Connecticut, and a hard working, successful federal employee; but back in Jamaica, he was a journalist and reporter for over two decades.

He is also a part-time DJ and has played at countless parties and over two hundred weddings. But writing has always been his gift, his passion, his talent, his mission, his message.

He wrote and produced three mega-staged drama productions in Jamaica (*Moon River*, *Dream Merchant*, and *House Arrest*) between 2008 and 2011.

His retirement plan in twelve years is to be a novelist, but he says that against all odds, he got a message one night in a dream that led him to write this novel: *Church Boy Love*. There is a message—in fact, there are so many—that the voice told him could not wait all of twelve years to be told.

Brace yourself. This is his story.

CPSIA information can be obtained
at www.ICGtesting.com
Printed in the USA
FSHW010110190521
81586FS

9 781649 52849